gta papers 7

Care

Torsten Lange and Gabrielle Schaad (eds.)

gta Verlag

Introduction
Torsten Lange and Gabrielle Schaad

Torsten Lange is a Cultural and Architectural History Lecturer at the Lucerne School of Engineering and Architecture (HSLU).

Gabrielle Schaad is a postdoctoral researcher at the Chair for Theory and History of Architecture, Art and Design at the Technical University of Munich (TUM).

Care work is at once omnipresent and invisible. It permeates our most important relationships and commitments, encompassing all forms of socially necessary—or reproductive—labor: raising children, cooking, cleaning, shopping, looking after the ill and elderly, and many other tasks typically performed by women daily at home and within society. In general, care revolves around work that aims at the well-being of people. It allows for and sustains productive labor, including architectural labor.

Capitalist accumulation relies on discounting care. Regardless of its social, material, and monetary value, care work remains mostly unpaid. It is also—perhaps due to a kind of collective bad conscience—frequently pushed out of sight. Its performance by women is often naturalized by alluding to the allegedly more caring, nurturing female character or body. As the Swiss economist Mascha Madörin points out, care work has never been of interest to economic theory; only feminist economists have taken up the topic. [1] Even today, regardless of cultural differences, most care work, paid or not, is done by women.

The gendered division of labor is one of the biggest obstacles in thinking and developing economic theory concepts and terms that could lead to relevant political-economic insights into the care economy. At the same time, in spite of its relative invisibility, the care economy has been in tremendous flux. Much of the Western world has undergone a transition from the "family wage" model that underpinned postwar state-managed capitalism to the "two-earner family" ideal of contemporary globalizing financialized capitalism. While the former institutionalized "androcentric understandings of family and work, [and] naturalized heteronormativity and gender hierarchy, largely removing them from political contestation," the latter caused a "crisis of care" as debt-driven economies are "systematically expropriating the capacities available for sustaining social connections." [2] This issue of gta papers argues that, in light of the current "crisis of care" brought about by neoliberal financialized capitalism, [3] it is high time for architecture and the architectural humanities to turn to care. Doing so requires reorientation. As the philosopher Sara Ahmed reminds us, orientations matter. What and whom we attend to, we tend to. What we consciously perceive in front of us is determined by the things and actions that affect us and that we value. But do we attend to those who tend to us? Ahmed illustrates this by describing the domestic setting from within which Edmund Husserl's phenomenological thinking about our directedness toward the world unfolds. [4] Starting from his writing desk, an

1 Mascha Madörin, "Die Logik der Care-Arbeit—Annäherung einer Ökonomin," in Ruth Gurny and Ueli Tecklenburg, eds., Arbeit ohne Knechtschaft: Bestandesaufnahmen und Forderungen rund ums Thema Arbeit (Zurich: Edition 8, 2013), 128–45, here 131, https://www.denknetz.ch/wp-content/uploads/2017/07/arbeit_ohne_knechtschaft_madoerin.pdf (accessed February 12, 2022). See also Ina Praetorius, The Care-Centered Economy: Rediscovering What Has Been Taken for Granted, Economy + Social Issues Vol. 16 (Berlin: Heinrich Böll Stiftung, 2015), https://www.boell.de/sites/default/files/the_care-centered_economy.pdf (accessed August 25, 2022).

2 Nancy Fraser, "Contradictions of Capital and Care," New Left Review, no. 100 (July/August 2016), 99–117, here 111, 115–16.

3 Fraser, "Contradictions of Capital and Care," 104.

4 Sara Ahmed, "Orientations: Toward a Queer Phenomenology," GLQ: A Journal of Gay and Lesbian Studies 12, no. 4 (2006), 543–74, here 547.

object placed immediately in front of him and located within the topography of the home, Husserl faces only certain things, while others remain "known" in the background. The latter remain undeserving of any specific attention (determining what is rendered visible and invisible in this process). Ahmed names "domestic work" that which allows for Husserl's desk to be kept clear and turned into a philosophical object. [5] Ahmed's observations about the situatedness of intellectual work may sound familiar to architects, perhaps even more so after the experience of working from home in the context of COVID-19. Given the extent to which architecture creates and establishes the spatial conditions for care work to take place, Ahmed's observations bear critical relevance for those tasked with designing the built environment. Tending to the back of architecture can offer a necessary corrective to our discipline's obsession with the "front of the house."

Since the 1990s, political scientists Joan Tronto and Berenice Fisher have worked on definitions and terminology to analytically grasp an "ethic of care." [6] As a result of the close ties of care to everyday practices of the domestic sphere and its division of labor, Tronto and Fisher note that public acknowledgment tends either to understate care almost exclusively as an emotional and intellectual act, and hence to undervalue the amount of active work that goes along with it, or to "overemphasize ... care as work at the expense of understanding the deeper emotional and intellectual qualities." [7]

The goal of this issue of *gta papers* is not to provide a false sense of an overview but to highlight how deeply entangled the discourses of care and architecture are. With few exceptions, architectural history as a discipline has not afforded much attention to reproductive labor, the ceaseless efforts of maintaining human and more-than-human life-worlds. Indeed, most of the discipline's (white male) protagonists have celebrated architects as the autonomous inventors of likewise autonomous stable structures, forms, styles, and so on. However, "[g]iven the degree of brokenness of the broken world," as Shannon Mattern writes, a shift in public discourse is necessary: away from the dominant paradigm of innovation—including the modern focus on economists, engineers, and policymakers—toward practices of maintenance and "the collective project of repair." [8] The essays assembled here offer points of departure in this direction. In this introduction we do not try to address all the perspectives contained in the issue—this would hardly be possible—but a few strands can be brought forward.

To begin pragmatically, architecture needs care, repair, and maintenance. Maintenance, or "the back half of life," [9] as artist

5 Ahmed, "Orientations," 547.

6 Berenice Fisher and Joan C. Tronto, "Towards a Feminist Theory of Caring," in Emily Abel and Margaret Nelson, eds., *Circles of Care: Work and Identity in Women's Lives* (Albany NY: SUNY Press, 1990), 35—62, here 35.

7 See Joan C. Tronto, "An Ethic of Care," *Generations: Journal of the American Society on Aging* 22, no. 3 (1998), 15—20, here 16, http://www.jstor.org/stable/44875693 (accessed February 12, 2022). Tronto points out four ethical elements of care: attentiveness, responsibility, competence, and responsiveness.

8 Shannon Mattern, "Maintenance and Care," *Places Journal*, November 2018, https://doi.org/10.22269/181120.

9 Cited in the program notes to the exhibition *Mierle Laderman Ukeles*, Matrix 137, September 20—November 15 1998 (Hartford, CT: Wadsworth Atheneum, 1998), 2.

10 Mierle Laderman Ukeles, "Manifesto for Maintenance Art 1969! Proposal for an Exhibition CARE" (1969), in Andrea Phillips and Markus Miessen, eds., *Caring Culture: Art, Architecture and the Politics of Public Health* (Berlin: Sternberg Press, 2011), 137—44.

Mierle Laderman Ukeles calls it, has been a lens to look at her artistic and spatial practice in urban and institutional environments. Half a century after issuing a "Manifesto for Maintenance Art 1969!," her critique, initially aimed at institutions, affects and stretches the architectural discourse in direct and indirect ways. **10**

The enactment of maintenance and its performative potential are what guides the curatorial project *The Power of Mushrooms: Berta Rahm's Pavilion for the Saffa 58* by Milena Buchwalder, Sonja Flury, and Dorothee Hahn. In their article reflecting on this project, the authors underline the role of collaboration and care in reevaluating historic women architects by rescuing and tending to a material object. Their commitment to an almost derelict pavilion architecture designed and built by the neglected Swiss architect Berta Rahm (1910—1998) for the 1958 *Swiss Exhibition for Women's Work* (*SAFFA 58*) is instrumental to the reevaluation of the architect who made it. We are familiar with the idea that historical monuments and buildings require care for their preservation. But performative preservation can also constitute a kind of curatorial activism. In the case of Rahm's *SAFFA* pavilion, the expression of care becomes a manifesto for the assertion of value. Tending to the material object draws attention to the pavilion's history and the impact of women architects. Because the pavilion was repurposed to house the canteen of a mushroom farm over the years, the maintenance performed through its transfer and restaging at gta exhibitions at ETH Zurich loosely revolved around the mushroom, both as actual and intellectual nourishment or thought model. In this context, mycelia's entangled and persistent lives became an emblem for the ecologies of care the pavilion itself created and continues to unfold. The curators both exceeded the classical activities of preservation specialists and transcended the frame of a conventional architecture exhibition, ultimately projecting different futures—not only for the pavilion they set out to reconstruct (at a location still to be found)—but also for women and LGBTQIA+ architects in the profession following in Rahm's footsteps.

Tethered to the question of maintenance is the question of who does the maintaining. Architecture establishes separate spheres and enclosed spaces within which labor is performed, and this contributes to the invisibility of care work; indeed, makes it literally structural. Such spaces range from the domestic sphere to environments of institutionalized care. The built environment structures relations between bodies; places caregivers and care receivers in specific, often separate, environments; and, just as it denies care as work, often denies those providing care work any space of their own within which they do not have to work. Care is thus closed off from productive labor and public discourse, physically as well as symbolically.

Theorists like Silvia Federici were already denouncing the feminization and concomitant undervaluation of all the necessary and life-sustaining activities of the domestic sphere in the 1970s. [11] For years, such remarks left the field of architecture untouched. Then, in the early 1980s in her now legendary essay "What Would a Non-sexist City Be Like?," [12] Dolores Hayden drew a concrete connection between urban design, architecture, and care (work). Hayden's historical analysis uncovered the radical proposals of nineteenth-century "material feminists" for revolutionizing the domestic sphere through the commoning of reproductive labor, [13] directly informing her recommendations for redressing the gendered and racialized spatial inequalities produced by US postwar suburban housing. To challenge and change the established relationship between private life and public responsibilities, with their false opposition between "home and work," she envisioned the creation of collective services to support the private household. Communal childcare, cooking, washing, and transportation were all part of a new system of small participatory organizations to be tested through experimental residential centers that she called HOMES (Homemakers Organization for a More Egalitarian Society). [14]

Meanwhile, in much of the world, the outsourcing and monetized transfer of care work within the neoliberal care economy has resulted in the precarious conditions encountered by caregivers—often racialized women—and care receivers alike. [15] Architecture may not affect these "external" factors, but it operates within them. Valentina Davila's contribution to this issue illustrates how architecture can provide a lens for the critical examination of these conditions. Her article focuses on the *quinta*, an upper-middle-class housing type in Venezuela whose extensive footprint and material comforts demand constant maintenance. Their owners' lives depend on the extraction of care work from impoverished, often indigenous, rural migrant domestic workers, who are frequently confined to tiny, meager back rooms adjacent to the service area of the house, rooms that are kept small as much for symbolic as for practical reasons. Davila traces the workers' discretely performed daily duties through her ethnographic practice, redrawing the proximate yet hidden spaces within the *quinta* to capture some trace of those who perform this care work.

The blindness within today's architectural discipline to unregulated domestic work is in part attributable to the influence of the lively debates and technical inventions of the early twentieth century—debates around domestic reform, household

11 Silvia Federici, *Wages Against Housework* (London: Power of Women Collective; Bristol: Falling Wall Press, 1975), 1.

12 Dolores Hayden, "What Would a Non-sexist City Be Like? Speculations on Housing, Urban Design, and Human Work," *Signs* 5, no. 3 (1980), 170—87, here 174.

13 Dolores Hayden, *The Grand Domestic Revolution: A History of Feminist Designs for American Homes, Neighborhoods, and Cities* (Cambridge, MA: MIT Press, 1981), 3—29, here 3.

14 Hayden, "What Would a Non-sexist City Be Like?," 181.

15 Arlie Russell Hochschild and Barbara Ehrenreich, *Global Woman: Nannies, Maids, and Sex Workers in the New Economy* (New York: Metropolitan Books, 2003), 1—14, here 2.

engineering, and labor-saving devices—spawned by what was then called the "servant problem." Frequently informed by Taylorist thinking, as well as an unshakable faith in technological fixes, the work of influential American household scientist Christine Frederick and the German economist Erna Meyer conceived of household labor as a form of work open to rational analysis and improvement. [16] The design and material construction of domestic space, amplified by the discourse of hygiene and cleanliness, was discussed not only by women reformers but also by critical proponents of modern architecture such as Bruno Taut, whose 1924 book *The New Dwelling* addresses women as "creators" of domestic space, albeit in their role as modern housewives. [17] Barbara Penner's short article makes a significant contribution here. It points away from these canonized examples of streamlined modern design envisioned for urban homemakers, turning instead to an unknown history of experimental plans for farmhouse kitchens in the American West. The requirements of busy farm women drastically differed from women who lived in the city. Penner notes how, in contrast to the disembodied silhouette that determined the scale of the modular kitchen and its mass-produced appliances, farmhouse women were encouraged to alter the standardized plans for farmhouse kitchens developed at Oregon State College to fit their own bodies. She thus unearths a hitherto unexplored prehistory of ergonomics.

The contemporary built environment works as an effective system of prosthetics for the standard human body (read: healthy, adult, male), but less so for everyone else. Judith Butler and Sunaura Taylor demonstrated this point succinctly by going for a walk in San Francisco. Navigating curbs and steps (Taylor is dependent on a wheelchair), they discussed the concept of interdependence. Responding to each other's thoughts and observations, they noted that the "idea that the able-bodied person is somehow radically self-sufficient" is itself something of a myth. "Disability" could be defined as a "social organization of [embodied] impairment" or "the disabling effects of society." [18] Only when we organized a roundtable discussion on spaces for interdependent care relationships between people with disabilities and their caregivers at ETH Zurich's Department of Architecture in 2018 did we become aware of the (invisible) administrative and physical constructional hurdles of the venue. Disability rights activist, performer, and scholar Nina Mühlemann advised us, the authors, on the organization of the event. Even though we all constantly depend on ergonomic support structures, society, politics, administration, and sometimes even architects declare assistance for non-normative bodies to be disproportionate.

16 See Mary Nolan, "'Housework Made Easy': The Taylorized Housewife in Weimar Germany's Rationalized Economy." *Feminist Studies* 16, no. 3 (1990): 549–77, here 549. See also Susan R. Henderson, "A Revolution in the Woman's Sphere: Grete Lihotzky and the Frankfurt Kitchen," in Debra Coleman, Elizabeth Danze and Carol Henderson, eds., *Architecture and Feminism* (New York: Princeton Architectural Press, 1996), 221–53; and Ruth Schwartz Cowan, *More Work for Mother: The Ironies of Household Technology from the Open Hearth to Microwave* (New York: Basic Books, 1983), 107.

17 Bruno Taut, *Die neue Wohnung: Die Frau als Schöpferin* (Leipzig: Klinkhardt & Biermann, 1924), 58.

18 Judith Butler with Sunaura Taylor, "Interdependence," in Astra Taylor, ed., *Examined Life: Excursions with Contemporary Thinkers* (New York: New Press, 2009), 185–230, here 195 (based on *Examined Life*, directed by Astra Taylor [Sphynx Productions, 2008], 1:28:00).

Think, for example, of the accessibility of emergency exits. As Mühlemann explains, because making space accessible "is deemed excessive and unreasonable," the use of an emergency exit "almost always involves a lot of extra labor from the side of the disabled person." [19] Disability studies scholar Margaret Price further specifies that justifications for lack of access — "this building was built before access standards were in place" or "we did the best we could" or "there is an accessible bathroom, just not on this floor" — shift the focus from the excluded disabled person onto those who are "doing their best" or onto the semi- or inaccessible spaces themselves. [20] Disability does not exist in a vacuum. It exists intersectionally with other markers of identity and with the surroundings that produce the social and political meaning of disability. The researcher Aimie Hamraie reminds us in this vein how "ugly laws," segregation politics, and the ideology of able-bodiedness have shaped public space by determining who accesses and hence inhabits it: "Denying non-normative access to shared space created the illusion of [the] nonexistence [of non-normative bodies], resulting in less-accessible environments." [21] The absence of non-normative bodies thus constantly feeds into how we imagine and project our environment. Physical access leads in turn to social access and the acceptability of "misfits." [22]

Architect, activist, and theorist Jos Boys is one of the pioneers among the growing number of designers attempting to confront and unbuild the disabling effects of the built environment. In her contribution to this issue of *gta papers*, Boys explores "how disability (and other corporeally framed identities) can be reframed, not in simplistic binaries but as a complex, intersectional, situated, and dynamic patterning of enabling and disabling practices and spaces." [23] By focusing on "difference as a creative generator," Boys's project seeks to reset how the built environment is taught and practiced. In collaborative drawing and mapping workshops, she reorients students and professionals to ideas of interdependent care that see access not as a service illiberally offered but as reciprocal generosity. Disability-led buildings in Berkeley, California, including the Ed Roberts Campus, serve as case studies to understand how the adaptation of a building can happen from the bottom up, sometimes even circumventing rules and regulations. In this process, the involved parties drop the assumption that the "needs" of different impairment groups "somehow add [up] to produce a 'universal design'" and privilege creative design solutions instead.

Whereas the work of disability scholars and crip practitioners confronts the disabling effects of the built environment, Meredith TenHoor's article highlights ways to conceive of space as

19 Nina Mühlemann, "Disability, Space, and Support" (paper presented at *Interdependent Bodies: Making Non-normative Spaces for Care*, panel discussion, October 29, 2018, ETH Zurich).

20 Margaret Price, "Un/shared Space: The Dilemma of Inclusive Architecture," in Jos Boys, ed., *Disability, Space Architecture* (New York: Routledge, 2017), 155–72, here 157.

21 Aimi Hamraie, "Normate Template: Knowing-Making the Architectural Inhabitant," in *Building Access: Universal Design and the Politics of Disability* (Minneapolis: University of Minnesota Press, 2017), 19–39, here 26.

22 Rosemarie Garland-Thomson, "Misfits: A Feminist Materialist Disability Concept," *Hypatia Special Issue: Ethics of Embodiment* 26 (2011), 591–609, here 595.

23 For this and further citations in this paragraph, see in this issue Jos Boys, "Care as Active Practice."

"enabling" — that is, as supporting the healing process of mental healthcare patients and easing their gradual return to social life. At the heart of her study is the pioneering 1963 design by French architect Nicole Sonolet for l'Eau Vive, a residential psychiatric hospital in Soisy-sur-Seine, a suburb of Paris , and Sonolet's later research into spaces for care conducted in collaboration with the psychiatrist Philippe Paumelle. Working in the context of institutional psychotherapy, a movement with origins in mid-twentieth-century decolonization theory and supported by key French intellectuals such as Frantz Fanon and Félix Guattari, Sonolet and Paumelle's goal was to "decarceralize" the old, centralized asylums with local, community-based care provision. Core to Sonolet's proposals were nonsegregated spaces where patients, rather than being closed off by walls or medication, could maintain close relations to others. Furthermore, such spaces should facilitate the transition into more independent forms of therapy whenever residents felt ready. Sonolet's project informed not only the 1967 discussions within the Centre d'études, de recherches et de formation institutionnelles but also later community-based care in Europe, the United Kingdom, and the United States. Underpinning Sonolet's designs was a nonmechanistic understanding of architectural spaces, resisting standardization and calculability, as TenHoor stresses in her contribution. The bodies of patients and carers were expected to always establish new and evolving relations with one another, as well as with the spaces surrounding them.

Max J. Andrucki's article — "Ceramics, Sex, and Sublimation" — takes its departure from the urban geographers who published groundbreaking studies of gay neighborhoods in the 1980s. Those researchers investigated the "material networks of infrastructure that enable queer life," a covert web of bars, clubs, saunas, and other meeting points that ultimately facilitated the emergence of a public political movement. Andrucki extends this discussion by talking about the subtle way in which the gay male body has always functioned as the definitive infrastructure of the neighborhood: a body that served, liberated, or desired the other bodies that it met, as part of a libidinal economy that permitted the desublimation of individual and radical notions of service. Intense sex, Andrucki argues, is also a kind of civil infrastructure. As a culmination to his account, Andrucki raises the example of two artists in London whose practice emphasizes relational aesthetics. The dual role of ceramics, both a material of public infrastructure and a familiar material of domesticity, comes into play in the artists' events. In a recent, key event — *Midsommar* — a seemingly innocuous garden party held at the end of the coronavirus lockdown, they demonstrated the extraordinary capacity of queer hospitality to offer renewal, solace, and conviviality in a time of isolation.

The questions "Who cares?" and "Who is cared for?" are complicated further when we move beyond anthropocentric scales. The environment, often conceived as a backdrop for human concerns, has in living memory become increasingly the object of them. Publications and exhibition projects such as Elke Krasny and Angelika Fitz's *Critical Care: Architecture and Urbanism for a Broken Planet* attest to the fact that the concept of care has become a central concern in architectural debates. [24] Demographic changes, growing mobility, environmental crises, and climate change increase the urgency for architecture to reflect upon its role in planetary questions. Natasha Baranow's study of terrariums persuasively reminds us that our consciousness of such questions now pervades our relationships even with miniature, isolated spaces—that is, anxiety has become inescapable. The realization that the construction industry is dependent on resource extraction at vast scales, leading to a scarcity even of sand, has become impossible to ignore, and some voices even controversially propose "a global moratorium" on new buildings to force us to take stock of the existing built environment. [25] On a planetary level, architecture not only finds itself entangled with the Anthropocene but also with geopolitical and economic interests, the result of asymmetrical struggles between what is usually abridged as the "Global North" and the "Global South."

Affective labor figures in different ways—and with a historical twist—in Alla Vronskaya's research. She unearths an overlooked figure in Soviet architectural history crucial in designing ideological and educational spectacles. Her article sheds light on Betty Glan, who—among other things—was vital in shaping Soviet spaces for leisure by conceiving and realizing the design of Moscow's Gorky Park (the Moscow Park of Culture and Leisure) while its director from 1929 to 1937. Vronskaya traces Glan's burning commitment to communism throughout her winding, decades-spanning career. In Vronskaya's account of Glan's life we might recognize glimmers of Hélène Frichot's "exhaustion as a methodology," theorized in her 2019 book *Creative Ecologies* as "offering a way of practising from the midst of the spaces and temporal paces of exhaustion." [26] Drawing on Gilles Deleuze's essay titled "The Exhausted," Frichot stresses that exhaustion is not to be confused with tiredness and that it can lead to forms of creativity. Glan understood "sacrificing one's life to the life of others" as the ultimate heroic gesture for a humanist member of the collectivist Soviet society. [27] Despite years of exile, prison, and forced labor, Glan retrospectively idealized her life as

24 Elke Krasny and Angelika Fitz, eds., *Critical Care: Architecture and Urbanism for a Broken Planet* (Cambridge, MA: MIT Press, 2019), 25—43.

25 See Charlotte Malterre-Barthes (interviewed by Alexander Stumm), "Wer definiert die Standards und zu welchem Zweck?," *Bauwelt* 16 (2021), 42—44.

26 Hélène Frichot, *Creative Ecologies: Theorizing the Practice of Architecture* (London: Bloomsbury Visual Arts, 2018), 69.

27 See Alla Vronskaya, "Affective Productivism" in this issue.

A Movable Feast. This leads Vronskaya to muse over the rhetorical tropes of romance and satire. In her romanticized autobiography, the cultural mediator and educator Glan imaginatively reclaimed what had been repeatedly revoked or put into question: the supposed rewards for the dedicated and unconditional care for others. Her commitment to the needs of school children, factory workers, and comrades went beyond the common demand for revolutionary enthusiasm, reaching something closer to an eschatological celebration of self-sacrifice. Glan appears to fully realize the longed-for political utopia only in the simultaneous experience of martyrdom by and for the party.

Science historian Donna Haraway paved the way for academic writing that allows the personal and private to enter the frame. She calls this "situated knowledges." **28** Haraway encourages writing that makes the researcher's subjective position traceable, allowing them to acknowledge their knowledge as partial, potentially biased through personal privilege, entangled in complex or asymmetrical power relations, or limited through resources and access, without surrendering the desire for knowledge in the process. Looking at one's research through the lens of care supports this type of writing by highlighting the temporal, spatial, and positional entanglements among researcher, researched subjects, and their respective working environments. Doing so requires the substitution of the modern Western individual subject for an interdependent human being that lives with and thinks with other body-minds. A narrative only partly sustained by historical testimonies, based primarily on one's horizon of personal experience, may be dismissed by some as unscholarly or as "first-person research." However, in stories of care, these tentative and self-critical contributions are necessary to clarify that the primary incentives, tribulations, and even fates of productive labor lie in the inseparable entanglement of our thinking bodies with built and social-emotional commitments that henceforth cannot be excluded from the picture without distorting it beyond any resemblance to "reality."

The contributions collected from the Society of Architectural Historians' workshop "Caregiving as Method" — convened by Annoradha Iyer Siddiqi during the global pandemic in 2021 — all acknowledge the affective dimension of our work as architectural historians, in contrast to the feigned detachment of scholarship. In preparing these oral accounts and testimonies for *gta papers*, the authors further developed and sharpened the methodological insights and conclusions presented during the event. An in-depth review of the workshop by Siddiqi and the other moderators introduces the individual contributions stemming

28 Donna Haraway. "Situated Knowledges: The Science Question in Feminism and the Privilege of Partial Perspective." *Feminist Studies* 14, no. 3 (1988), 575–99.

from panels that revolved around the topics of "Care," "Repair," and "Method." In various ways they note the fetishism around the built object that characterizes architectural history. To us, as editors, these short contributions read as a plea for mutually engaged scholarship. They seek to create solidarity and strategic alliances between researchers and their research subjects.

Milena Buchwalder is an independent curator, and practicing architect at Architekturgenossenschaft C/O, Zurich.

Sonja Flury is an independent curator, a practicing architect at Architekturgenossenschaft C/O, and a teaching assistant at the Department of Architecture at ETH Zurich.

Dorothee Hahn is an independent curator, editor, and architect, working in Zurich and Berlin.

1 *The Power of Mushrooms: Berta Rahm's Pavilion for the Saffa 58*, gta exhibitions, ETH Zurich, March 8 to December 23, 2021, https://ausstellungen.gta.arch.ethz.ch/veranstaltungen/the-power-of-mushrooms-berta-rahms-pavilion-for-the-saffa-58 (accessed April 24, 2022). The exhibition was presented in five iterations: "Material Evidence," "Entangled Histories," "Images of Berta," "Close Encounters," and "The Feast." The curatorial team comprised Milena Buchwalder, Sonja Flury, Dorothee Hahn, and Larissa Müllner on behalf of the ProSaffa1958-Pavillon association, together with the codirectors of gta exhibitions, Fredi Fischli and Niels Olsen.

fig. 1 a, b Views of the wooden framework of the pavilion in the exhibition *The Power of Mushrooms: Berta Rahm's Pavilion for the Saffa 58*. Photograph: Nelly Rodriguez, ETH Hönggerberg, Zurich, 2021

2 Throughout this article, we use *women* to refer to everyone who identifies with the female gender.

Caring to Know: Exhibition as a Technique of Feminist Preservation
Milena Buchwalder, Sonja Flury, and Dorothee Hahn

For slightly more than sixty years the building stood as an annex in an anonymous industrial park, about half an hour outside the city of Zurich. It was attached to, or almost leaned on, a nondescript building that could have been a manufacturing plant or a warehouse but was in fact a farm, a mushroom farm. The annex was utilitarian, dilapidated, but even at first sight it did not quite match its neighbors. Its construction was lighter and its detailing more careful than the buildings around it. We—Milena Buchwalder, Sonja Flury, Dorothee Hahn, along with Larissa Müllner—had the pleasure to curate the display of the pavilion at gta exhibitions on behalf of the association ProSaffa1958-Pavillon. 1 fig. 1 a, b

In March 2021 we installed surviving fragments of Berta Rahm's (1910—1998) pavilion for the 1958 *Swiss Exhibition on Women's Work* (*Saffa*) within the gta exhibition space at the Department of Architecture (D-ARCH) of the ETH Zurich. The installation was one step in a campaign to rescue and rebuild the structure permanently, which is the aim of the association ProSaffa1958-Pavillon, founded in 2020.

The pavilion fragments mostly consist of demountable wall elements clad in corrugated metal that we reconstituted within the gallery space. They became the central element of our year-long exhibi-

tion *The Power of Mushrooms: Berta Rahm's Pavilion for the Saffa 58*. Why take such efforts to save and valorize such fragments? For us, their preservation was both a way to recall the historical work of women architects and a stimulus for active collaboration. 2 The collective effort was itself both a monument to and an embodiment of collective practices.

The resonance of the building perhaps requires some explanation. The acronym SAFFA refers to the *Schweizerische Ausstellung für Frauenarbeit*. ₃ The first instance of the exhibition took place in 1928 in Bern and paid particular attention to the invisibility of domestic care work. Thirty years later, in 1958, the second iteration of the exhibition, organized by several women's organizations, including alliance F, focused on

voting rights and the status of domestic labor in postwar Switzerland. ₄ The exhibition was held in a symbolically prominent site: the grounds of the former Swiss National Exposition of 1939 on the shores of Lake Zurich. Women architects and designers were commissioned for the master planning and design of the individual exhibition pavilions, including their interiors. Berta Rahm's L-shape building, located on the periphery of the exposition site in Landiwiese park, was devoted to recreation and contemplation. It was not freestanding but served as an annex to the journalists' clubhouse, the so-called Club Pavilion.

3 The official title is *Saffa 1958 — Eine nationale Bühne für Schweizer Architektinnen und Gestalterinnen: Städtebau, Architektur, Ausstellungsdesign im internationalen Kontext.*

4 Prior to 2011, alliance F was known as the Bund Schweizerischer Frauenvereine (Federation of Swiss Women's Associations). For more on *Saffa*, see Dorothee Huber, "Die Tugend der Not: Zu den beiden historischen Ausstellungen für Frauenarbeit (Saffa 1928 und 1958)," in Petra Stojanik, ed., *Ausstellungen — Darstellungen, Beiträge zum Diplomwahlfach "Frauen in der Geschichte des Bauens,"* Vol. 3 (Zurich: ETH, 1996), 129–38.

The Club Pavilion was a demountable aluminum building designed by Milanese architect Carlo Pagani for another occasion. ₅ His structure was erected again under Rahm's supervision, whose original architectural work was restricted to the aluminum-clad annex that housed the restrooms, wardrobes, and a reading room. Not even depicted on the exhibition's site plan **fig. 2** , Rahm's extension is paradoxically the only surviving material structure of *Saffa 58*. Designed to be assembled and disassembled easily, the pavilion was moved after the end of the exposition to the village of Gossau near Zurich, where it was modified for use as the canteen for a mushroom farm. **fig. 3** Rahm herself supervised the reassembly on the new site. This work encompassed the laying of a concrete foundation, fitting of insulation, and the construction of an extension that contained a kitchen. The building was used for decades as a canteen and later as a show kitchen before becoming a storage shed for tires for the neighboring garage. Traces of this translocation and adaptation, not to mention years of neglect and dampness, are etched into the pavilion's material structure. Some of the columns have been partially disintegrated by colonies of wasps. In 2020, the new owner of the mushroom factory obtained a demolition permit, news of which triggered a rescue operation by a loose alliance of women.

5 For more information on Carlo Pagani, see the Rinascente archives, https://archives. rinascente.it/it/funds/ archivio_carlo_pagani (accessed 24 April, 2022).

The preservationists Eva Nägeli and Pietro Wallnöfer first raised the alarm when they heard about the imminent demolition of Rahm's pavilion. They contacted a research group at the Zurich University of Applied Sciences (ZHAW) led by art historian Eliana Perotti, who had recently embarked on a nationally funded

fig. 2 The annex is not represented on the official site plan accompanying the 1958 *Saffa* exposition. However, the Club Pavilion, to which the annex is attached, can be found under the site plan key "F." Image: Foldable pamphlet of the site plan for *Saffa 1958*, paper, 14.2 × 8.4 cm, 1958. Design: Franz Fässler. Source: Zürcher Hochschule der Künste / Museum für Gestaltung Zürich / Designsammlung, Zurich

project researching the context and impact of *Saffa 58*. Perotti and her team knew of a similar endeavor by the multidisciplinary association proSAFFAhaus (2002—2007) to relocate Lux Guyer's model house, designed for *Saffa 1928* in Bern. 6 With this precedent in mind, the ZHAW researchers turned to architects Sonja Flury and Kathrin Füglister, who had become known for their walking tours of buildings designed by women in Zurich as part of the 2019 Women's Strike. 7 Together, they brought in Barbara Buser from baubüro in situ, an expert on the reuse of building components. In total, twelve women from the fields of architecture and art history founded the nonprofit association ProSaffa1958-Pavillon in March 2020 for the purpose of preserving and restoring Rahm's pavilion. 8 Nearly 80,000 Swiss francs were raised from private donors and institutions to support the costs of careful removal and storage of the structure. **fig. 4**

6 The story of this relocation is well-documented in *Die drei Leben des Saffa-Hauses: Lux Guyers Musterhaus von 1928* (Zurich: gta Verlag, 2006).

7 For more information on the tour of buildings by women architects, see siebaut, https://www.siebaut.org/ (accessed April 24, 2022).

8 For the association's website, see https://www.prosaffa1958-pavillon.ch/ (accessed April 24, 2022).

Berta Rahm

Rahm was an ambitious architect and committed feminist. Like many of her female contemporaries, she had a particular interest in Scandinavian architecture. After her studies at the ETH Zurich, Rahm received a travel grant and visited the Netherlands, Scandinavia, and Finland. In 1940 she opened her own architectural practice, starting with small projects—or, as she described them in an interview with Radio Munot (1990), "the breadcrumbs that fell from the men's tables." 9 Besides planning several single-family and holiday homes or refurbishments, as she recalled in the interview, what attracted international attention was her progressive farm building (1951) in her hometown Hallau. In 1963 she represented Switzerland at the foundation of the Union Internationale des Femmes Architectes in Paris and displayed her successful projects in the accompanying exhibition.

When Rahm completed her architectural studies in 1934, eleven years after the first architecture degree was awarded to a woman in Switzerland, she entered a field dominated by men. From her diary entries, newspaper articles, and accounts in radio interviews we know how much she struggled against traditional gender roles. When she sought to establish an independent office in 1940 she not only experienced discrimination but remembered being systematically bullied and misled in the professional context: "They did not give me construction permits. They wrote for example that the property was lacking a sewage pipe. I knew for certain that a sewage pipe existed but they refused to let me see the plans." 10 Despite participating in and winning several prestigious competitions, Rahm never received a public commission. Repeatedly refused building permits in her home canton Schaffhausen, she finally gave up her architectural practice in 1966 and founded the ALA publishing house in Zurich, which specialized in feminist literature and re-editions of books by forgotten female authors.

The biographies of successful women architects of the time testify that, without either teaming up or having the support of a male peer, a career in the field was nearly impossible. Many women architects came from architectural dynasties; for example, Gertrud Brenner (1905—1995), the first woman to join the Swiss Society of Engineers and Architects (SIA). 11 While Rahm, together

with her colleague Lisbeth Sachs (1914—2002), applied for the position of chief architect of *Saffa*, Annemarie Hubacher-Constam (1921—2012) was ultimately appointed to the job. Rahm herself assumed that the reason for her rejection was her status as an unmarried woman and that she did not have the support of a male business partner.

9 "Unter vier Augen," with Berta Rahm, Radio Munot, August 27, 1990, audiocassette tape, in Archiv zur Geschichte der Schweizer Frauenbewegung, Archive Berta Rahm, AGoF 521, 1:0-01, 21:10; translation by the authors. Original: "Die Brosamen, die von der Herren Tische fallen." https://www.gosteli.anton.ch/objects/17514 (accessed April 24, 2022).

fig. 3 Exterior view of the pavilion after its translocation to Gossau, Zurich, in 1958. Photograph: unknown. Source: Berta Rahm Architectural Collection, Ms1998-011, Special Collections and University Archives, University Libraries, Virginia Polytechnic Institute and State University

10 "Unter vier Augen," 21:55; translation by the authors. Original: "Und häm mier also Baubewilliginge nid gää. Lüüt händ zaom Byspiel gschrybe es hägi kei Abwasserleitung aond ich ha gwüsst, es isch en Abwasserleitung dört. Dänn häns mier verweigerert d Planysicht."

11 Gertrud Brenner's grandfather, Johann Joachim Brenner, founded the SIA in 1838. See *Historisches Lexikon der Schweiz*, https://hls-dhs-dss.ch/it/articles/042237/2002-12-18/ (accessed 24 April 2022).

fig. 4 Constructed section through the pavilion before its disassembly by ProSaffa1958-Pavillon. Composite point-cloud scan, 2020. Source: Scanvision, Zurich

Curating as Caretaking

The physical remains of Rahm's pavilion in its state of disrepair act as a material evidence for the erasure of Rahm and stood emblematically for those women architects of her generation whose work remains overlooked to this day. The remnants also actualized and extended feminist engagements revolving around the pavilion. Our aim as guest curators was not to distill one reading of the pavilion's past but to involve the community of the D-ARCH in the discourse around the pavilion's present and future. We understand our work as both caring for the pavilion's historic fabric and also making visible its immaterial histories to a wider public. Among the association—a heterogenous group of women from various backgrounds, disciplines, and generations—the question of how to care has been a continual point of discussion. Could an educational project help create awareness and ultimately raise the prospect of reconstruction? Could exhibition-making even be a means to gain new understandings of how the pavilion could work in the past, present, and future? The exhibition format that we ultimately developed continued the historical narrative of uses and spatial adaptations. It gave it, in a sense, a new chapter.

That we were granted this opportunity to display Rahm's pavilion is not coincidental. In 2021 Switzerland celebrated the fiftieth anniversary of women's suffrage, which led institutions and organizations nationwide to support women and feminist projects. Public concern about structural discrimination against women and minorities had built up in the years preceding the anniversary. [12] Global movements such as #MeToo only amplified the trend. When claims of sexual harassment at D-ARCH surfaced in 2019, [13] the calls for change voiced by a grassroots activist organization known as the Parity Group became louder than ever. [14]

We conceived the exhibition as a work in progress with five iterations entitled "Material Evidence," "Entangled Histories," "Images of Berta," "Close Encounters," and "The Feast." Every iteration kicked off with an event that aimed at connecting people and learning from one another. In addition to these

12 According to estimates, half a million people took to the streets on June 14, 2019. See "Frauenstreik 2019 – Ein historisches Ereignis," Amnesty International, June 17, 2019, https://www.amnesty.ch/de/themen/frauenrechte/sexualisierte-gewalt/dok/2019/frauenstreik-ein-historisches-ereignis (accessed April 24, 2022).

13 See Palle Petersen, "Professor X," *Hochparterre*, February 6, 2019, https://www.hochparterre.ch/nachrichten/architektur/blog/post/detail/professor-x/1549267882/ (accessed April 24, 2022).

14 During the Parity Talks 2020 we and a group of students presented the initial results of our work on the *Saffa* pavilion and Rahm at the guerilla exhibition *Making Space for Berta Rahm* (a precursor to the gta exhibition) that took place in an unoccupied office at the Department of Architecture (D-ARCH) at ETH Zurich. The Parity Group itself is a fluid group of students, assistants, and professors from the D-ARCH who meet to discuss issues around gender and diversity, organizing yearly Parity Talks. For a summary of the Parity Group's history, see Charlotte Malterre-Barthes and Torsten Lange for the Parity Group, "Architects Who Make a Fuss: A Speculative Investigation into the Archive of a Grassroots Initiative for Gender Parity at the Department of Architecture ETH Zurich, 2014–2017," *Site Magazine*, 2018, https://www.thesitemagazine.com/read/architectswhomakeafuss (accessed April 24, 2022). In 2021, the executive board of the D-ARCH answered these requests by commissioning the artist-led collective Engagement Arts (https://www.engagementarts.be/en, accessed April 24, 2022) to help the department analyze and tackle the systematic structures that were failing to sufficiently deter sexual harassment, sexism, and abuse of power. The results of the collective's work were presented in November 2021 as the ENGAGE D-ARCH Report, which is accessible only by ETH members. For more information, see Simon Zogg, "Ein Kulturwandel geht nicht auf Knopfdruck," ETH Zurich Staffnet, November 19, 2021, https://ethz.ch/services/de/news-und-veranstaltungen/intern-aktuell/archiv/2021/11/ein-kulturwandel-geht-nicht-auf-knopfdruck.html (accessed April 24, 2022).

five events, the space stayed open for informal gatherings or workshops, initiated by D-ARCH students and teachers.

Displaying Material Evidence

Not being preservationists by training, we had to develop an approach toward the careful conservation of the material. To minimize harm, the wood frames were purposely not joined together but individually attached to rails along the ceiling by a support system of rods and ratchet straps. **fig.5** To fit the large walls into the exhibition space, parts of the ceiling panels had to be removed. The wooden frame walls, each a self-contained structural element, traced the original constellation of the pavilion's floor plan. Yet we shifted them slightly, altering the distances between them, to create new rooms of differing shapes and sizes between the pavilion and the limits of the gallery. These mediating zones helped to open the pavilion conceptually and performatively to manifold uses. Since the inner paneling was not reassembled for the exhibition, the walls revealed how the Fural facade system of dovetailed corrugated aluminum sheets was rolled onto its fixtures. The sixty-three-year-old aluminum cladding proved to be durable and had lost little of its appearance and functionality. The translucent panels of a Scobalit wall (made of glass-fiber-reinforced polyester resins developed in the 1950s) diffusely illuminated the space behind. We did not assemble the interior fittings or the roof, only setting up the original wardrobe next to the entrance of the exhibition space.

fig.5 View of the support system of rods and ratchet straps stabilizing the pavilion in the exhibition *The Power of Mushrooms: Berta Rahm's Pavilion for the Saffa 58.* Photograph: Nelly Rodriguez, ETH Zurich, Hönggerberg, 2021

Unearthing Entangled Histories

The second iteration focused on the pavilion's history of use as a staff canteen and show kitchen at a mushroom farm in Gossau. The mushrooms proved to be a useful metaphor. Our investigation drew on the work of anthropologist Anna Lowenhaupt Tsing and biologist Merlin Sheldrake, who write economic histories of friction in an increasingly globalized world through the figure

fig. 6 a, b Clara Richard and Nicolò Krättli, *Family Portraits*. Photography, paper on aluminum, 2020, Gossau, Zurich. Courtesy of the artists

of mycelia. Mushrooms are made up of tiny threads (mycelia) that travel underground, connecting the roots of different plants and even different species in an area, allowing them to exchange nutrients and information that might be missing in their immediate surroundings. In our exhibition they came to stand for the often covert organization of feminist, women, and LGBTQIA+ networks and the unpredictable offspring of activism that sprout when conditions

are right and that survive if conditions are ideal. In the case of Rahm's pavilion, a chain of individual efforts culminated in collective action. In stark contrast to this connective nature, we added photographs of the interior spaces of the mushroom factory to the exhibition. The photographs by Clara Richard and Nicolò Krättli, titled *Family Portraits*, capture the industrialized process of breeding mushrooms from inoculated substrate packages.   **fig. 6 a, b**

Projecting Images of Berta

Iteration three built on the diaries and other surviving records from the archive of Berta Rahm held at the International Archive of Women in Architecture (IAWA) at Virginia Tech in Blacksburg, Virginia. These traces were brought into conversation with present-day experiences of women in architectural practice. While some things have changed since Rahm's time, others have not. Aspects of Rahm's own accounts of her professional and private life still sound familiar: sexism at work, barred access to

fig. 7 a, b Two views into the reading room of the *Saffa* pavilion Zurich. Left, from 2021. Photograph: Urs Siegenthaler. Right, from 1958. Source: Berta Rahm Architectural Collection, Ms1998-011, Special Collections and University Archives, University Libraries, Virginia Polytechnic Institute and State University

15 Eliana Perotti and Katia Frey, "Images of Rahm," from the untitled exhibition handout for *The Power of Mushrooms: Berta Rahm's pavilion for the Saffa 58*, iteration 2.

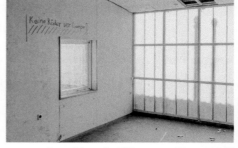

power positions, the income gap between women architects and their male colleagues, among others. Looking closely at her biography, we tried to contextualize these struggles. We asked ourselves to what extent Rahm's experience stood for an entire generation of women architects. To do so, we invited Eliana Perotti and Katia Frey from the "Saffa 1958" research group to discuss the challenges that archival absences and a lack of sources pose for reconstructing the careers of Swiss women architects active in the interwar and postwar eras. **15** **fig. 7 a, b**

Enabling Close Encounters

Until the semester break in summer 2021, access to the exhibition was restricted by COVID measures on the grounds of the ETH campus, and the first three events thus took place online. The last two stages, set for the autumn 2021 semester, finally offered a chance to inhabit the spaces of the exhibition, to be with one another. "Close Encounters" celebrated the publication of Rahm's diaries, edited by architecture student Friederike Merkel and the curatorial team. **16** **fig. 8 a, b, c** In the summer of 2016, Merkel had visited Rahm's holiday house, Laueli, in Hasliberg on an excursion as part of her studies at ETH Zurich. The owner of the house, Iris Kaufmann, brought along one of Rahm's diaries, in which she describes her work. This fired Merkel's curiosity and led her to study all of Rahm's diaries in the hope of shedding light on the architect's relation to her profession from 1935 to 1950. With the aim of creating a more intimate setting for the encounter with Rahm's personal accounts, we invited HOTMAILHOTNAIL to set up a pop-up nail studio in the exhibition space. Visitors could dive into Rahm's inner life within an intimate atmosphere of bodily well-being. Known for their collaborations with artists, HOTMAILHOTNAIL uses the guise of a nail studio to appropriate and redefine city spaces and create meeting places. They develop nail art with clients as a form of artistry and self-expression. With deck chairs and a view of the waterfront, the nail studio itself referenced the sun deck that was part of the *Saffa 58* pavilion.

Coming Together: The Feast

Finally, the last iteration, "The Feast," unified the *Power of Mushrooms* exhibition with the Annexe project, which in the summer of 2021 had toured Switzerland with a reinterpretation of the interior of Rahm's pavilion. Annexe was led by fellow association members Elena Chiavi, Kathrin Füglister, Amy Perkins, and Myriam Uzor. During its tour to Geneva, St. Gallen and Zurich, Annexe had supported lectures, discussion rounds, readings, workshops, film screenings, and cooking evenings. It had consisted of a reproduction and abstraction of four pieces of furniture Rahm specifically designed for the pavilion: the generous built-in kitchen, two long tables on a raised platform on either side of the reading room and the quiet room, and an L-shape table with shelving. For "The Feast" we brought Annexe's furniture into the pavilion and celebrated the merging of its exterior with its interior by inviting the collective Kitchuan to facilitate a cooking session and subsequent feast of mushroom dumplings on the opening evening. The kitchenette became the kitchen, the shelf turned into a bar, and the table served as a workstation.

16 Friederike Merkel et al., eds., *Berta Rahms Diaries 1935–1950* (Zurich: gta Exhibitions, 2021).

fig. 8 a, b, c View of the exhibition installation for the event and exhibition iteration "Close Encounters" within the exhibition *The Power of Mushrooms: Berta Rahm's Pavilion for the Saffa 58*. Photograph: Jana Jenarin, ETH Zurich, Hönggerberg, 2021

Milena Buchwalder, Sonja Flury, and Dorothee Hahn Caring to Know

On the evening of the opening of "The Feast," many of the people who had become active in rescuing the pavilion or had contributed to the exhibition program gathered around a table for the first time. The hope was that their bonds would remain and grow through the future task of reconstructing the pavilion in a visible, accessible public space. **fig.9 a, b**

Ongoing use of any building is ambivalent, as it both preserves and consumes the building's material and its context. Had Rahm's pavilion not been in continuous use since *Saffa 1958*, it likely would have disappeared a long time ago, as institutional and soci-etal attention to the legacy of Swiss women architects has been sparse, periodic, and partial. The publicity around the rescue mission and the subsequent actions of our association raised awareness of the pavilion's historical context, and today it is no longer perceived as a mere functional space but as a potential future (counter-)monument to Rahm, *Saffa 1958*'s historical legacy, and its engaged women protagonists. The pavilion is a reminder of

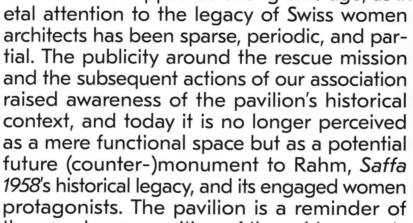

fig.9 a, b View of the exhibition installation for the event and exhibition iteration "The Feast" within the exhibition *The Power of Mushrooms: Berta Rahm's Pavilion for the Saffa 58*. Photograph: Simona Mele, ETH Zurich, Hönggerberg, 2021

the overdue recognition of the achievements and biographies of these and other women in architectural historiography. In re-erecting and reusing the Rahm's pavilion, we took on the responsibility not only to reopen this rare artifact to a larger public but also to maintain and embed the legacy of *Saffa 1958* and its women pro-tagonists in the collective memory by creating a space for the untold histories, presences, and futures of women in architecture. We are currently amid advocating politically and contacting the authorities whose approvals are necessary for the pavilion's re-erection. Still pending are questions about an appropriate location and future use of the pavilion, the quantity of original structure we will be able to keep, and how to add new material.

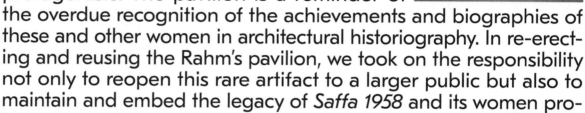

In analogy to rhizomatic networks, the pavilion within the exhibition acted as a con-nective tissue within a wider network of knowledge production. It became a physical anchor that enabled us to address and highlight current initiatives supporting feminism in the field of architecture. Beyond preserving the past, our work of caring for Rahm's pavilion is concerned first and foremost with the imagi-nation of, and performative enactment of, a more equitable and diverse profession.

The Servantful House
A Case Study of Venezuelan *Quintas*
Valentina Davila

Homes

Modern Latin America's colonial past, with its marked inequality in the distribution of wealth, has resulted in a segregated population and service relationships based on gender, race, and class. This pattern has proved strikingly persistent across different times and political systems: democracy, authoritarian military rule, popular revolutions, and socialist experiments, including Venezuela's own socialist experience since the late 1990s. A tradition of hiring impoverished domestic workers to care for the middle and upper classes has long persisted. Beginning in the middle of the twentieth century, a period of oil-infused economic prosperity magnified Venezuela's socioeconomic differences. In contrast to other economies, the number of impoverished women entering domestic service multiplied. [1] This dynamic strengthened a culture of dependence upon service workers, materializing in a vernacular bourgeois housing type locally known as the *quinta*, a general term of uncertain origin that implies affluence, land, property, walls, and, within them, the trappings of status. **fig.1**

Quintas are large, detached homes surrounded by gardens, picturesque vegetation, and diverse interior and exterior spaces for social events and private life. The interior architecture of a *quinta* typically follows a pattern that separates the core family's living spaces from those prescribed for women hired to perform maintenance and care work. For service areas, including the kitchen, laundry, and domestic workers' bedrooms, homeowners use cheaper, lower-quality materials, which amplify a sense of displacement from the rest of the house. This combination of spatial segregation and austere materiality reflects an unspoken need to separate the middle-class's domestic experiences from those of "others." Depending on their place in the building, employee and employer have markedly different personal stories. While inextricably linked through the dynamics of space and care work, the workers' and the employers' experiences are two sides of a multilayered reality.

This article focuses on the relationship between domestic architecture and care work from the perspective of Venezuelan domestic workers. It looks at *quintas* to highlight how the figure of the domestic care worker has influenced Venezuelan architecture and material culture. By placing these domestic workers at the center rather than at the margins of the narrative, it asks

Valentina Davila is a doctoral candidate at the Peter Guo-hua Fu School of Architecture at McGill University in Montreal.

1 According to 2001 census statistics from the Instituto Nacional de Estadística de Venezuela, some 5.7 percent of the workforce is employed as domestic servants. For comparison, the United States has around 0.5 percent of its workforce so employed, and Australia 0.1 percent. See *Domestic Workers across the World: Global and Regional Statistics and the Extent of Legal Protection* (Geneva: International Labor Office, 2013), 126.

how architecture shapes the dynamics of labor, especially care work. Inversely, to what extent does the figure of the domestic worker shape architecture?

My own starting position, with all its attendant bias, is what makes my observations possible: I grew up in the 1980s inside a beautiful *quinta* located in an upper-class neighborhood. My unquestioned privilege hinges on multiple generations of exploitative domestic labor relations. Our four-bedroom, 300-square-meter house was home for me, my brother, my mother, and a domestic worker named Mariana and her two children. From my vantage point, ours was a happy childhood. In hindsight, however, precisely those differences that were most successfully normalized now seem to me to be most jarring. These retrospective insights are at the core of my ethnographic method. Today, my memories of growing up as a member of the employer's family transform when I shift the narrative to fit Mariana and her children's perspectives. From an early age, labor dynamics teach Venezuelan children to differentiate between those who serve and those who are served, perpetuating an ideology in which race, gender, and labor correlate in specific ways. **fig. 2**

2 See Juhani Pallasmaa, "Identity, Intimacy and Domicile — Notes on the Phenomenology of Home," in David N. Benjamin, David Stea, and Eje Arén, eds., *The Home: Words, Interpretations, Meanings and Environments* (Aldershot: Avebury, 1995), 131–47, here 131.

3 See Mary Romero, *The Maid's Daughter: Living Inside and Outside the American Dream* (New York: New York University Press, 2011).

Architecture frames a set of rituals, routines, and everyday relations that inform people's standing in society. [2] The position of care workers' children inside the house determines their status in the broader social world, not least through the privileges visibly denied to them but given to employers' children. [3] Housing is therefore both a model and a crucible of the country's situation, an essential contributor to the social conflicts that have fueled Venezuela's ongoing turmoil.

Shortly after obtaining my architecture degree in Venezuela, I collaborated with a small domestic workers' co-op working to obtain federal funding to build their homes. This professional engagement permitted me to enter the *quintas* from the service entrance, both literally and figuratively: my experience as the domestic worker's "guest" stood in sharp contrast to my previous position at the receiving end of care. This was the moment at which I began to realize the different ways domestic space could be inhabited and that, in Venezuela, separate personal stories develop depending on their subject's place in the building. This interaction marked the beginning of my research into the territory of the Venezuelan domestic worker.

A decade later, from 2017 to 2020, I spent several months studying domestic workers' laboring and living conditions through multisited ethnographic work in private homes. To ensure that domestic workers were not forced to participate, I approached them informally in public spaces in the late afternoon hours after they had finished their work. In my hometown, Merida, I visited areas (e.g., La Mara, Las Tapias, Alto Chama, and Belensate) where I knew domestic care workers were employed. Once they left the *quintas*, these women became hypervisible on the empty streets. **fig. 3**

Only after the domestic workers agreed to participate in my research did I contact their employers. I asked for a short interview and permission to access and photograph their homes. Most willingly opened their doors to me because of our shared class status. Once inside the *quintas*, I focused on domestic workers' spatial experiences, following in their steps, entering the buildings through the back, and remaining with them at all times. I acknowledge the limitations of my own practice to map and document the workers' embodied experiences. In many ways, I am attempting to act as a translator and commentator navigating between the two extremes of labor dynamics. **4**

Despite the fact that the *quinta* presents a form of housing for the upper and affluent middle classes, this type is not a European import but is part of the vernacular building tradition of Latin America, and in some crucial regards it spatially reflects particular local relationships. The act of ethnographic (re)drawing of these particular buildings captures the spaces of those serving and being served in their entanglement. Drawings have the capacity to archive undocumented and invisible labor even in the spaces between objects and in the relation of sites of care, labor, and

4 See Debī Mahāśvetā and Gayatri Chakravorty Spivak, *Imaginary Maps: Three Stories* (New York: Routledge, 1995), xxiii.

fig. 1 A Venezuelan *quinta* built in 1971 and impeccably maintained by its architect-owner. Merida, Venezuela. Photograph: Valentina Davila, 2020

fig. 2 The employer and domestic worker's grandchildren find common ground to play and jump at the back of the house. Merida, Venezuela. Photograph: Valentina Davila, 2017

fig. 3 Domestic workers walking in the streets of La Mara, an upper-class neighborhood populated with *quintas*. Merida, Venezuela. Photograph: Valentina Davila, 2020

5 Huda Tayob, "Subaltern Architectures: Can Drawing 'Tell' a Different Story?," *Architecture and Culture* 6, no. 1 (2018), 203–22, here 214.

refuge. **5** My method included dimensioned drawings of floor plans that illustrated spatial relations such as those of the constrained service areas. I annotated these plans with subjective observations based on my field notes, seeking out seemingly insignificant details that are revealing nevertheless. **fig. 4 a**

Later, I translated the initial drawings into architectural plans for the *quinta*. They form an atlas of domestic care workers' spaces. **fig. 4 b** In Venezuela, the consultation of public records frequently depends on partisanship, favoritism, or corruption, and the infrastructures for storing and maintaining documents are often in a poor state. In the context of the flawed bureaucratic control of municipal building records (including architectural plans), my decision to draw the buildings and publicize these drawings is also politicized.

Oil

Before turning to the workers' everyday experiences of *quintas*, we need to understand how the socioeconomic developments in twentieth-century Venezuela created a proliferation of middle-class households that hired domestic workers as symbols of status and wealth. In the early twentieth century, Venezuela transformed from an agricultural economy with few substantial exports other than coffee and cacao to become, for some decades, the world's largest exporter of oil. [6] The switch from an almost feudal society to a progress-oriented rentier state profoundly impacted the country's urban landscape and domestic architecture. However, the transformation of the built environment, the modernization of architecture, and urban development provided only the illusion of progress and did not result in prosperity across population sectors. Instead, the growing

6 For episodes in this well-studied history, see Franklin Tugwell, *The Politics of Oil in Venezuela* (Stanford, CA: Stanford University Press, 1975); and Edwin Lieuwen, *Petroleum in Venezuela: A History* (Berkeley and Los Angeles: University of California Press, 1955), 116.

fig. 4 a *In situ* sketch showing the drawing process and personal notes and codes. Field notes, Valentina Davila, 2020

fig. 4 b Re-drawn using architectural conventions. Valentina Davila, 2020

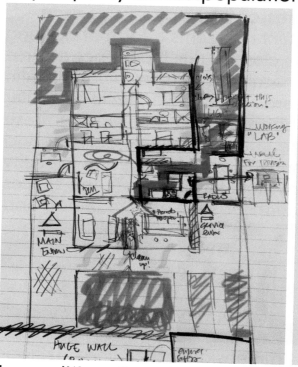
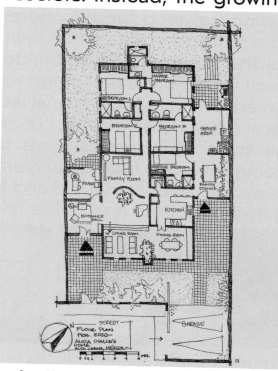

inequalities disrupted the modernization process, which could not resolve the contradictions of the unwavering colonial structure clinging to social, political, and economic power. [7]

The radical change of economic structures caused a rural exodus and an unprecedented influx of people into the urban centers, which underwent a housing shortage. From 1941 to 1971, the rural areas in the Andes became almost depopulated. In addition, poverty pushed numerous underage and adult women, many of them of indigenous origin, to leave their homes "just as much as men did," [8] usually to procure a position as domestic workers in nearby urban centers.

For thousands of disenfranchised girls and women in Venezuela, domestic care work is the only form of wage labor that

7 Penélope Plaza-Azuaje, *Culture as Renewable Oil: How Territory, Bureaucratic Power and Culture Coalesce in the Venezuelan Petrostate* (Abingdon, UK: Routledge, 2019), 3.

8 Elizabeth Gackstetter Nichols and Kimberly J. Morse, *Venezuela* (Santa Barbara, CA: ABC-CLIO, LLC, 2010), 158.

provides immediate access to the even more urgent prerequisites of food and shelter. In one of my case studies, Elena left her home at age nine to clean, cook, wash, and iron for a middle-class family; she had to combine these responsibilities with caring for the family's two children, who were only a couple of years younger than herself. Elena explained that her family's agricultural production barely sufficed for domestic consumption. When her mother gave birth to another baby, Elena's entering the workforce meant at least one less mouth to feed and the possibility of earning a meager income to help relatives back home. **fig. 5**

Quintas

The prestigious materials and desirable location of *quintas* broadcast the financial means of their middle- and upper-class owners. These spacious buildings come with high maintenance costs for gardening, repair, and restoration. In addition to the material conditions of the house, which demand onerous cleaning, dusting, polishing, waxing, and washing, everyday life requires someone to cook, serve, and care for the family. From the beginning, architects and homeowners planned these labor-consuming buildings with the expectation of support from a full-time resident domestic worker.

Life inside the large, clean *quintas* keeps employers and workers entangled in an exploitative dynamic of labor. The typology of the *quintas* embodies architecture's ability to limit women's freedom. On average, each *quinta's* footprint encompasses 200 to 500 square meters divided into public, private, and service areas. The public spaces include the dining and living rooms and, at times, a sunroom, allowing ample space for social gatherings of family and friends. The private zone is the family's most intimate environment and usually consists of three or four bedrooms, an equal number of bathrooms, and a den. Finally, the service area consolidates all the reproductive and life-sustaining activities at the back of the house. Homeowners and architects conceive it as a space for domestic workers to live near and work for, but away from, the hiring family. **fig. 6**

Middle-class families hire an outsider to take over the household's care work and reproductive labor. Although these housing dynamics awkwardly pierce the nuclear family's private bubble, they do not trump the benefits of outsourcing the strenuous domestic tasks. For gender theorist Judith Butler, "up againstness" expresses this type of extreme interpersonal proximity. [9] Architects and homeowners rely on space and material strategies to establish proper distancing and alleviate the anxieties brought about by "unwilled cohabitation." [10] An established

[9] Judith Butler, "Precarious Life, Vulnerability, and the Ethics of Cohabitation," *The Journal of Speculative Philosophy* 26, no. 2 (2012), 134–51.

[10] Butler, "Precarious Life, Vulnerability, and the Ethics of Cohabitation," 134.

catalog of standard design elements—remote location, walls, small windows, and swiveling doors—offers the necessary tools to separate the coexisting domestic realities: well-being and conviviality from hard work and solitude. Much like the spatial relations of domestic housing under South African apartheid described by Rebecca Ann Ginsburg, *quintas* enclose two "different social and physical spheres" within a limited radius. 11 These spheres are supported by spatial rules and material regulations that separate the family and the resident domestic worker. For example, traditional designs limit the service bedroom to around 2 by 3

11 Rebecca Ann Ginsburg, "At Home with Apartheid: The Cultural Landscapes of Suburban Johannesburg, 1960–1976" (PhD diss., University of California, Berkeley, 2001), 4.

fig.5 Elena's employer gave her a white first Communion dress and a party to celebrate the sacrament of Confirmation. Clara and Sara, her employer's children, stand next to Elena, who is only a couple of years older than them but is employed as their carer. Merida, Venezuela, ca. 1962. Photograph: private collection

meters, allowing barely enough space for a single bed, closet, and old TV set. Inside, cheap materials and worn furniture characterize the room and the en suite bathroom, and the spaces are usually deprived of daylight or natural ventilation. The service area's marginal location in the building and its below-standard materials solidify the class-formation process. 12

12 Elise van Nederveen Meerkerk, "Introduction: Domestic Work in the Colonial Context: Race, Color, and Power in the Household," in Dirk Hoerder, Elise van Nederveen Meerkerk, and Silke Neunsinger, eds., *Toward a Global History of Domestic and Caregiving Workers*, Studies in Global Migration History (Leiden: Brill, 2015), 245–53, here 248.

According to a simplistic reading, the spatial distribution in the house relegates the domestic workers to a subordinate position with no possibility of social connections or recreation with their employers. The home becomes a vector that extends colonial encounters through space and time. Strict spatial limitations cinch the workers' alienation and guarantee their psychological, ideological, and social distance. 13 This particular narrative is well-known; however, the actual mechanisms of exploitation are both more internalized and more complex. I found that all *quinta* residents expect clear limits and follow the established spatial cues to separate themselves. That is, the need for privacy

13 Elsbeth Locher-Scholten, "'So Close and yet So Far': European Ambivalence toward Javanese Servants," in *Women and the Colonial State: Essays on Gender and Modernity in the Netherlands Indies 1900–1942* (Amsterdam University Press, 2000), 85–120, here 101.

goes both ways. For example, Patricia and her employer, Nancy, are the only residents in the house; therefore, they keep each other company in front of the TV at night. However, respecting the strict rules of deferential behavior compensates for breaching the spatial hierarchies. While Nancy sits on the den's sofa, Patricia stands behind the ironing board folding clothes or ironing bedding. "I like keeping busy during our nightly routine. I wouldn't feel right sitting next to her on the sofa; it would be weird. I have my bedroom for that, and I enjoy resting in my own time inside my space; when I work, I work, and when I rest, I rest." 14 Following the established spatial patterns helps these women navigate unprecedented forms of intimacy.

Inside the home, small-scale spatial metaphors reflect a strict social organization. Feminist anthropologist Shirley Ardener argues that design elements such as walls, corridors, and doors are not neutral but influential components that delimit space and determine people's domestic realities. 15 For example, the construction materials differ inside Elena's *quinta* depending on their positioning. The public and private areas' windows have thick, carved wood frames, while the service part has simple, black metal ones. The long, lateral party wall has natural brick veneers throughout the front yard, but the veneers are unmaintained once they cross the threshold to the servant's quarters, and consequently stained. The carefully maintained exterior terra-cotta floors transform into cement surfaces past the service entrance. The house's wood or marble floors halt at the kitchen door and switch to ceramic or terrazzo. These abrupt material changes reinforce the front and back divide, thus creating a phenomenology of service. The service area's consistency, size, and neglected nature speak of profoundly ingrained class arrogance that assumes domestic workers' needs and wants are different from their employers. From employers I often heard, "this is a good space for them; they wouldn't appreciate finer things, and if given to them, they would break or damage them." 16 The construction embodies the employers' conception of their workers' character as humble, improvident, lazy, ignorant, and unappreciative of quality. 17 Another factor, however, was the underlying anxiety that, if the difference between worker and employer was not actively maintained, it might collapse into a threatening overfamiliarity. **fig.7**

14 Patricia, interview by author, Merida, January 21, 2020.

15 Shirley Ardener, "The Partition of Space," in Jane Rendell, Barbara Penner, and Iain Borden, eds., *Gender Space Architecture: An Interdisciplinary Introduction* (London: Routledge, 1993), 112–17, here 113.

fig.6 A typical domestic worker's bedroom. Merida, Venezuela. Photograph: Valentina Davila, 2020

16 Leticia, interview by author, Merida, February 8, 2020.

17 These coincide with some of the attributes that Venezuelan musician, educator, and diplomat Manuel Carreño attributed to the poor. In 1853, Carreño published his "Manual of Civility and Good Manners," a book that, in Latin America and Spain, became the quintessential guide in lessons and instructions on how educated people should behave in public and private places, such as home, family, school, and work. See Manuel Antonio Carreño, *Compendio del Manual de urbanidad y buenas maneras: Arreglado [por el mismo] para el uso de las escuelas de ambos sexos* (New York: D. Appleton, 1860).

Working, Not Living, Inside the *Quintas*

Interacting with domestic workers, I soon identified the employer's proximity concerns as unfounded. For the working women, *quintas* represent nothing more than a workplace and a means to generate income and support their own families. Immediately after emerging from the service bedroom in their work outfit, domestic workers are constantly moving, following a strict self-crafted routine to maximize time and increase their productivity. In our exchanges, live-in domestic work-

ers never considered their employers to be family. While most participating employers and workers appeared to have excellent relations based on mutual respect and even feelings of love, workers clearly understood their contractual relations, sometimes better than their employers. As a result, domestic workers circumscribed their relationship with employers to the perimeter of the *quintas*, where they occupy a subordinate position. On the other hand, they enjoyed describing their own houses and spatial interventions, such as kitchens, large altars, and bedroom additions. Workers talked lovingly about their own absent homes, where they belonged, center stage, next to their children, grandchildren, animals, and flowers. They laughed or cried when sharing their expectations for the future or their concern about their relatives' bad choices. Many would break off our conversation when employers entered the kitchen, demonstrating how they sharply divide their personal and professional lives. **fig. 8**

Domestic workers keep pictures and small family tokens inside their purses instead of exposed in their *quinta* bedroom, even if they sleep there six out of the seven days of the week. Sometimes, live-in domestic workers erect small, portable altars

next to their beds; however, they keep the spatial interventions to a minimum. **18** For example, they place their clothing in the closet and their personal care items in the bathroom but never personalize or decorate their surroundings. Next to a typewriter and a rotary phone, I observed a pair of golden high heels in the closet in Dora's bedroom; when I asked who they belonged to, she shrugged, no idea, but still she did not move them. This attitude reflects their mercantile relationship with the house, a place they would never consider a home.

Inside the *quintas*, employers expect workers to coordinate their movements around the house so as to avoid awkward interactions with guests and family members. However, the domestic worker's invisibility sows a problematic seed; delegating

fig. 7 The exterior area at the back of the house. Merida, Venezuela. Photograph: Valentina Davila, 2020

fig. 8 A domestic worker and her employer inside the kitchen. When the employer came in to check on her, the worker said to her son on the phone, "I have to go, call me after work." Merida, Venezuela. Photograph: Valentina Davila, 2020

18 For more on the domestic workers' altars, see Valentina Davila, "Altars of Hope: Venezuelan Domestic Workers and the Material Culture of the Divine," *Buildings and Landscapes: Journal of the Vernacular Architecture Forum* 29, no. 1 (2022), 67–93.

socially reproductive labor breeds an idea of a nuclear family exempted from any care work, erasing the physical and emotional effort required to fuel households and societies. [19] The standard architectural practice of segregating the kitchen and the service area at the back of the house disconnects living from working, cooking from eating, cleanliness from scrubbing, building from maintaining, and loving from caring.

Domestic workers keep a strict distance from their employers' personal choices. Employers see *quintas* as a home worth protecting, while workers perceive it only as a place of employment worth preserving. This internalized perception prevents them from fostering strong feelings of attachment or assuming any responsibility for the building's arrangement. For example, I asked Sioly if she would like to sleep somewhere else in the house. After giving me a confused look, she said,

"What do you mean? I come here to work, not to sit and enjoy the view! I have my house for that. There, I make all the decisions: the color of the walls, the size of the furniture, and the kitchen's shape; here, my only responsibility is to clean. The rest is up to the owners." [20]

Contrary, then, to the employer's belief that the distinction in spaces refers to the character of the worker, it is clear to domestic workers that the *quinta*'s architecture and material culture reflects the employers' values and prejudices. I learned from domestic workers that they prefer having a designated space

away from or invisible to the family. The possibility of operating away from the employer's private life corresponds with their professional stance and limits interruptions. Workers prefer to operate in an enclosed kitchen and remote service area, a layout that responds to their need for concentration and privacy. The back of the house is a center of operation with reduced opportunities for interruptions or monitoring, a zone to organize their work and regain professional agency. fig.9

Domestic workers have ample professional experience. For most, a lifetime in domestic service offers a profound understanding of the processes necessary to maximize efficiency. I noticed that each domestic worker I interviewed was a highly organized individual who systemized her tasks, developed a mental map of the house, and coordinated it with the available resources to complete her work efficiently. Workers calibrate their movements around working patterns, rotating between the large service area at the back and ephemeral cleaning and polishing

19 See bell hooks, *Feminist Theory: From Margin to Center,* 3rd ed. (New York: Routledge, 2015).

20 Sioly, interview by author, Merida, February 21, 2020.

fig.9 Inside the service area, domestic workers feel free to be themselves, away from the family's gaze. Here, Amanda shows me how clean her hands are after using her home-made soap. Merida, Venezuela. Photograph: Valentina Davila, 2020 stations, consisting of a bucket and rag or brush, at the front of the house. For instance, workers handwash the clothes in different stages: soak, treat stains, submerge under stones for an hour, swish, scrub, rinse, and repeat. They move away from the laundry station to wash bathrooms or clean bedrooms between the handwashing steps.

Employers often disassociate from everything maintenance-related, including the spaces at the back of the house, which they perceive as dirty, ugly, and disorganized. They expect workers to make sense of and operate in those precarious spaces. They also limit the employees' demands for additional brushes, rubber gloves, a specific detergent, or a new bucket. Hence, care workers become master administrators operating with restricted technology, supplies, and space. They repurpose shirts into rags, fill wine bottles with cleaning detergents, employ large receptacles as buckets, and polish mirrors and windows with old newspapers. Domestic workers transform the back into a maintenance hub organized by activity. Their bodies move confidently from one station to another, honoring a process that relies on simultaneity, coordination, and organization to achieve daily tasks.

fig. 10 Cleaning at the back of the house. Merida, Venezuela. Photograph: Valentina Davila, 2020

Domestic workers understand the back as an area free from the employer's control or concern. This power void allows workers to provisionally control space, make changes, and develop specific processes. For example, they keep buckets full of water around the laundry area; these reserves are vital during the frequent water outages to boil, cook, wash, clean, and flush.

Workers use their practical knowledge to solve all sorts of domestic matters and construct allegiances both licit and illicit, with materials, animals, and human beings. Betty secretly feeds a stray cat she named Peluda; it hangs around the house and hunts rats and mice.

"Señora doesn't like animals, and she wouldn't like to know I've been feeding a cat. But I know for sure she would die if the house's rat population kept growing. So Peluda and I have an agreement, I feed her, and she gets rid of pests. She especially loves cockroaches. Now I need to teach her to stop killing the birds too!" [21]

21 Betty, interview by author, Merida, January 28, 2020.

Josefina fig. 10 prepared a large stone to sharpen the knives at the back. Nearby the kitchen, she also assembled a "secret" garden to grow herbs and spices that she affirms taste better because they grow in soil she brought from her hometown.

Inside their sphere, domestic workers recreate a world of their own, a bubble that they can mostly control. They tune the radio to their favorite station to connect with their social worlds, humming to familiar music, checking on bus schedules, or learning about issues important to their communities. In the privacy of the service area, they take microbreaks to answer their families' text messages or respond to personal phone calls. Inside

their realm, workers take small but significant steps to improve the *quinta's* state without explaining them to anyone—except me. For example, Ingrid boils and grinds the plantain peels to enhance the plants' health. Alicia sews discarded linen shirts into filters for the "imported" drip coffee maker to solve the shortage of paper filters. And Olga offers a piece of cake or lemons from her home to the trash collectors in exchange for them not throwing and breaking the plastic rubbish bins. Domestic workers do not take anything from the *quinta* to use in their home unless the employer has discarded it or given it to them. For instance, Betty freezes animal bones and other organic residues to feed her animals and plants back home. And most workers save half of their assigned meals to take home to their families. All this would perhaps not be possible but for their invisibility.

Luz is a fifty-five-year-old worker, one of the few specializing in ironing. Unlike regular domestic workers, ironing workers are hard to find and keep. Therefore, employers tend to comply with their needs and increase their salaries. She claimed to accept work only in houses with a service area at the back where she could plug in the iron, turn on her radio, and "disconnect" from the world. 22 fig. 11

"I need my space. Somewhere where I set the ironing table on one side and a pile of clothes on the other. That way, I can sort my work and settle into my routine. I can't iron with people around me, looking, asking questions, and demanding that I do other things. I need to maximize my time, and I need isolation from the family's hustle." 23

Luz explained that working in the back of the house guarantees the required space and time to accomplish her tasks. She is a perfectionist who takes pride in her work and does not like changes. "I do things a certain way. Ironing requires lots of light and ventilation, two electric outlets, and space to hang the clothes. I like to work in the same houses because I know what to expect." Pepa and I listened to Luz speak while following her hand movements, mesmerized by how she perfectly ironed what seemed like thousands of pleats in one of the employers' skirts. Pepa smiled and nodded to Luz's comments. She then said,

fig. 11 Luz explains that ironing is an activity that requires light, ventilation, and… music. Merida, Venezuela. Photograph: Valentina Davila, 2020

22 Ironing is one of the most time-consuming and difficult activities in the house. I found that most workers dislike doing it, and some even specify upon hiring that they will not iron the family's clothes. Therefore, employers either hire women who specialize in ironing to come weekly or monthly, or they bring their delicate garments to the drycleaners.

23 Luz, interview by author, Merida, February 4, 2020.

"I agree. I did not enjoy the times I worked in small apartments or one of those new houses that muchachas—young girls—*now like with the open kitchen to cook in front of everyone. I don't have a place to change or shower, and I can't turn on the radio; I feel like everyone is watching me. It is too uncomfortable. I usually avoid working in those places. There is no space for one to do one's job freely."* [24]

24 Josefa, interview by author, Merida, February 10, 2020.

Thus, domestic workers understand the space at the back as an essential part of their contract. A reconfiguration of the home that eradicates the service area but still employs domestic workers disrupts the spatial dynamics that allow a separation between living and working.

The Postrevolutionary Home

Today, Venezuela is far from the wealthy country in which the *quintas* proliferated. Two decades have passed since the beginning of the Bolivarian Revolution, a new political era inaugurated by the late president Hugo Chavez and characterized by opposition to American "imperialism" and a robust ideological connection and trade relationship with Russia, China, Iran, and Cuba. Regardless of intentions, Chavez's planned economy, antipoverty campaigns, and social policies all collapsed under the weight of corruption and plummeting oil prices. [25]

25 For a recent book on the topic, popular rather than scholarly, see Raúl Gallegos, *Crude Nation: How Oil Riches Ruined Venezuela* (Lincoln: University of Nebraska Press, 2016).

Venezuela's economic and political crisis affects all social strata. The economic crisis has severely limited the middle class's disposable income, but domestic workers are among the most stricken group. Hundreds of thousands of women, around 15 percent of the female workforce, [26] continue to rely on domestic work as their primary source of income. Many of them earn between one and two dollars per day, and some trade one of their workdays for their meals. Marcela explains,

26 "Who Are Domestic Workers," International Labour Organization, https://www.ilo.org/global/topics/domestic-workers/who/lang--en/index.htm (accessed April 26, 2022).

fig. 12 Throughout economic and political crisis, *quintas* continue to require large amounts of work for their maintenance. Merida, Venezuela. Photograph: Valentina Davila, 2020

"I thought I was poor before Chavez, but I was so wrong! I didn't have much additional money, but I still managed to go to the store, find everything I needed and eat well. Twenty years ago, if I only had ten bolivares, I would buy ten bolivares worth of rice or cheese from the store. Now, even if I had ten bolivares, the supermarkets are empty! There's nothing I could buy. And did you hear Señora? Did she tell you she needs to pay for her cancer treatment in dollars? She cannot afford that! So it turns out that now we are all poor! She pays for two of the three days I work here. On the third day, I come, eat breakfast and lunch, and we divide the leftovers, so I have something to take home for

my husband. I am lucky that I found work the remaining two days and some Saturdays cleaning a private hospital." [27]

27 Marcela, interview by author, Merida, February 28, 2020.

The middle class's diminished economic power eliminates the possibility of hiring a full-time domestic worker. Moreover, the decline in service demand coincides with high rates of male and female unemployment, directly affecting domestic workers and lowering their already dismal possibilities of negotiating salaries and working conditions. This study's participants had all at some point fulfilled the common ambition of moving out of the employer's house and into their own homes. However, gas shortages and the increasing price of public transportation have pushed many domestic workers out of their homes and back into live-in work. "What can we do with a house of our own and no money? For us, being a poor women means either working or dying. Luckily, I love working as much as I love living." [28] **fig. 12**

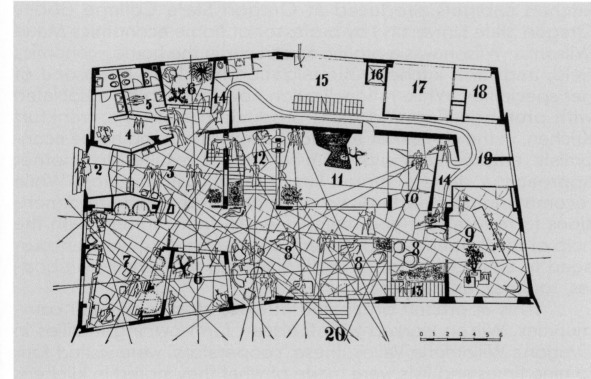

28 Betty, interview by author, Merida, January 28, 2020.

fig. 13 The social arrangements of the contemporary *quinta* is also mirrored in the villas of the wealthiest strata of society. This line-of-sight diagram for Gio Ponti's *Villa Planchart*, built for a wealthy Cadillac dealer in Caracas (1957) shows the ground floor criss-crossed by social gazes. Only the service rooms (numbered 14–19) are unmarked, invisible to the guests. "Una villa fiorentina," *Domus 375*, (February 1961), 1–39, here 3

The once desirable middle- and upper-class homes have degraded from privilege to burden, especially for aging home-owners. The large *quintas* have become increasingly hard to maintain and almost impossible to sell or trade. Once symbols of economic prosperity, this housing type has become a liability, forcing the declining middle class to financial expenditures beyond their capabilities. However, while many middle- and upper-class women have drastically reduced their housekeeper's hours, they have not entirely abolished the outsourcing and monetizing of domestic labor, as they lack the necessary skills to maintain their own homes. **fig. 13**

Farm Kitchens and Home Economy: Demonstrating Care
Barbara Penner

Barbara Penner is Professor of Architectural Humanities at the Bartlett School of Architecture, University College London.

We open with six staged kitchen photographs. **fig.1** These were clearly taken for demonstration purposes, but just what are they demonstrating? At first glance, the kitchens look neat but unspectacular, a world apart from the streamlined glories of the mid-century American technokitchen. But, if we look more closely at the details (the pull-out boards, that meat grinder!), we glimpse something else: an alternative version of modernity emerging from rural rather than urban or suburban lives, stressing thrift, self-build, home production, and adaptation. And, at the heart of this alternative modernity lies an engaged, active consumer and designs centered on the female body.

This page of photographs comes from a 1947 study of kitchen cabinets produced at Oregon State College (today Oregon State University) by professor of home economics Maud Wilson. [1] Wilson was a prolific researcher in the home economics field, and farm kitchen rationalization had long been one of her specialties. While rationalization now tends to be associated with prefabrication and mass production as in the Frankfurt Kitchen, in the context of American university-based home economists' engagement with farm families, it resulted in another approach: a strategy more akin to mass customization. While recommending standardized principles and minimum dimensions to reduce cost and material waste, farm women, with the help of family members or other home carpenters, were encouraged to adapt these plans and equipment to fit their own bodies, routines, and spaces.

This approach originated in close studies of rural communities. Wilson worked with fourteen farm-owning families in Oregon's Willamette Valley: these "cooperators" were visited four to nine times and lists were made of what they stored in kitchens and the activities that took place there. How many people typically sat down for meals? How many miles were traveled each year to make common dishes? How much canning was done annually? (A formidable 387 quarts.) [2] Although we should not assume that farm women were oppressed drudges—they themselves rejected such a view—Wilson's study confirms their labor was not easy. The centralized services available in cities were not typically available to even better-off farm women, who lived on farms of 20 to 300 acres and looked after extended households. They did their own butchering, canning, churning, cooking, baking, cleaning, childcare, and laundering. They hauled wood and water, cultivated gardens, and tended poultry for additional income. [3]

1 Maud Wilson, *Considerations in Planning Kitchen Cabinets*, Oregon State Agricultural Experiment Station no. 445 (Corvallis: Oregon State College, November 1947), 442, https://ir.library.oregonstate.edu/concern/administrative_report_or_publications/k0698788d (accessed July 6, 2022).

2 See Maud Wilson, *The Willamette Valley Farm Kitchen*, Oregon State Agricultural Experiment Station Bulletin no. 356 (Corvallis: Oregon State College, August 1938), 11.

3 As of 1930, 85 percent of farmhouses still did not have running water or electricity; only 37 percent had refrigerators; 60 percent had wood stoves. As late as 1947, Wilson still did not assume readers had electricity, piped hot and cold water, or a refrigerator, though she predicted these would arrive "eventually." Wilson, *Considerations in Planning Kitchen Cabinets*, 19.

Thus, the urban middle-class model of a full-time homemaker/consumer was never realistic for productive farm women. 4

Increasingly influenced by industrial engineering, university-based home economists sought to ease housework and rationalize domestic workspaces from the 1910s on. Their engagement with farm communities, however, inflected their advice in specific ways. First, they saw that isolated spaces such as the Frankfurt Kitchen would not do for multitasking farm women. Instead, they promoted "living kitchens" with compact work spaces inserted into existing large rooms that hosted social activities, such as dining and children's play. Second, even though they advocated the use of labor-saving devices, home economists were aware that cash-strapped farm families made improvements only as resources allowed. Rather than wait for ready-made solutions, they exhorted these families to take matters into their own hands. Simple and inexpensive hacks to enhance a kitchen's serviceability might include repurposing washstands to act as mix centers, setting ranges and sinks up on blocks, or reorganizing existing equipment for easier workflow. To reduce trips and "kitchen mileage," home economists also encouraged families to build movable furnishings of all kinds, from step-saving dinner trolleys to wheeled work tables. **figs. 2 and 3**

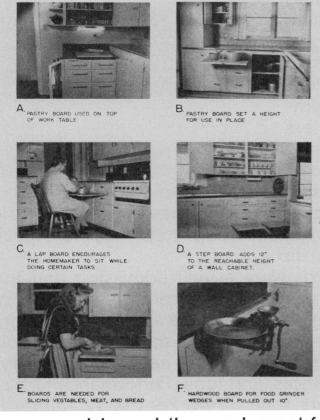

A. PASTRY BOARD USED ON TOP OF WORK TABLE

B. PASTRY BOARD SET A HEIGHT FOR USE IN PLACE

C. A LAP BOARD ENCOURAGES THE HOMEMAKER TO SIT WHILE DOING CERTAIN TASKS

D. A STEP BOARD ADDS 12" TO THE REACHABLE HEIGHT OF A WALL CABINET.

E. BOARDS ARE NEEDED FOR SLICING VEGTABLES, MEAT, AND BREAD

F. HARDWOOD BOARD FOR FOOD GRINDER WEDGES WHEN PULLED OUT 10".

Wilson's farmhouse kitchen studies were a more systemic response to these same conditions. Building on her studies of farm women's routines, Wilson devised rules, equipment prototypes, and plan variations for the refurbishment of "cooperator" kitchens. These were publicized through her landmark bulletin *Willamette Valley Farm Kitchen* (1938) and refined in later bulletins, such as the 1947 example with which we began. Although Wilson rationalized plans and standardized cabinet dimensions with input from agricultural engineers, these were offered as possible, not final, solutions. Her primary goal was to share good design principles with remodeling farm owners to inform *their*

4 Katherine Jellison, *Entitled to Power: Farm Women and Technology, 1913–1963* (Chapel Hill: University of North Carolina Press, 1993), xxi.

fig.1 "Placement and use of pull-out boards." Source: Maud Wilson, *Considerations in Planning Kitchen Cabinets*, Oregon State Agricultural Experiment Station Bulletin no. 445 (Corvallis: Oregon State College, November 1947), 42, https://ir.library.oregonstate.edu/concern/administrative_report_or_publications/k0698788d (accessed March 1 2022) adaptations. The seated worker in the opening page of photographs, for instance, demonstrates the well-established "sit when you can" principle drawn from fatigue studies. **fig. 1** But how to account for the rather crazy proliferation of pull-out boards slotted into base cabinets? In addition to pastry and food chopping boards, we now have lap boards and standing boards that allow women to step up and reach the highest cabinets. The kitchen seems equal parts laboratory and climbing frame.

Although they appear excessive, multilevel pull-out boards had a distinct rationale in Wilson's work. For the previous two decades, home economists had taught women how to measure their work curves, consisting of elbow and shoulder reaches, in order to customize their kitchens. They rejected the streamlined kitchen's use of counters of uniform height (36 inches, the industry standard) and instead sought to ensure working surfaces and storage were placed at a "comfortable reach" for the operator (within the elbow circle) and not beyond maximum reach ("shoulder-to-grasping-finger-tip"). **fig. 4**

Yet the pull-out boards were a tacit admission that the performance of domestic tasks regularly exceeded the ability of any one arrangement to meet them. Even the simplest task might consist of dozens of discrete actions—wash, scrub, pare, sift, roll, knead, beat, pat, spread, scrape, and so on—each requiring varying degrees of physicality, stances, and tools. Performance further differed according to factors such as worker ability, handedness, and sightedness. And even if farm wives were the kitchen's main operators, they were likely not to be the only ones. Influenced by John Dewey and Lillian Gilbreth, home economists were great believers in "teamwork" and in training children to do domestic tasks. Accepting that no fixed kitchen—even a customized one—could accommodate this broad range of uses and users, home economists relied on features such as pull-out boards and trolleys to give additional "flexibility of use." [5]

Much more can be said about home economics kitchens and their research-derived design principles, which became astonishingly detailed in the postwar period. But the pull-out boards alone begin to tell the story of a different and less top-down mode of engaging modernity, one not governed by advanced technology, mass production, or consumption. Rather it was driven by a situated and scientifically informed understanding of

fig. 2 A step-saving dinner wagon "can be made by any one who knows how to handle tools at all." Source: Leah D. Widtsoe, "Labor Saving Devices for the Farm Home," *Utah Agricultural College Experiment Station Circular*, no. 7 (June 1912), 61, https://digitalcommons.usu.edu/uaes_circulars/6/ (accessed March 1 2022)

5 Wilson, *Considerations in Planning Kitchen Cabinets*, 12.

the exigencies of use, labor, and care, specifically those involved in female homemaking. As opposed to the glamorized and gadget-filled vision of housewifery circulated in the mass media of the period, home economists insisted on treating homemaking as *work* with physical and psychological costs and rewards for productive farm women. Their attention to female bodies and routines meant they highlighted how life cycles, aging, infirmity, even the wearing of bifocals, could impact home environments at a time when such concerns were not even blips on the radar of mainstream architectural modernism.

That this distinct — and, let us not forget, female-led — mode of practice has not been widely recognized is also easy to understand. These designs do not *look* modern, at least in comparison to the established canon. Yet, if we look closely, we can find residues of other modernisms even in the most canonic of projects. In an important study parallel to this one, Sophie Hochhäusl points to the hay box located to the right of the Frankfurt Kitchen's gas stove but rarely mentioned by historians or shown with its lid open. 6 The hay box was a type of fireless cooker that saved on fuel costs and labor, as it cooked food gently over many hours without needing the housewife's constant attendance. And, as home economists on both sides of the Atlantic liked to point out, users could easily fabricate hay boxes themselves. **fig. 5 a, b**

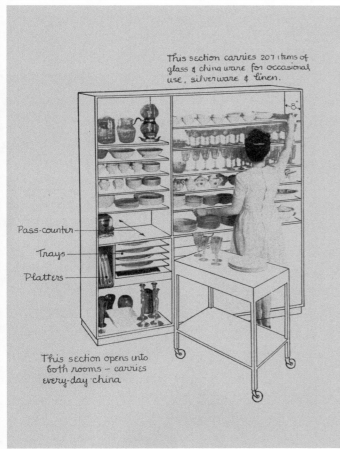

This section carries 207 items of glass & china ware for occasional use, silverware & linen.

Pass-counter
Trays
Platters

This section opens into both rooms — carries every-day china

fig. 3 Double-sided storage wall, showing utility service cart. Source: Mary Koll Heiner and Helen E. McCullough, "Functional Kitchen Storage," *Cornell University Agricultural Experiment Station Bulletin*, no. 846 (June 1948), 64

6 Sophie Hochhäusl, "From Vienna to Frankfurt inside Core-House Type 7: A History of Scarcity through the Modern Kitchen," *Architectural Histories* 1, no. 1 (2013), Art. 24, http://doi.org/10.5334/ah.aq. Figure 8 of the article is a photograph of the Frankfurt Kitchen hay box, lid open.

The presence of the hay box disturbs the usual account of the Frankfurt Kitchen, which ties its modernity to its embrace of industrial construction, equipment, services, and theories. Instead, Hochhäusl's study traces another genealogy for the kitchen, re-enmeshing it in discourses of scarcity, self-help building movements, and alternative technologies. (And by allowing for supervision-less cooking, it makes evident that Margarete Schütte-Lihotzky did not assume women were or should be full-time homemakers/consumers either.) In a similar way, pull-out

boards lead us to another strand of modernism in America, one that was resourceful, cooperative, and female-centered. In contrast to Schütte-Lihotzky, however, who ultimately turned to prefabrication as a solution, American university-based home economists resisted the pull of mass production well into the 1950s.

fig. 4 Marjorie Knoll teaches a home economics student to measure her work curve, n.d., in New York State College of Home Economics records, #23-2-749, Box 77, Folder 25. Courtesy: Division of Rare and Manuscript Collections, Cornell University Library, Ithaca, NY

fig. 5 a, b Image DD-HEM-19, from "Series of photographs showing how to make a fireless cooker at home. Taken in 1921 by Troy for Miss Blinn for Bulletin H-135, 'Fireless and Steam Pressure Cookers,'" 1921, in Cornell University, Human Ecology Historical Photographs, http://he-photos.library.cornell.edu/index.html/

They standardized construction and design principles, but, in turning these over to farm owners for customization, they went beyond prescription, opening kitchens to differentiated bodies, flexible uses, and unanticipated adaptations.

Meredith TenHoor
is Professor of
Architecture at Pratt
Institute, New York.

The Design of Community Mental Healthcare: Nicole Sonolet in Postwar France
Meredith TenHoor

What role can architects play in the delivery of care? Is there a theory of care provision in architectural form that does not resort to behaviorism? How can care spaces be programmed? Designs for two mental hospitals and a body of theoretical work from the 1950s to 1970s by the French architect Nicole Sonolet (1923–2015) offer potent and understudied responses. Rather than imagine that architectures of care would themselves directly produce healing, Sonolet believed that careful programming, collaboration among architects, patients, doctors, and staff, and an understanding of architecture's potentials and limits would improve spaces for care.

Sonolet's hospitals were developed in the context of institutional psychotherapy (IP). Elaborated by the Catalan psychiatrist François Tosquelles in the 1940s at the clinic of St. Alban, further developed by Frantz Fanon in the context of colonial Algeria and, much later, by Jean Oury and Félix Guattari in postcolonial France, IP sought to decarceralize the provision of mental healthcare and empower patients to direct more of their own processes of healing. [1] This would be done by allowing both patient and analyst to rethink the relationship between the patient and the institution, activating the creativity of both doctors and patients in this process to understand the social forces at work on the patient. Institutional psychotherapists considered that not only doctors and nurses but also care workers, staff members, other patients, family members, and even the spaces of care themselves could intervene in a process of healing. This would assist patients in obtaining care according to their own needs, rather than following patterns of care predetermined by overly rigid treatment protocols or even the state. As Meike Schalk, Susana Caló, and Godofredo Pereira have discussed, the focus on space in processes of treatment in IP opened important avenues for understanding the roles that architecture can play in mental healthcare more broadly. [2] What is particular about Sonolet's design and theory work in this context is its explicit focus on designing and theorizing care (*"soin"* in

1 See Valentin Schaepelynck, *L'institution renversée: Folie, analyse institutionnelle et champ social* (Paris: Eterotopia, 2018); and Camille Robcis's new intellectual history of the movement, *Disalienation: Politics, Philosophy, and Radical Psychiatry in Postwar France* (Chicago: University of Chicago Press, 2021).

2 See, in particular, Meike Schalk, "The Urban Mental Hospital and the State of Research," *SITE* 2 (2002), 15–16; and Susana Caló and Godofredo Pereira, "CERFI: From the Hospital to the City," *London Journal of Critical Theory* 1, no. 2 (May 2017), 83–100. An analysis of Sonolet's work in the 1960s and 1970s appears in Meredith TenHoor, "State-Funded Militant Infrastructure? CERFI's Équipements Collectifs in the Intellectual History of Architecture," *Journal of Architecture* 24, no. 7 (2019), 999–1019, https://doi.org/10.1080/13602365.2019.1698638. In addition, Julie Mareuil has recently completed an excellent master's thesis on the architectural history of l'Eau Vive in which she reads not only archival material but also building permits to document its construction history. Julie Mareuil, "Une clinique-pilote de la sectorisation psychiatrique: L'hôpital de l'Eau Vive et son évolution de 1959 à 1977" (MA thesis, ENSA Paris-La Villette, 2020). Work on the architectures of community-based care in other national contexts is developing as well. For a UK-based history, see Christina Malathouni, "Beyond the Asylum and before the 'Care in the Community' Model: Exploring an Overlooked Early NHS Mental Health Facility," *History of Psychiatry* 31, no. 4 (December 2020), 455–69. For a US-based history, see Joy Knoblauch, *The Architecture of Good Behavior* (Pittsburgh: University of Pittsburgh Press, 2019).

French). Some of the most crucial formulations of that term in IP emerged through her collaborations from the late 1950s until the early 1980s with the psychiatrist Philippe Paumelle. Sonolet designed two hospitals directed by Paumelle: l'Eau Vive residential mental hospital in the Parisian suburb of Soisy-sur-Seine, which opened in March 1963 after five years of planning and construction; and the Center for Mental Health of the Association de Santé Mentale 13 (or ASM 13) in Paris, which Sonolet designed conceptually during the 1960s before collaborating on site with architects Maria Baran, Olek Kujawski, and Tristan Darros from 1973 to 1982. This article focuses on the former, as it is an important yet underrecognized prototype for this new form of hospital.

Sonolet became involved with architectures for mental healthcare as somewhat of an expert. A close family member had been hospitalized, and she knew intimately the architectural and organizational challenges of the French mental healthcare system. As a student at the École de Beaux-Arts in Paris during the Second World War, she had studied modernist design with Henri Larrieu, André Leconte, and Georges-Henri Pingusson, and her thesis project was a design for a psychiatric hospital with three hundred beds, which she completed after resuming her studies in 1954. In the early years of her career, she was, through her thesis research, in conversation with many leading figures in the institutional psychotherapy movement, and these conversations helped her to develop her own ideas for how new complexes for mental health services could be designed. 3

In these years, mental health in France was in a state of crisis, with patients confined to overcrowded asylums. During the Vichy regime, some patients had been subject to deliberate neglect and starvation. 4 There were too few beds for too many

patients; patients were housed in asylums far from where they lived and thus severed from communities that could assist with healing; outpatient facilities were uncommon and preventative treatment even more so. Beyond these material conditions, patients were stigmatized. The sheer number of people who needed treatment, coupled with a lack of doctors, meant that care was often routinized, with patients and their families disempowered to intervene in the course of treatment. IP emerged as an alternative. Institutional psychotherapists wanted to offer care outside the context of the asylum and to do so, whenever possible, in outpatient settings in the patient's own communities.

3 My research on Sonolet draws on interviews with her family members and from her personal archive of letters, plans, pamphlets, and notes, shared with me by her family. I am deeply grateful to Christine de Bremond d'Ars, without whom this work would be impossible. Because Sonolet's work was not collected by the primary architectural archives in France, and because Sonolet herself was not particularly concerned with self-promotion, her work is not as widely known as that of many male architects who have realized a similar quantity of projects.

4 Philippe Paumelle was particularly critical of this and contributed a strong condemnation of the state of French psychiatry to Esprit, publishing under a pseudonym: Philippe Langlade [pseud.], "Qui sommes-nous?," Esprit 197 (December 1952), 797–800. For more on this text, see Serge Gauthier, "Philippe Paumelle, homme de pensée et d'action, et la fondation du Treizième," in Colette Chiland, Clément Bonnet, and Alain Braconnier, eds., Le souci de l'humain: Un défi pour la psychiatrie (Toulouse: Érès, 2010), 9–30.

fig.1 Nicole Sonolet, plan of the grounds and buildings of l'Eau Vive hospital, Soisy-sur-Seine, France, 1960s. Archives of Nicole Sonolet, collection of Christine de Bremond d'Ars

After years of agitation from doctors and patients, laws reforming mental healthcare in France were passed in the early 1960s, which broke up the asylum system into locally organized "sectors" and facilitated a transition to more locally directed care with consistent teams of doctors for residents in a given geographic area, as well as other reforms in the treatment of patients.

Community-based care was particularly important to Paumelle. Starting in the mid-1950s, he began to organize urban mental health services in Paris, hoping to provide people with access to intensive psychiatric services within their neighborhoods. The system of community-based care he envisioned would include outpatient psychotherapy and free clinics, as well as occupational and movement therapies, and would provide support to patients and their families before and after hospitalization. With funding from a donor who wanted to improve treatments for alcoholics, he founded the Association de Santé Mentale 13 (ASM 13), intended to serve the population of the 13th arrondissement in Paris. Thanks to this funding, starting in 1958 Sonolet and Paumelle were able to work together to plan l'Eau Vive, which was intended to be an experimental pilot project that

figs. 2 and 3 Exterior views of l'Eau Vive hospital, Soisy-sur-Seine, France, 1960s. Archives of Nicole Sonolet, collection of Christine de Bremond d'Ars

would test the strategy of sectorization, allowing care to shift from its previous "hospital-centrism" to a more open model. 5

While Paumelle had hoped to be able to establish a hospital within Paris and to explore the possibilities for designing urban mental healthcare centers, he accepted the opportunity offered to develop one in Soisy, a small suburb south of the capital, as a first and crucial step in improving care for Parisian residents. Following tenets of community-based care, he imagined a hospital where patients would be seen by a consistent team of doctors, nurses, and caregivers rather than switching from

5 Simone Paumelle in the brochure *1963–2003: Les 40 ans de l'eau vive* (ASM 13, June 2003), 6.

clinician to clinician. He planned for an open campus where patients of different genders could interact rather than be segregated and in which patients would not be confined to their rooms, as if in a prison, but would be free to move around the grounds. At Soisy, patients, families, and doctors would also be able to collaborate in developing a course of treatment. Over several years, Sonolet and Paumelle worked together to develop plans for the hospital. Sonolet's design for the complex integrated a few extant buildings and ten new pavilions in the 5-hectare, park-like setting of a former theological center. **fig.1**

The hospital was designed to accommodate 175 patients suffering from either alcoholism or psychological challenges. These patients were organized into treatment groups of seven, who were to be monitored by one consistent nurse rather than a rotating team of staff, as Paumelle and Sonolet believed that

deeper and more therapeutic relationships could form with consistent staff and doctors. They also recognized that every relationship a patient had—whether with other patients or with staff at the hospital—would be part of the patient's recovery. This was an essential tenet of IP dating from Tosquelles's work at St. Alban: all interactions with people, objects, and buildings could be opportunities for patient-initiated exchange that could untangle the relationships between patients and their social and political environments, and these interactions could assist with resocialization and reintegration. At Soisy, the staff would consist of artists and craftspeople who would work with patients in studios; people in charge of animating the collective life of patients; physical therapists; and housecleaners, all of whom would be involved with therapeutic interaction.

Processes of Healing

Sonolet's designs for l'Eau Vive were modernist and elegant: a series of long, low pavilions, often raised on pilotis, with long expanses of windows opening onto verdant grounds. **figs. 2 and 3** These buildings were formally and materially similar to the architectural designs of her Corbusian-inspired professors at the École de Beaux-Arts and to "organicist" modern architects such as Alvar Aalto and Aino Aalto, who, in the 1950s and 1960s, similarly designed concrete and steel-framed buildings with abundant use of natural materials in their interiors, and whose work Sonolet admired. Like these precedents, Sonolet's pavilions could be economically built with flexible floor plans, wood and stucco on the interior, and were planned with great consideration of how patients, doctors, and staff would move through them. Yet Sonolet's designs went far beyond design logics that privileged the economical use of materials, organized circulation or movement through space, or highlighted views between interiors and landscapes. They also exceeded Alvar Aalto's attempts to bring physical comfort to patients through careful calibration of ergonomics, materials, and light. Sonolet's focus at l'Eau Vive was on *processes of healing*.

fig. 4 a, b Nicole Sonolet, diagrams of socialization patterns in mental hospitals, ca. 1964. Archives of Nicole Sonolet, collection of Christine de Bremond d'Ars

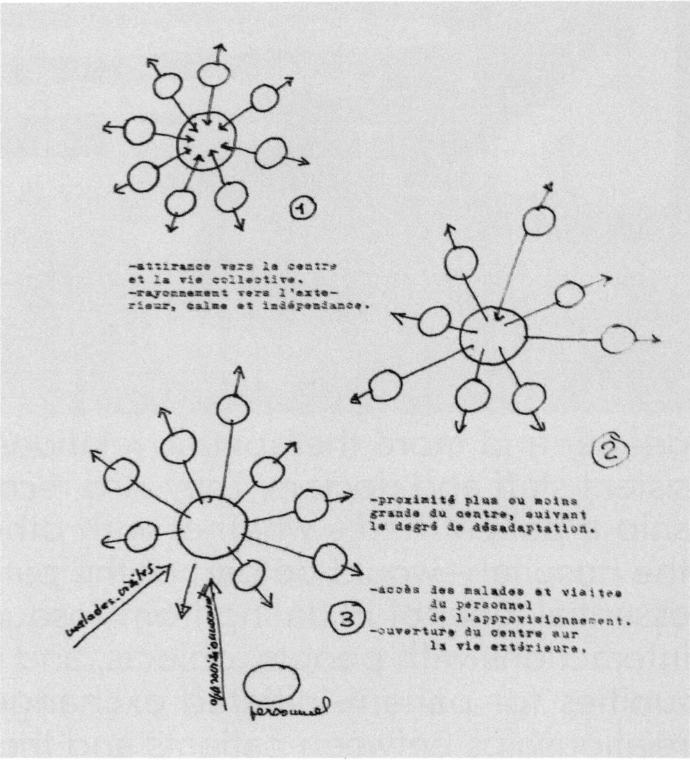

The degree to which patients desired and were capable of socializing with others in the course of their treatment was a major driver both of Paumelle's treatment strategy and of Paumelle and Sonolet's conception of the hospital. Diagrams based on notes Sonolet compiled on care and architecture conceptualize different ways that social interactions — orientation toward or away from others — might inform the organization of space. Sonolet considered not only the staff's need for access to and distance from the patients **fig. 4 a** but also the various needs of the patients **fig. 4 b** whose groupings were far more fluid and intermingled because they would vary depending on where they were in the course of their treatment. Yet Sonolet's diagrams were not intended to be directly spatialized. Instead, they were a conceptual tool for understanding how the space(s) could be planned. To render her diagrams in built form, Sonolet carefully planned a variety of services (*équipements*) — for food preparation and eating, for gathering, for quiet repose, for treatment, for enjoying nature — and distributed them throughout the complex. These were intended to support not only patients but also visitors and staff.

While some programmatic components for patients were fixed, others were intended to be as flexible as possible, built with the understanding that one space might have to serve multiple purposes and that the patient's ability to transform that space

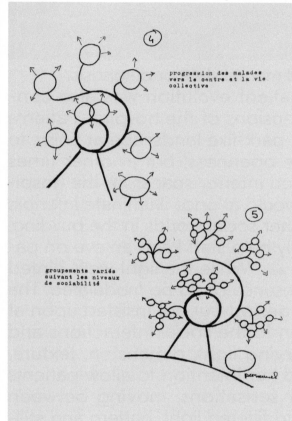

progression des malades vers le centre et la vie collective

groupements variés suivant les niveaux de sociabilité

could also be an instrument in the patient's healing. Describing her understanding of this process in notes she took on the planning of the clinic, Sonolet wrote that architectural and interior design might help to "condition" spaces to provide a variety of experiences: of openness to the world or of enclosure; of stimulation or of repose; of warmth or of coolness. The staff and the patients would orchestrate movements through these variously conditioned spaces as a way to provide therapeutic experiences, which would either help them maintain ties to communal life or gradually prepare them to reintegrate into their

communities. Photographs of the interior of the hospital show Sonolet's attention to the design of communal spaces: chairs could be grouped and regrouped to offer flexible possibilities for socialization, for example. They comprised an active environment intended to be used in the course of treatment. **fig. 5**

In Paumelle and Sonolet's programmatic plans for l'Eau Vive, patients would not be segregated according to gender, as they often had been in asylums, and would have more ability to choose whom to spend time with. Doctors would not use straitjackets or tranquilizing "neuroleptic" drugs that rendered patients inert or catatonic, and they hoped to avoid closed doors that would evoke prisons. As patients recovered, those ready for reintegration into collective life could have social experiences at Soisy; those who were not ready would have spaces for solitude and repose. In a text she wrote on mental health consultations,

Sonolet underscored the importance of privacy, noting that it was especially important in waiting areas in the clinic's entry, where patients would be nervous as they entered the complex. She recommended the construction of several private waiting areas, and designed the bedrooms to offer patients visual

fig.5 Patient lounge at l'Eau Vive. Archives of Nicole Sonolet, collection of Christine de Bremond d'Ars

privacy even when their doors were open. She wanted patients to have quiet corners that they could be comfortable in, where they could observe but not be observed. Most of all, she insisted that patients had the right to evolve — not to be fixed in one space in the hospital or in one fixed mental state or diagnosis.

Sonolet's conception of patient evolution was also concerned with visual and aural dimensions of the hospital. Patients might sometimes want to see the park-like landscape at Soisy, to have an experience of expansive openness, but at other times they might prefer to be in enclosed interior spaces. In the hospital, she designed light wells that would at once illuminate interiors and also signal the presence of other social worlds in the building. These views could also presumably help staff keep an eye on patients in a less obtrusive manner. **fig.6** While the light wells hinted at the presence of others, their presence could be modulated. The possibility of community was suggested but not insisted upon at every moment. Sonolet's attention to the social interactions and social sensations enabled by varying light, dimension, texture, and spatial organization reflected her intention to allow patients and caretakers to manage their sensations, moving between enclosure and exposure, bright and filtered light, pattern and stillness. Spaces would have clearly different qualities, ones Sonolet called "hot" or "cold," which could correspond to patients' moods and desires. Overall, the hospital would have a kind of legibility that would be important for patients who might feel nervous upon entering and whose perceptual capacities might be altered due to their illness. Sonolet insisted that patients should feel oriented in the hospital: they should know where nurses and doctors were, and these caretakers should be accessible. In this sense, the building would allow patients to care for themselves through their use of different spaces, but it could also model a world with more accessible forms of care — a place where people offering care would be responsive and available, with this availability facilitated through the design of the building.

Soisy's organizational schema — one where patients move through different spaces to become progressively more socialized in the course of their treatment—became more widely used later in the 1960s, as community-based case services were developed in the United States, the United Kingdom, as well as in other European countries. After the passage of the 1963 Community Mental Health Act in the United States, for instance, national funding and support were made available for a similar process of de-institutionalization and for community-based facilities. As Joy Knoblauch documents, architect Clyde Dorsett was put in charge of coordinating and supporting the development of architectural typologies for community mental health for the US National Institute of Mental Health. **6** Dorsett and Sonolet were friendly colleagues, visiting each other's families and projects in Washington, D.C., and in France and exchanging yearly cards and letters. After the construction of l'Eau Vive, several of the schemes Dorsett helped promote were explicitly designed to support socialization processes in ways similar to those Sonolet had earlier designed. Hospitals he supported used various materials, lighting, color, and other techniques of spatial differentiation. This was especially true of a 1967 plan by Kiyoshi Izumi for the Rice Design Fete in which, as Knoblauch describes, "diverse residents could be encouraged, slowly, to interact with each other in increasingly larger groups." **7** This gradual exposure to social interaction was not invented by Sonolet, but she was one of the first architects to translate these goals into architectural form. She published commentary on her experiences at l'Eau Vive in international psychology journals

in 1966 and 1967, drawing from her work designing the facility to explain how urban mental health complexes, including the one she and Paumelle would later build in Paris, should be planned. **8** Because l'Eau Vive was one of the first community mental health centers to be realized by IP practitioners in France, Sonolet became known in community mental health circles as the French expert on the architecture of IP. She consulted on international projects throughout the 1960s, sharing many conclusions derived from her work, especially about the role of spaces conditioned for various forms of sociability in the design of mental health centers.

However, Sonolet did not have a mechanistic understanding of the hospital's impact on socialization. She did not believe that the hospital itself would guide socialization but rather that the hospital would make it possible for patients to use different

6 Knoblauch documents the architectural dimensions of this work in great detail. I am grateful to her, as well as to my father, William TenHoor, who worked with Dorsett in the 1970s, for discussions about the architecture of community mental health centers in the United States during this period. See Joy Knoblauch, "Better Living through Psychobureaucracy? Community Mental Health Centers," in *The Architecture of Good Behavior*, 57–96.

7 Knoblauch, "Better Living through Psychobureaucracy?," 69–71.

fig. 6 Light wells at l'Eau Vive. Archives of Nicole Sonolet, courtesy of Christine de Bremond d'Ars

8 Nicole Sonolet, "Un centre de santé mentale: Point de vue et proposition d'un architecte," *Information psychiatrique*, no. 6 (June 1966), 527–32; and Nicole Sonolet, "An Urban Mental Health Center: Proposal for an Experimental Design," *Social Psychiatry* 2, no. 3 (1967), 137–43, https://doi.org/10.1007/ BF00578330. These texts also describe Sonolet's forthcoming urban projects.

9 Michel Foucault, in an interview with Paul Rabinow and Gwendolyn Wright in these years, came to a similar conclusion: the architecture of the panopticon reflected techniques of power, but ones that depended on use. Architecture alone did not guarantee freedom. "Liberty is a practice," he argued. See Paul Rabinow and Gwendolyn Wright, "'Space, Knowledge and Power' [Interview with Michel Foucault]," *Skyline*, March 1982, 16–20.

spaces as techniques or *dispositifs* in their own healing. The spaces offered by the hospital were enabling rather than prescriptive, following the thinking of IP practitioners. **9** Sonolet's conceptual models for hospitals show how hierarchical models of care common in past asylum designs could be replaced with the more fluid arrangements promoted by practitioners of IP, where social interactions with anyone physically present in the clinic would offer an opportunity for social support. The clinic would become a kind of city in miniature, or a model for the city, a space of potentially healing social interactions that would be available for patients as they were ready for them. Just as community-based clinics would make mental healthcare a standard part of the city, Sonolet's plans made the clinic into a space of socialization. This was an important departure from the more behaviorist readings of architecture espoused by the American architects who developed the field of environmental psychology in subsequent years and would search for standard bases for architectural sensations or, more flagrantly, argue that urban design decisions shaped things like crime statistics in cities. **10** Sonolet did not believe that care could be guaranteed through architectural plans. Rather, careful research and programming and the deployment of spaces attuned to the psychology of patients could make the experience of hospitalization less frightening and more healing.

10 One could trace this tendency in Christopher Alexander's work, and Oscar Newman's work was widely received in this manner, leading to the development of the theory of "crime prevention through environmental design," which delineated design features that would supposedly deter criminals. See also Joy Knoblauch, "Defensible Space and the Open Society," *Aggregate* 3 (March 2015), https://doi.org/10.53965/AKNV9163.

Sonolet's concerns about privacy and socialization were also reflected in the aspects of her designs focused on supporting the hospital's staff by improving their working conditions both materially and psychologically, which was also a preoccupation of Paumelle's. This was reflected in her designs for each pavilion's facades, which were oriented to different uses or types of patient. Some entrances were designated for staff, away from the view of the patients, whereas another side of the building might offer patients open views onto the park, and still others would offer enclosed spaces. For example, in the entry building located closest to the street, one facade features a guardian's quarters, garages, and spaces for occupational therapy, while gathering spaces facing the street occupy a separate facade. While separation of functions along the facade was common in other forms of hospital design, the facades at Soisy were organized according to the specific needs communicated to Paumelle and Sonolet by those working at the clinic. Sonolet's extensive interviews with hospital staff made clear to her that she needed to offer workers relief from constant interaction with patients. The staff would have use of a chateau, which already existed on the site, with dormitory-style bedrooms, teaching rooms, and a laboratory, and some could access special larger living quarters. Two houses for doctors had their own gardens and were separate from both the patients and the staff quarters, allowing for additional privacy. Over time, it became clear that staff at the center needed spaces to rest from providing care, spaces separate from those of the patients, and further accommodations were organized a few kilometers from the hospital. Some of Sonolet's plans were meant to gently push doctors to provide better care: she planned one central cafeteria for all staff, as this would require doctors to interact and work together, thus preventing them from assuming too much unchallenged power over their small domains within the hospital. [11] Sectorization promoted consistent care but made exchanges between doctors and staff even more essential. Since Soisy was also a teaching hospital, spaces for staff sociability would ensure that it was a place of learning and discovery.

Like all designs, Sonolet and Paumelle's work was modified over time. Chronic underfunding of mental health services meant a shortage of hospital beds in the 1970s and 1980s , and the number of beds at Soisy was increased, which changed the character of the hospital, eliminating many of the spaces for solitude that Sonolet had planned. And as patients with less debilitating conditions began to receive treatment in Paris in newly-built day clinics, l'Eau Vive began to serve more seriously ill patients. While the hospital was planned so that patients would never be forcefully isolated, after this change some patients apparently requested or required a "closed" pavilion for their own healing, and one was established in the early 1970s. Paumelle had strongly opposed this idea and put himself in charge of this pavilion (whose door was designed to give the sense of enclosure without being truly carceral) to ensure that patients in it were well cared for and could leave if they were able to, though after his death in 1974 the character of this pavilion did change. [12] The violence of some psychotic patients also required procedural modifications. After a patient brought a gun to a different clinic, the staff at l'Eau Vive decided to create procedures to gently search patients before they entered Soisy, though not in a "police-like manner." [13] Patients and activists have also raised concerns about how one prominent doctor in the hospital treated transgender patients. Though this has little to do with the architecture of the clinic, it shows that the rhetoric of liberation at l'Eau Vive was not always in alignment with what patients and activists demand for their own communities. [14]

Research as Care

In the mid-1960s, as Sonolet completed planning of l'Eau Vive, she continued to work with Paumelle to plan an urban mental health center in Paris, the Center for Mental Health, and began to publish

[11] Paul Béquart, the first medical director of the clinic, underscores this point. See *1963–2003*, 28.

[12] Béquart writes that some patients chose this space in pavilion 7, but I cannot substantiate this. See *1963–2003*, 25. In spring 2022, a former patient relayed to me how traumatic the experience of isolation was at l'Eau Vive, and I hope that future work on the history of this clinic can include testimonials from patients.

[13] *1963–2003*, 25.

[14] Colette Chiland, one of the doctors who worked at the hospital for many years, has been criticized by Act-up Paris and the group Activiste Trans for imposing binaristic and regressive definitions of trans identities not based on trans experiences, especially in her book *Changer de sexe* (Paris: Odile Jacob, 1997). The website Transgender Map documents the critique of Chiland in greater detail: https://www.transgendermap.com/politics/psychiatry/colette-chiland/ (accessed March 1, 2022).

15 Sonolet, "An Urban Mental Health Center"; Nicole Sonolet, "Un centre de santé mentale urbain: Proposition d'une expérience," in "Programmation, architecture et psychiatrie," special issue, *Recherches* 6 (June 1967); Sonolet, "Un centre de santé mentale: Point de vue et proposition d'un architecte"; and Phillippe Paumelle and Nicole Sonolet, "Le dispensaire d'hygiène mentale," *Techniques hospitalières* 12, no. 133 (1956), 51—53.

her findings from years of research on mental health facilities. [15] Writing for IP-focused psychology journals, as well as the more widely read *Esprit* (for which she wrote an article on social housing, which she had designed during the 1950s and 1960s) and, later, for the journal *Recherches*, Sonolet described how healthcare facilities could be planned. Whereas care *practices* could be flexible and attuned to the patient, architecture could not be made infinitely changeable; a firm and fixed understanding of the requirements and qualities caregivers desired for patients was necessary. Accordingly, while some of Sonolet's recommendations could be derived from data about desired doctor/patient/space ratios and the populations of each sector, others were more ineffable. They had to do with how care spaces could inflect and allow access to social and natural environments, altering phenomenological qualities of space so as to create a varied palette of spaces for treatment, as Sonolet had done at Soisy. In her texts, Sonolet clarified that these two sets of knowledge were necessary to consider when building a community mental health center.

The other part, however, could be elicited only through conversations with those using the clinic themselves: patients and doctors. For Sonolet, then, both of these forms of research—understanding architectural typologies and possibilities, then undoing and modifying them based on feedback from users—were forms of care. Speaking at an event celebrating forty years of l'Eau Vive, Sonolet clarified this process:

"Doctors explain what they want as a mode of life for their patients, what they need. Architects try to find types of space and connections between spaces that favor care—in the life of patients and of the staff. It is evident that architecture isn't care, but it can support or inhibit care (a very good team in bad spaces is better than a bad team in good spaces). You need a constant back and forth between proposals and critiques between doctors, architects, social assistants, and nurses." [16]

16 These talks were later published in a pamphlet. See *1963–2003*, 39 (author's translation).

These feedback loops between programming and design had parallels with the patient-specific treatment protocols that doctors involved with IP developed as they worked against the idea of a uniform and standardized formula for treating different illnesses. Sonolet seemed to modify the psychoanalytic practice of providing care to derive a process for designing the hospital. Following the principles of IP, this would yield designs that were guided by a set of common principles but were specific to each situation and team of staff members and also to the community from which they issued. Designing these spaces required close collaboration between architects and doctors. Simply creating a formula that would directly translate health into space was impossible. This irreducibility to type helps to account for the formal variations in Sonolet's work, as well as the careful intentionality of her designs. Ideally, Sonolet implied, the kind of care that generated variety might be deployed in the planning of all collective facilities.

The importance of variety is a theme of Sonolet's text for *Esprit*, published in 1969, in which she argues that collective housing should be made more humane and that different qualities of spaces should be created by enabling more forms of programming and human interaction in collective social housing developments. [17] Indeed, Sonolet's understanding of l'Eau Vive as a variously programmed space in which patients could comfortably live while receiving treatment aligns well with her understanding of an ideal form for residential projects. IP attempted to make mental healthcare less carceral—the opposite of which was to make it more domestic—but Sonolet did not maintain this opposition, understanding that even the most domestic spaces could themselves be carceral if not based on a design process organized around experience, desire, and need. The best escape was liveliness and the possibility of unexpected and felicitous interaction, if so desired, or safe repose if not. [18]

In 1967, the Centre d'études, de recherches et de formation institutionnelles (CERFI, led officially by Guattari and practically by Anne Querrien), a research institute devoted to investigating the politics and potential designs of collective facilities, received a state-funded contract to investigate the relationships between architecture and psychiatry, the results of which were published in an issue of CERFI's journal *Recherches*. [19] Guattari, already friendly with Sonolet, tapped her as a key protagonist in the meetings and discussions about this project, centering her work at Soisy as essential to understanding how collective facilities for mental health could be designed. Sonolet's contribution reprised those she published in *Social Psychology* and *Information psychiatrique*, outlining challenges, processes, and formal considerations when programming hospitals, along with a menu of programmatic possibilities and several charts explaining how such a scheme could work under different population densities. She stressed that long-term success (rather than flexibility that would be impossible in architectural design) could be achieved only after considerable research and conversation. [20] A few years later, Sonolet participated in another Guattari-led CERFI project about planning mental healthcare in French New Towns. A transcript of a colloquium on this topic was preserved in a CERFI report. [21] Sonolet, along with the architect Alain Schmied, resisted creating fixed typologies for hospitals, working against the idea of creating a

17 Nicole Sonolet, "Logements Sociaux?," *Esprit*, no. 385 (October 1969), 464–74.

18 Sonolet's focus on the user and on animation in social housing parallels critiques of French housing projects from the 1950s and 1960s that Kenny Cupers documents in *The Social Project: Housing Postwar France* (Minneapolis: University of Minnesota Press, 2014). Sonolet was in conversation with many of the protagonists (alas, mostly male and, in the world of postwar French architecture, thus better documented) in Cupers's book.

19 "Programmation, Architecture et Psychiatrie," special issue, *Recherches* 6 (1967). For more on this aspect of Sonolet's work, see TenHoor, "State-Funded Militant Infrastructure?"

20 A brief analysis of this text appears in Caló and Pereira, "CERFI: From the Hospital to the City," 95–97.

21 CERFI, *La programmation des équipements collectifs dans les villes nouvelles (Les équipements d'hygiène mentale): Rapport sur l'exécution de la convention d'études entre le CERFI et le Ministère d'équipement et du logement (Direction de l'aménagement foncier et de l'urbanisme) du 4 mai 1971* (Paris: Centre d'études, de recherches et de formation institutionnelles, 1972).

standardized and repeatable architectural "solution" to a problem. While a gospel of mechanization and architectural standardization was part of Sonolet's architectural training, and certainly a technical interest of hers as someone who had to create public buildings on tight budgets, Sonolet did not feel that standardization would work in the case of programming, which she argued needed to emerge in response to the specific needs of a community and the specific practices of doctors. During these years, Michel Foucault, who worked on CERFI-funded projects and was very much part of the conversations about psychiatry, power, and planning that Sonolet helped to shape, argued that French liberalism was based in part on biopolitics; that is, calculations about the value of life. By theorizing care as an incalculable practice, one valuable in and of itself, CERFI and Sonolet developed an antibiopolitical understanding of how the state could tend to mental health needs by destigmatizing care and allowing for healing to happen through multiple channels. The IP model might itself appear neoliberal to modern ears, with its focus on individualizing patient desires and letting these desires drive healing processes, but when viewed in the context of midcentury French mental healthcare overall, which was one of great austerity and underfunding and alarming routinization of care, this turn toward the individual can clearly be seen as corrective rather than paradigmatic.

In plan and facade, in the design of interior spaces and exterior gardens, Sonolet's architectures for IP offer a simultaneously detailed and open-ended model of how institutions can be designed to support the provision of care and how they can become one of many therapeutic media through which patients might interact as they shape a path toward recovery. Architecture could assist in the practice of IP, and architects, Sonolet demonstrated, could adapt some of the conversational practices of IP to drive design research.

Acknowledgements
This article is based on talks I gave about Nicole Sonolet's work at the Princeton-Mellon Initiative at Princeton University in spring 2019 and at the Heyman Center for the Humanities at Columbia University in spring 2020, and on an article I recently published in French on Sonolet's collaboration with Philippe Paumelle: "Des architectures du soin: Philippe Paumelle et Nicole Sonolet," *Terrain* 76 (Spring 2022), ed. Christine Langlois and Baptiste Moutaud, 146–63. I am grateful to the editors for their support for revising this work in the context of care.

Care as Active Architectural Practice
Jos Boys

How might we understand care and care work as something that starts from our own bodyminds, [1] both as architectural or other kinds of workers and through our various ordinary lived social, spatial, and material experiences and encounters? What does it mean to conceptualize architecture as an explicitly embodied practice? What kinds of work do we each do that perpetuates or challenges which bodyminds are valued and which marginalized or ignored? [2] What are the everyday, unnoticed social, material, aesthetic, and spatial practices that perpetuate one particular normality—including one version of care or its lack? How can we critique normative practices that reproduce the world to the benefit of some rather than others? And what kinds of collective and personal shifts can move architectural, social, and individual practices toward valuing the vital richness of human and non-human bio- and neurodiversity?

In this article I explore "care" by opening up difficulties in how architecture as a discipline talks to and about itself; most particularly around who and what gets left out, how such gaps

Jos Boys is Senior Lecturer in Environments for Learning, University College London, co-founder of Matrix and The DisOrdinary Architecture Project.

1 Margaret Price, "The Bodymind Problem and the Possibilities of Pain," *Hypatia Special Issue: Conversations in Feminist Disability Studies* 30, no. 1 (2015), 268–84.

2 See Jos Boys, "Invisibility Work? How Starting from Dis/ability Challenges Normative Social, Spatial and Material Practices," in Hélène Frichot et al., eds., *Architecture and Feminisms* (London: Routledge/AHRA, 2017), 270–80, here 270.

fig.1 Matrix feminist design collective cofounder Anne Thorne with her son, negotiating a North London underpass in the 1980s. Image used for the front cover of the Matrix book *Making Space: Women and the Man-Made Environment* (London: Pluto Press, 1984). Photographer: Liz Mullen

come to be both unnoticeable and unconsidered (not worth considering), and the effects this has on how architecture is inculcated and practiced. I have previously suggested that the Western architectural canon has a tendency for slippage *away from* the difficult implications for design processes of actual, diverse, and complex embodiments. This slippage can occur through reliance on general concepts such as user or community (or even care) when these rely on commonsense notions of "the people as a whole," unproblematically sharing characteristics, attitudes, or interests in common—concepts that, by obscuring relational and differential effects of power, ultimately hide as much as they reveal. It can come about through theoretical frameworks that locate care away from actual messy bodyminds, projecting it instead into the "body" of the built environment; for example, in notions of a "sense of place" where this is assumed to be based on a shared communality, which is then literally read into certain kinds of "familiar" spaces, rather than through engagement with different kinds of bodyminds or their complex and sometimes conflicting histories, trajectories, needs, preferences, and desires. [3]

Finally, the Western architectural canon's slippage away from the difficult implications posed by the multitude of human embodiments can occur through valuing "care-full" design; that is, creative approaches that explicitly express care in how buildings are made material. Again, instead of analyzing how caring happens (or could happen) through and in the *occupation* of built space, this kind of care predominantly comes to reside in the designers' own intentions and actions and is thus judged through their perceived sensitivity and "carefulness." While this is not wrong—and can produce beautiful buildings and spaces—it acts to blur other ways of conceptualizing an architecture of care. [4]

This is not meant to underplay the considerable difficulties in finding ways to design that can support the complex—and often contested and contradictory requirements of—human and nonhuman bio- and neurodiversity. [5] In fact, starting from a commitment to embodied practice, to the valuing of non-normative bodyminds, and to human and planetary flourishing is ridiculously idealistic and radical and ultimately demands a complete rethinking of the modes of education and practice around the built environment. Despite this, I will start things rolling by discussing some small-scale provocations and interventions that stem from exploring care as an active practice. These are based both on the work of The DisOrdinary Architecture Project [6] —of which I was cofounder in 2008 with disabled artist Zoe Partington—and on occasional references to Matrix, a feminist design collective I helped cofound in London in the 1980s. [7] Key themes center on developing new kinds of terminology and alternative design methods and on reframing access and inclusion as social, spatial, and material justice. [8]

Toward a New Language: Fitting and Misfitting
DisOrdinary Architecture is an informal platform that brings together disabled artists with built environment students, educators, and practitioners (both nondisabled and disabled) for creative

3 See Jos Boys, ed., *Doing Disability Differently: An Alternative Handbook on Architecture, Dis/ability, and Designing for Everyday Life* (New York: Routledge, 2014), 127–28.

4 See Jos Boys, "Space, Place and 'Careful' Designing for Everyday Life," in Charlotte Bates, Rob Imrie, and Kim Kullman, eds., *Care and Design: Bodies, Buildings, Cities* (London: Wiley-Blackwell, 2016), 155–77; and Jos Boys, "Cripping Spaces? On Dis/abling Phenomenology in Architecture," in Bryan E. Norwood, ed., "Phenomenology against Architectural Phenomenology," special issue, *LOG* 42 (2017), 55–66.

5 And, of course, considerably affected by the lack of power of architects and other built environment professionals within larger economic, political, and social contexts.

6 See https://disordinaryarchitecture.co.uk/ (accessed February 12, 2022).

7 See the prototype online Matrix archive at http://www.matrixfeministarchitecturearchive.co.uk/ (accessed February 12, 2022).

8 Understanding access as a matter of justice is central to much contemporary disability activism and scholarship, with associated concerns that it will be co-opted by nondisabled people and undermined. For more on design justice, see Sasha Constanza-Chock, *Design Justice: Community-Led Practices to Build the World We Need* (Cambridge, MA: MIT Press, 2020), 52, 68, 100.

and critical dialogue and action that coexplores how disabled and other nonnormative bodyminds offer a valuable and generative force in design, rather than being merely a technical and legalistic "problem" for designers. Informed by the vital contemporary work of disabled artists, activists, and scholars, we explore how disability (and other identities) can be reframed, not in simplistic binaries but as a complex, intersectional, situated, and dynamic patterning of enabling and disabling practices and spaces. This means there is no such thing as simple, "universal" access design solutions, added on at the end of a process of designing for "normal people" in order to include those who have already been excluded [9] —what Jay Dolmage calls "retro-fitting." [10] Instead, we need to start codeveloping collective and emergent design practices deeply informed by disabled and other nonnormative people's experiences and expertise, a process that looks for shared affinities in how we occupy space but also accepts tensions and contradictions by introducing variety and multimodality. [11]

In talks and workshops with built environment students, educators, and practitioners, DisOrdinary Architecture often starts from participants' own embodied assumptions and experiences. Building on the work of Rosemarie Garland-Thomson, [12] a feminist disability studies scholar, we refuse the artificial binaries of "able-bodied" or "disabled" by instead using the concepts of "fitting" and "misfitting." Rather than characteristics of ability (or gender, race, class, or sexuality) being located "in the body," these are always relational—dependent on the dynamic intersections between particular bodyminds, spaces, objects, and encounters. To "fit" is to find the normal world unproblematic, to be able to operate smoothly in it, without needing to take much notice of it. As Tanya Titchkosky writes,

"Language recommends that we conceive of the able-body as something that just comes along 'naturally' as people go about their daily existence. People just jump into the shower, run to the store, see what others mean while keeping an eye on the kids, or skipping from office to office and, having run through the day whilst managing to keep their noses clean, hop into bed. All of this glosses the body that comes along while, at the same time, brings it along metaphorically. Speaking of 'normal bodies' as movement and metaphor maps them as if they are a natural possession, as if they are not mapped at all." [13]

As Garland-Thomson explains, such fitting occurs in "a world conceptualized, designed, and built in anticipation of bodies considered in the dominant perspective as uniform, standard, majority bodies." [14] In contrast, misfitting occurs whenever your needs, preferences, or desires are unmet (whether unnoticed,

9 Tanya Titchkosky, "'To Pee or Not to Pee'? Ordinary Talk about Extraordinary Exclusions in a University Environment," *Canadian Journal of Sociology* 33, no. 1 (2008), 37—60, here 48.

10 Jay Dolmage, "Mapping Composition: Inviting Disability in the Front Door," in Cynthia Lewiecki-Wilson and Brenda Jo Brueggemann, *Disability and the Teaching of Writing: A Critical Sourcebook* (Boston: Bedford/St. Martin's, 2008), 14—27.

11 See M. Remi Yergeau et al., "Multimodality in Motion: Disability and Kairotic Spaces," *Kairos: A Journal of Rhetoric, Technology, and Pedagogy* 18, no. 1 (2013), https://kairos.technorhetoric.net/18.1/coverweb/yergeau-et-al/ (accessed February 20, 2022).

12 Rosemarie Garland-Thomson, "Misfits: A Feminist Materialist Disability Concept," in "Ethics of Embodiment," special issue, *Hypatia* 26 (2011), 591—609.

13 Tanya Titchkosky, *Disability, Self and Society* (Toronto: University of Toronto Press, 2003), 103.

14 Garland-Thomson, "Misfits," 595.

marginalized, misinterpreted, or deliberately excluded) by the design of built space and by its other occupants. You become (however momentarily) "the odd one out":

"In one moment and place there is a fit; in another moment and place a misfit. One citizen walks into a voting booth; another rolls across a curb cut; yet another bumps her wheels against a stair; someone passes fingers across the brailled elevator button; somebody else waits with a white cane before a voiceless ATM machine; some other blind user retrieves messages with a screen reader. Each meeting between subject and environment will be a fit or misfit depending on the choreography that plays out." [15]

So we ask our DisOrdinary Architecture workshop participants—and you the reader—to think about how smoothly *you* fit within your social and built surroundings. When and how often do you have to negotiate a failure to take notice, a lack of care, or experience thoughtless assumptions about who you are or what your needs are? This might only be about noticing uneven floor surfaces, awkward steps, and a lack of lifts when you are looking after a baby in a pushchair. **fig.1** Or it might be about negotiating the complexities of being the only woman or person of color at a formal meeting; or it might be about hiding ("passing" or "masking") the experiences of chronic pain or sight loss or neurodivergence as an architectural student, educator, or practitioner because disclosing is likely to adversely affect your studies or employment and because fighting for even reasonable adjustments is so often itself exhausting and unproductive. [16]

As Sara Ahmed writes, bodies take shape as they move through a world that either directs (orientates) them toward or away from themselves. [17] The experience—and unpleasant discomfort of—being directed away from yourself is one of the mechanisms through which power and privilege continually enact everyday discriminations, by undermining nonnormative ways of being—what feminist Sheila Rowbotham tellingly describes as "lumber(ing) around ungainly like in borrowed concepts which do not fit the shape we feel ourselves to be." [18] Together with Julia Dwyer, I have written elsewhere about how we are each implicated in experiencing, perpetuating, and/or contesting unequal and normative practices through both our personal and professional lives. [19] This is underpinned by commonsense assumptions that constitute the "normal" body as an unencumbered, mobile, autonomous, white, and well-resourced subject, as well as the preference in architectural education and practice for body-minds that are similarly unencumbered, but also obsessive and endlessly energetic and focused. [20] Nearly forty years ago,

15 Garland-Thomson, "Misfits," 595.

16 See, for example, Margaret Price et al., "Disclosure of Mental Disability by College and University Faculty: The Negotiation of Accommodations, Supports, and Barriers," *Disability Studies Quarterly* 37, no. 2 (2017), http://dsq-sds.org/article/view/5487 (accessed February 20, 2022). See also Margaret Price, "Everyday Survival and Collective Accountability" (University of Utah Disability Studies lecture, University of Utah, School for Cultural and Social Transformation, March 23, 2021), https://transform.utah.edu/dslecture-2021/ (accessed February 20, 2022). Similar studies of built environment education and practice have not yet been undertaken.

17 Sara Ahmed, *Queer Phenomenology: Orientations, Objects, Others* (Durham, NC: Duke University Press), 25.

18 Sheila Rowbotham, *Woman's Consciousness, Man's World* (Harmondsworth: Pelican, 1973), 35.

19 Boys, "Invisibility Work?," 270.

20 Challenging existing overwork processes in built environment education and practice are becoming more common. See, for example, the United Voices of the World Section of Architectural Workers: https://www.uvwunion.org.uk/en/sectors/architectural-workers/ (accessed February 20, 2022).

Matrix—through both its practice and book-writing group—also asked how built environment practices and built space design were gendered so as to create and perpetuate just such uncomfortable misfitting for women. 21 What has changed since then and by how much?

Analyzing our own assumptions about whose bodyminds are noticed and valued in conventional design processes and whose experiences are misrepresented or invisible also illuminates missed creative and critical opportunities. During the COVID-19 pandemic, for example, DisOrdinary Architecture worked with Fem_ArcSTUDIO from Berlin as part of a workshop series in which students challenged existing power structures in the built environment and explored new design tools. fig.2 COVID-19 shifted conventional relationships of public/private, inside/outside, visible/invisible, and included/excluded for "normal"

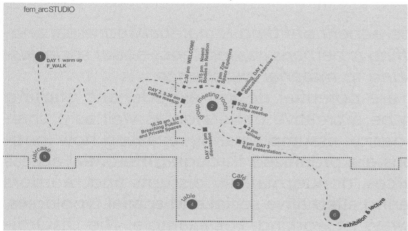

people by creating unpredictability and uncertainty in such everyday acts as going to the shops or the park. Such disruptions of "smoothness" demanded new creative skills in navigation and negotiation—an expertise many disabled people would say they already have just by living in the *normal* world. By working with disabled artists, students creatively and critically investigated their changed everyday practices as a means to explore how to design differently. 22

DisOrdinary Architecture artists also aim to open up invisibilities in designing for access, asking that built environment students, educators, and practitioners take more notice of how space is experienced not just differently but differently. In her seminal article "Lying Down Anyhow: Disability and the Rebel Body," disabled artist Liz Crow explores how the act of lying down in public (an essential access requirement for her as someone with chronic pain) becomes a story of external constraints, as societal assumptions about what is "proper" behavior are enacted and she is endlessly assumed to be homeless or drunk and moved on. 23 Both through her own practice and in DisOrdinary workshops, Liz has coexplores how built space might better offer informal places of rest.

21 Matrix (1984), *Making Space Women and the Man-Made Environment* (London: Verso, 2022), 1–11.

fig.2 Map of fem_arcSTUDIO's online collaboration with DisOrdinary Architecture, November 2020. Source: fem_arcSTUDIO, http://studio.fem-arc.net/

22 "Developing an Embodied Practice with DisOrdinary Architecture," *Fem_ArcSTUDIO 1*, November 2020, http://studio.fem-arc.net/ (accessed February 20, 2022).

23 Liz Crow, "Lying Down Anyhow: Disability and the Rebel Body" (2013), in Jos Boys, ed., *Disability, Space, Architecture: A Reader* (Oxford: Routledge, 2017), 42–47. Also available online at http://www.roaring-girl.com/work/lying-anyhow-disability-rebel-body/ (accessed October 23, 2021).

Difference as a Creative Generator

For a DisOrdinary design project at the University of Westminster, London in 2017 entitled "Tilted Horizons," Liz Crow and Julia Dwyer asked students to explore the effects and potential of lying down in public spaces. **24** **fig.3** This project started from the expertise that creative disabled people already have in negotiating spaces and encounters not made for them and in opening up new spaces of accessibility:

> "[T]he experience of misfitting can produce subjugated knowledges from which an oppositional consciousness and politicized identity might arise. So although misfitting can lead to segregation, exclusion from the rights of citizenship, and alienation from a majority community, it can also foster intense awareness of social injustice and the formation of a community of misfits that can collaborate to achieve a more liberatory politics and praxis. ...
>
> So whereas the benefit of fitting is material and visual anonymity, the cost of fitting is perhaps complacency about social justice and a desensitizing to material experience." **25**

Misfits, then, are potential design experts, and starting from difference can be a creative generator, as well as a challenge to normative design assumptions. By revealing how inequitable social relations are organized through differential access to space and resources, nonnormativity disrupts and reorders these relations—offering alternative social and spatial typologies, as well as different ways of working. For example, The DisOrdinary Architecture Project uses nonconventional drawing/mapping techniques—developed out of diverse disabled artists' own creative practices—to investigate experiences of embodiment that often disappear in conventional (visually oriented) orthographic techniques. This might be by changing our bodies to draw differently **fig.4** or by reframing the development of a design brief as an embodied process. **26** With Architectural Association (AA) tutors Manijeh Verghese and Inigo Minns, Deaf artist Aaron Williamson worked with students to explore how his creative practice could critique the normative forms of production of architectural projects. **27** This is one of several current DisOrdinary Architecture collaborations that start from the positive qualities of Deaf Gain, starting from the spaces that learn from the social, spatial and performative character of sign language. **28**

Another project aims to challenge the very nature of architectural education. Called Architecture Beyond Sight (ABS), it is a foundation-level one-week residential intensive study program to enable blind and partially sighted people to study architecture. It was originally commissioned in 2018 by the then dean

24 "Disabled Artists Making Dis/Ordinary Spaces," Liz Crow and Julia Dwyer, 2018, https://vimeo.com/showcase/4562223/video/215407274 (accessed February 20, 2022).

25 Garland-Thomson, "Misfits," 597.

26 *Narratives of Difference: A Collaboration between Rachel Gadsden, Judit Pusztaszeri and Students of the School of Architecture and Design, Brighton University,* dir. Tim Copsey for The DisOrdinary Architecture Project, posted as "Brighton University Case Study," Vimeo, March 6, 2019, https://vimeo.com/showcase/4562223/video/321870384 (accessed February 20, 2022).

27 *Disrupting Behaviors: A Collaboration between Aaron Williamson, Manijeh Verghese and the Students of the Architectural Association, London,* dir. Tim Copsey for The DisOrdinary Architecture Project, posted as "Architectural Association Case Study," Vimeo, July 17 2019, https://vimeo.com/showcase/4562223/video/348571812 (accessed February 20, 2022).

28 Todd Byrd, "Deaf Space," in Boys, *Disability, Space, Architecture,* 241–46. The term *Deaf Gain* originated with Aaron Williamson. See, for example, H-Dirksen L. Bauman and Joseph J. Murray, eds., *Deaf Gain: Raising the Stakes for Human Diversity* (Minneapolis: University of Minnesota Press, 2014), xv. The DisOrdinary Architecture Project is also developing a foundation course called "Vibrant Spaces" for Deaf people wanting to study architecture and a Deaf Space—informed temporary festival pavilion for Theater Formen in Germany.

of the Faculty of the Built Environment at the Bartlett School of Architecture, University College London, and has run once with fifteen participants (and again in August 2022, post-pandemic). Program development and implementation has been disability-led throughout, starting with a one-year development process,

with the course itself led by blind and partially sighted architects, makers, and artists. Like conventional foundation courses, studies are centered on conceptual thinking, design making, spatial and atmospheric mapping, and interpretation and design communication. But tutors and students also codevelop ways of designing beyond the visual, including audio description, large-scale sketching, and tactile and performative communications. This, in turn, suggests methods that all architectural students and practitioners could use to design

differently. **29** **fig.5** ABS thus works at multiple levels. It provides blind and visually impaired people with the confidence, skills, and portfolio to apply for further educational opportunities conventionally unavailable to them; it challenges normative assumptions about what disabled people are capable of creatively; it opens up alternative ways of designing space beyond the norms of standard orthography; and it models best practices for providing truly accessible design education. As one of the participating blind students writes,

I went on the Architecture Beyond Sight course at the Bartlett School of Architecture in London, with no expectations and I've gained far more than I could ever have imagined. ... We had been asked to make a box inspired by our time at the British Library, I've ended up making two, one made of driftwood, that's texture and smell links back to the library's architectural links to ships and there for the sea. ...

On Saturday [the day after the workshop finished] I woke up and realised I've spent years making art accessible for others but no one has ever made anything accessible for me in my entire life, this was a very emotional realisation.

I realised that being excluded or only getting half the information had become the norm. As recently as last year I was told it didn't matter if I learnt things properly because I couldn't see anyway, it was at that moment that I decided I needed to find a new way of learning because these tutors only see my visual impairment, they don't see me as an artist who exhibits and does art residencies unlike the tutors [sic] attitudes this week. **30**

fig. 3 "Tilted Horizons," a design project codeveloped by disabled artist Liz Crow and architect Julia Dwyer, who invited interior design students from the University of Westminster, London, to explore the conditions of, and adapt existing spaces for, lying down. Screenshot from video by Tim Copsey, 2017

29 *Architecture beyond Sight*, dir. Tim Copsey, posted as "Architecture beyond Sight 2018," Vimeo, October 24, 2018, https://vimeo.com/showcase/4562223/video/296974975 (accessed February 19, 2022; and Anna Ulrikke Andersen, *Architecture beyond Sight* (dir., 2019), https://annaulrikkeandersen.com/2019/08/23/architecture-beyond-sight/ (accessed February 20, 2022).

fig. 4 Exploratory device for drawing differently, developed by students at the Royal Academy of Design, Copenhagen KADK, for the *Alternator* project, created by disabled artist David Dixon. Photograph: Jos Boys, 2018

30 Fae Kilburn, "Architecture Beyond Sight," *Disability Arts Online (DAO)* [blog], August 6, 2019, https://disabilityarts.online/blog/fae-kilburn/architecture-beyond-sight/ (accessed February 19, 2022).

To me, this is the closest DisOrdinary Architecture has come, to date, to implementing care as active practice.

Access Is Love

As Leah Lakshmi Piepzna-Samarasinha writes in their seminal work *Care Work: Dreaming Disability Justice* (2018), the first Creating Collective Access network started in the United States in 2010, aiming to break away from normative "'access as a service begrudgingly offered to disabled people by non-disabled people who feel grumpy about it' to 'access as collective joy and offering we can give to each other.'" **31** Since then, many disabled activists and scholars, such as Sins Invalid (2017), the Disability Visibility Project, **32** and Aimi Hamraie's Critical Design Lab **33** —all always working intersectionally—have been exploring ideas of collective care, developments that can vitally inform built environment education and practice

31 Leah Lakshmi Piepzna-Samarasinha, *Care Work: Dreaming Disability Justice* (Vancouver, BC: Arsenal Pulp Press, 2018), 16–17.

32 Alice Wong, ed., *Disability Visibility: First Person Stories from the 21st Century* (New York: Vintage Books, 2020), xv–xvii. See also the "Access Is Love" project, https://disabilityvisibilityproject.com/2019/02/01/access-is-love/ (accessed February 17, 2022).

33 See https://www.mapping-access.com/lab (accessed February 20, 2022); and Aimi Hamraie, *Building Access: Universal Design and the Politics of Disability* (Minneapolis: University of Minnesota Press, 2018), here xiii–xiv.

if the discipline just takes time to listen. Care is here framed as responsive, reciprocal, emergent, dynamic, and adaptive. It is not split along caregiver/care receiver, active/passive, normative/non-normrative divides or "solved" through mechanical design solutions added onto the end of a design project conceived originally for bodies not needing care. As Piepzna-Samarasinha asks,

fig. 5 A partially sighted "Architecture Beyond Sight" participant explains her one-week foundation design project to one blind and one sighted tutor in an "under-the-table" crit. Photograph: Jos Boys, 2019

34 Piepzna-Samarasinha, *Care Work*, 33.

"What does it mean to shift our ideas of access and care (whether its disability, childcare, economic access or many, many more) from an individual chore, an unfortunate cost of having an unfortunate body, to a collective responsibility that's maybe even deeply joyful?" **34**

Mia Mingus also explores such an understanding through the concept of access intimacy:

"Access intimacy is that elusive, hard to describe feeling when someone else 'gets' your access needs. The kind of eerie comfort that your disabled self feels with someone on a purely access level. Sometimes it can happen with complete strangers, disabled or not, or sometimes it can be built over years. It could also be the way your body relaxes and opens up with someone when all your access needs are being met. ...

It doesn't mean that our access looks the same, or that we even know what each other's access needs are. ... Sometimes access intimacy doesn't even mean that everything is 100% accessible. Sometimes it looks like both of you trying to create access as hard as you can with no avail in an ableist world.

Sometimes it is someone just sitting and holding your hand while you both stare back at an inaccessible world." 35

Accessibility understood like this is an always emergent, partial, and shared activity. Of course, such a way of articulating access causes problems for conventional architectural forms of thinking and doing. It is less focused on the "bright new shiny thing" of the next building or project and more on the slow and particular, on diverse people finding creative ways to occupy space through negotiation and adaptation.

Care as Repair, Adaptation, and Maintenance

Kim Kullman's research on the Ed Roberts Campus, a well-known disability-led building in Berkeley, California, 36 offers clues about how interpreting care as repair, adaptation, and maintenance can challenge normative built environment practices. fig. 6 The original building design for the campus grew out of a campaign by mainly physically disabled people—a particular historical moment of disability activism 37 —but its ongoing value to diverse disabled people means that it has adapted to the needs of more recently self-advocating groups, such as autistic people and those with environmental sensitivities. For these newer generations of disability activists, impairment is not so obviously framed around identity categories such as wheelchair users, blind or deaf people, or focused on "barriers" that can be designed out. Kullman suggests that the people with environmental sensitivities he talked to were much more concerned to explore the intersections between their vulnerabilities and the requirements of other disabled people in the building—recognizing tensions and multiple needs as a means to develop improvements—rather than by first defining the "needs" of different impairment groups and then somehow adding these together to produce a "universal design."

This research also highlights the vital role of ongoing service support in managing these tensions productively and illustrates how building maintenance and caretakers—mostly learning-disabled people at the Ed Roberts Campus in a supported employment scheme—respond to complex differences positively and creatively. This is ongoing detailed work that is often framed as problematic—as a "wasted" resource in conventional building services and management—because it takes time and connection to support individual adaptation of, for example, building-wide ventilation, heating, and lighting systems. This project's continuing commitment to meeting diverse needs is a great illustration of both access as collective care and care as embodied practice. To conceive of built space like this requires moving access out of its normative location as an "add-on" technical and

35 Mia Mingus, "Access Intimacy: The Missing Link," *Leaving Evidence* [blog], May 5, 2011, https://leaving evidence.wordpress.com/2011/05/05/access-intimacy-the-missing-link/ (accessed February 26, 2022).

36 Kim Kullman, "Politics of Dissensus in Geographies of Architecture: Testing Equality at Ed Roberts Campus, Berkeley," *Transactions of the Institute of British Geographers* 44, no. 2 (June 2019), 284—98, https://doi.org/10.1111/tran.12276.

37 The building is named in honor of Ed Roberts (1939—1995), a pioneer of the disability rights movement in the United States. After his death, a disabled group came together to develop an inclusive campus for organizations that provide services to disabled people.

38 See Mia Mingus, "Access Intimacy, Interdependence and Disability Justice" (Paul K. Longmore Lecture on Disability Studies, San Francisco State University, April 11, 2017), https://sfpirg.ca/wp-content/uploads/2017/08/Access-Intimacy-Mia-Mingus.pdf (accessed October 31, 2021).

39 Yergeau et al., "Multimodality in Motion," https://kairos.technorhetoric.net/18.1/coverweb/yergeau-et-al/pages/index.html (accessed December 8, 2022).

legal solution, "out of the realm of only logistics and into the realm of relationships and of understanding disabled people as human beings, not burdens." [38]

In addition, centering care in this long term and adaptive way requires a generosity of investment (of both capital and revenue) in spaces, resources, and services, not just one accessible toilet but several with different facilities, corridors spacious enough for comfortable passing, doors wide enough to get through easily in a mobility scooter or with children or when carrying packages. This demands a major shift from normative allocation (where a grand commercial foyer is value for money but a lift is "too expensive"). And it requires multimodality as a core design principle. Multimodality—the layering of multiple access requirements—needs to be underpinned by what Yergeau and colleagues call an ethics of accessibility, requiring responsible and respectful attention paid to the differences people bring to a situation "that allow[s] the broadest possible range of people to make meaning in ways that work best for them." [39] Yergeau particularly discusses how multimodality needs to be more than just the additive combination of different elements (particularly if this retains a "retrofitting" mentality). We need always to be exploring how those access layers can be commensurable, however varied, without a differential quality of experience. Committing to multimodality, then, is a deliberate redistribution of resources toward those who currently face barriers and away from those who already occupy space smoothly.

Toward Care as an Active Practice

In the 1970s and 1980s, I was one of many feminists trying to better understand how space was gendered rather than neutral (the common assumption) at a time when sexism was not a concept in everyday use, let alone in architectural discourse. Matrix worked to enable women and other disadvantaged groups to imagine and actively be involved in creating new building types (e.g., women's centers and refuges and radically different forms of shared childcare). It did this by developing equitable design methods (e.g., explaining the arcane language of architectural drawings, working with easily manipulated physical models, and by creating straightforward techniques for understanding scale); by aiming to break down boundaries across construction and design so as to bring more women into the built environment sector; and by creating multiple sites of discussion and development. The DisOrdinary Architecture Project continues in that vein, starting this time from disability-led creative arts practices to develop a similar range of tactics to help us better understand how our built surroundings disable (not just in relation to impairment but also beyond it) and how we might begin to productively "crip" not just built space but — as Matrix did — the normative modes of practice across built environment disciplines that (re)produce inequalities. We agree that "when disability activists enter ... the profession of architecture, they show ... that architects do not just design buildings, they also design curricula, licensing requirements, research, and fields of discourse that give meaning to their work." [40] This means everything from rethinking employment and continual professional development practices, to building in ways of engaging with the creativity of disabled people across all aspects of the discipline, to exploring alternative design methods and forms of representation.

40 Matthew Allen, "Designing for Disability Justice: On the Need to Take a Variety of Human Bodies into Account," Harvard Graduate School of Design, February 10, 2021, https://www.gsd.harvard.edu/2021/02/designing-for-disability-justice-on-the-need-to-take-a-variety-of-human-bodies-into-account/ (accessed March 4, 2022).

Again, the intention here is ridiculously idealistic. But it starts with each of us and our own embodied practices and moves toward an ongoing, slow, but increasing accumulation

fig. 6 Internal view of the Ed Roberts Campus, University of California, Berkeley, 2011. Designed by Leddy Maytum Stacy Architects. Photograph: Tim Griffith

of changed mindsets and new kinds of actions, an accumulation that can snowball into a real paradigm shift. For built environment professionals, educators, researchers, and students this means recognizing and acting against the normative assumptions of privilege (we are already privileged in being able to read this). The intent is not to create feelings of guilt, blame, or embarrassment or to ask "What shall I do?" or "What is the solution?" (questions that nonnormative people have been fielding for many, many years). It is instead about listening to those most impacted by social, spatial, and material inequalities, finding ways to be an ally across diverse forms of misfitting and discrimination, and intervening when needed to call out inequalities. For the built environment industries, it is about paying attention to the sheer oddness of designing for "normal" people and then adding on access "solutions" for those you have already left out. It also means critically reflecting on current ways of working within architecture as a discipline. This could include challenging professionalism as "neutral" consensus, compromise, and balance instead of looking to social, spatial, and material justice. It could be about rethinking design techniques that are still stuck in the limitations of orthography. Wherever you focus, caring, in this understanding, is to explore how—within the very real constraints of contemporary architectural education, theory, and practice—normative practices and spaces might be critically and creatively rethought and redesigned. As David Graeber writes, "the ultimate, hidden truth of the world is that it is something that we make, and could just as easily make differently." [41]

41 David Graeber, *The Utopia of Rules: On Technology, Stupidity, and the Secret Joys of Bureaucracy* (Brooklyn: Melville House, 2016), 89.

Ceramics, Sex, and Infrastructure:
A Queer Erotics of Urbanism
Max J. Andrucki

Queer Urban Infrastructure

What makes a queer city? How should we understand the inter-section of desire, bodies, and nonhuman objects that continuously makes and remakes it? Geographers and other social scientists have attended to the spatiality of urban queer life since the 1980s, if not before, but in comparison to their quantification and elucidation of the bounded sites and spaces of gay life, little attention has been paid within queer urban studies to the net-works of material infrastructure that actually enable queer life. The dominant method geographers have used to study the gay and lesbian—and, later, queer—urban is derived from what is some-times called the "ethnic" model of urban clustering. John D'Emilio traced the emergence of gay urban subcultures in the United States to histories of urbanization associated with wage labor and thus the ability of people with same-sex attractions to live independently of families for the first time. Earlier studies, like that of Catalan sociologist Manuel Castells, pioneered the con-vention of treating gay men's urban land-use patterns as simi-lar to the 1920s Chicago School's urban ecology framework for understanding how ethnic groups successively invade, take over, and then depart from particular zones of urban space. [1] For Castells, San Francisco's Castro and similar neighborhoods that flourished and became visible in the 1960s marked the radical territorial claims of a highly stigmatized and marginalized pop-ulation and served as sites for the entry of gay people as sub-jects into the formal order of politics, embodied most famously by San Francisco supervisor Harvey Milk. At the same time, Castells argued that white gay men contributed to the rescue and rebirth of cities devastated by economic restructuring and white flight. [2] Generations of geographers have focused on the role of neighborhoods, homes, and other bounded entities as contain-ers for queer urban sociality. [3]

Many subsequent geographers and urban historians have deployed Castells's model to map not just the presence but the evolution of gay neighborhoods in various cities within the glo-balizing economy. The implications of imbrication with forces of neoliberal capitalism and, by extension, gentrification are never far away, but scholars are focused on attending to the extent to which gay neighborhoods are being selectively and problem-atically incorporated into the urban entrepreneurial strategies

Max J. Andrucki is an Associate Professor in the Department of Geography and Urban Studies at Temple University in Philadel-phia, Pennsylvania.

1 John D'Emilio, "Capitalism and Gay Identity," in Henry Abelove, Michèle Aina Barale, and David M. Halperin, eds., The Gay and Lesbian Studies Reader (New York: Routledge, 1993), 467–76, here 470; and Manuel Castells, The City and the Grass-roots: A Cross-cultural Theory of Urban Social Movements (Berkeley and Los Angeles: University of California Press, 1983), 138–70, here 156–58.

2 Castells, The City and the Grassroots, 166.

3 See, notably, David Bell and Gill Valentine, eds., Mapping Desire: Geographies of Sexualities (London: Routledge, 1995), 8.

4 See David Bell and Jon Binnie, "Authenticating Queer Space: Citizenship, Urbanism and Governance," *Urban Studies* 41, no. 9 (2004), 1807–20, here 1807.

5 See Christina B. Hanhardt, *Safe Space* (Durham, NC: Duke University Press, 2013), 188; and Camila Bassi, "Riding the Dialectical Waves of Gay Political Economy: A Story from Birmingham's Commercial Gay Scene," *Antipode* 38, no. 2 (2006), 213–35. See also the preface to Jen Jack Gieseking, *A Queer New York: Geographies of Lesbians, Dykes, and Queers* (New York: NYU Press, 2020).

6 Jason Orne, *Boystown* (Chicago: University of Chicago Press, 2017), 4; and Amin Ghaziani, *There Goes the Gayborhood?* (Princeton, NJ: Princeton University Press, 2014), 2.

7 See Michael Brown and Larry Knopp, "Queering the Map: The Productive Tensions of Colliding Epistemologies," *Annals of the Association of American Geographers* 98, no. 1 (2008), 40–58, here 45.

8 See Christopher Castiglia and Christopher Reed, *If Memory Serves: Gay Men, AIDS, and the Promise of the Queer Past* (Minneapolis: University of Minnesota Press, 2012), 77. See also Michael Kimmelman, "Sculpture, Sculpture Everywhere," *New York Times*, July 31, 1992.

by which cities attempt to position themselves within the international spatial division of consumption—by attracting gay tourist dollars and branding themselves as tolerant in the struggle to attract capital, as has been documented in cities such as Manchester, Singapore, and Tel Aviv. 4 A second and contrasting strain of research focuses on the apparent demise of urban gay neighborhoods. Scholars have noted that gay ghettos remain dependent on the contradictions of the capitalist space-economy and that, in the face of hypergentrification, as in New York, they disappear into myth and live on as constellations of memory. 5 Other scholars have attributed the demise of gay neighborhoods to processes of homonormativity, whereby upwardly mobile gay men, some of whom form nuclear families, invest in properties elsewhere in urban areas as they lose interest in spaces of queer politics, nightlife, and hedonism. The depressed property values that gay men raised through painstaking efforts of restoration in declining inner-city neighborhoods led directly to a process of hollowing out of the character of gay neighborhoods through their colonization and desexualization by curious tourists and other straight interlopers. 6

Recognizing that gay venues and neighborhoods are always in flux, geographers have turned to oral histories and archival materials to record palimpsests of urban gay space for posterity. 7 In a similar vein, a sense of transience and loss, and the imperative to unpick queer practices of traumatic amnesia in the wake of the HIV-AIDS crisis, has led to new spatial practices of memorialization; that is, to the production of new, ostensibly permanent sites in urban landscapes commemorating gay civil rights struggles and the memory of gay and queer people murdered by fascism and taken by AIDS. Particularly notable are George Segal's 1980 Gay Liberation Monument (finally installed in 1992) in New York City and Karin Daan's Homomonument in Amsterdam (1987). The former has been the subject of intense criticism for how it whitewashes and cis-washes the legacy of the Stonewall Riots—and also for just being bad art. 8

In this article I propose an alternative vocabulary for the queer urban, one that is anchored less to fixed sites and spaces. I ask how queer artistic and sexual practices might perform a queer urban infrastructure, and I explore a theory of queer infrastructure that takes seriously the performative materiality of the city.

If we want a history of the visualization of bodies as the infrastructure of the city, we do not need to look much further than the work of situationist Guy Debord. For his piece *Naked City*, he cut up a map of Paris and rearranged it to give a sense of the way the logics of the capitalist city channel our bodies, often unaware, through space. 9 The places we come together he calls "*plaques tournantes.*" This is the French term for the rotating plates that reposition trains at depots, but for Debord they are psychogeographic "pivot points" — the most frequently used English translation of the term — where multiple logics and inhabitations of the city converge. For Debord, the meeting points occupy and substitute for the role of heavy industrial infrastructure. The city, rendered naked, is a place where capitalist urbanism is exposed as a force that brings bodies together in infrastructural moments. These moments have a latent capacity to create collective possibilities of reimagining; that is, infrastructures for unlearning.

For AbdouMaliq Simone, bodies themselves are infrastructure. His focus is on the ways that individual bodies improve the provision of public goods in cities such as Johannesburg and Abidjan, where the physical infrastructures that provide public goods are not reliable and where states lack the power to enforce a modernist division of spatial functions and assignment of bodies into them. As Simone writes, "The accelerated, extended, and intensified intersections of bodies, landscapes, objects and technologies defer calcification of institutional ensembles or fixed territories of belonging." 10 Simone argues that such "infrastructure" is not merely provisional but actively resists the inscription of institutional power in the urban landscape. This process is particularly marked in African postcolonial contexts in which material deprivation combines with an imperative to celebrate the indigenization of urban patterns and processes. In the present article I draw from psychoanalysis and its critiques to suggest that thinking through desire as a mode of infrastructure can help us move past fantasies of the queer urban as a legible series of discrete and organically coherent utopian counterpublics. Emphasizing desire becomes a way to think queer urbanism as a messy set of caring practices that exceed individuals and couples, households and families.

Gay male writers such as Edmund White have articulated a sense in which bodily traces and viscosities of public and non-monogamous sexual encounter work as the "sticky semen-glue that binds [gay men] together." 11 The work of Samuel Delaney on Greenwich Village in the 1960s, for example, vividly presents the queer urban as a space of care that is performed through the management, exchange, and disposal of bodily surpluses. During the orgies that took place in trucks on the West Side Piers, he writes, "cock passed from mouth to hand to ass to mouth without ever breaking contact with other flesh for more than seconds. Mouth, hand, ass passed over whatever you held out to them, sans interstice." 12 For Delaney, this is a moving and deeply

9 Guy Debord, *The Naked City: Illustration de l'hypothèse des plaques tournantes en psychogéographique,* lithographic map (Loire Valley: FRAC, 1957).

10 AbdouMaliq Simone, "People as Infrastructure: Intersecting Fragments in Johannesburg," *Public Culture* 16, no. 3 (2004), 407–29, here 408.

11 Edmund White, *The Farewell Symphony* (New York: Vintage, 1998), 396.

12 Samuel Delaney, *The Motion of Light in Water: Sex and Science Fiction Writing in the East Village* (New York: Arbor House, 1988), 226.

human scene. Crucially, for him, it signifies a mode of "being for others" that is not prefigurative of utopia but is a mode of enacting urbanism as a form of conscious, engaged, and fleshy copresence and exchange. These queer infrastructures constitute what Thomas Strong calls "vital publics": "forms of embodied association elicited through the generalized exchange of body." Strong focuses on blood and the politics of gay men's blood donation in Canada (specifically, some blood's selective exclusion from the Canadian national bloodstream), pointing to how the circulation of bodily fluids "draw[s] persons into reciprocal relations peculiarly characterized by an intimate strangerhood." [13]

We can think of the nonmonogamous gay male body, among other urban bodies, as itself a *plaque tournante*, a public space, one where multiple, strangely intimate bodies are brought together, where intensities are performed and lived, connections made and broken, where the residue of temporary residence and mundane mobilities accumulates. As I have written elsewhere, [14] embodiments of care that range queerly across the boundaries of platonic and erotic, and of public and private, have been central to the way gay men have continued to reproduce themselves in urban contexts such as San Francisco that have been beset with repeated rounds of social and economic conflict since the middle of the twentieth century, particularly the ongoing response to the tragedy of HIV. Note that my intention here is not to argue that gay men's intimate body-publics are to be ontologically privileged as central to the constitution of the city. Saidiya Hartman's *Wayward Lives, Beautiful Experiments* is just one example of careful historical work that places women's, in this case Black women's, sexual experimentation and nonmonogamous and queer practices as central to a rendition of the emergence of American urban modernity at the turn of the twentieth century. [15] As Hartman demonstrates, many, if not most, of the Black women whose lives she limns paid dearly for their sexual nonconformity, even as they constructed new worlds of experience in the emerging ghettos of America's northern cities before and during the Harlem Renaissance. Contemporary gay men provide a different kind of example for several reasons. We now live in an age in which formal legal equality for gays and lesbians has been attained in most jurisdictions of the developed world. Pharmaco-capitalism has, in the guise of PrEP and combination therapies, obviated the immediate threats of the AIDS crisis for many if not most. New digital technologies have massively expanded possibilities of access to multiple sexual partners (as well as infinitely multiplying the force of sexual rejection). Most significant, the messy and playful queering of

13 Thomas Strong, "Vital Publics of Pure Blood," *Body and Society* 15, no. 2 (2009), 169–91, here 173.

14 Max J. Andrucki, "Queering Social Reproduction: Sex, Care and Activism in San Francisco," *Urban Studies* 58, no. 7 (2021), 1364–79.

15 Saidiya Hartman, *Wayward Lives, Beautiful Experiments: Intimate Histories of Riotous Black Girls, Troublesome Women, and Queer Radicals* (New York: W.W. Norton, 2019), 161–92.

distinctions between the erotic and the platonic, public and private, that so indelibly shapes gay men's urban socialities also "inoculates" gay communities from supposed threats of assimilationist deradicalization that, according to some, are always threatening gay libertine existence. [16] Saunas, bathhouses, sex parties, and dark rooms pepper the urban landscape in a way that is qualitatively different from that of many other urban subjects — after all, gay men continue to manifest forms of privilege vis-à-vis women, whose sexuality remains policed in very different ways, whose lives are constrained by lower incomes and economic restructuring, and whose vulnerability to violence sometimes precludes spontaneous engagements with strangers.

Ceramic World Building

If queer infrastructure is an infrastructure of improvised care, then urbanists might attend to the gay male body's material traces, which circulate through urban space, as the infrastructure of a queer city. One arena of materialization of those traces is how ceramics emerges not just as an assemblage point through which bodies and urban materials intersect and pass but specifically how ceramics materialize an erotics of care that simultaneously embodies and radically resists the normative sublimation of homoerotic libidinal energy. What follows is less an empirical claim than a set of reflections on the work of two gay male craft ceramics artists/producers in London, which I read through the postpsychoanalytic work of Guy Hocquenghem and Herbert Marcuse. I turn to the work of craft ceramicists for several key reasons that constitute their work as emblematic examples of a queer infrastructure. First, on a literal level, ceramics actually do constitute infrastructure. As Paul Mathieu in his book *Sex Pots: Eroticism in Ceramics* suggests, ceramics cannot be abstracted from the traditional close association with the body. He argues that "pottery is part of the cycle of life (and death) sustained by food, and pottery functions are closely related to bodily functions: pottery contains, preserves and excretes food and liquids, then receives the waste the body rejects." He continues,

"The scatological aspect of clay is reinforced not only by its appearance, colour and tactile qualities, but by its commonality, its availability, its cheapness, its crudeness, as well as its domestic nature, in relation to food primarily but also, and importantly here, to body functions. After all, the bathroom is an almost completely ceramic space." [17]

Like bodies, ceramics can be hard or soft. Whether fired or not, they may crack or crumble. If glazed, they have a kind of skin that is smooth; if not glazed, they are rough and can

[16] See, for instance, Timothy Stewart-Winter, "The Price of Gay Marriage" *New York Times*, June 26, 2015, SR1.

[17] Paul Mathieu, *Sex Pots: Eroticism in Ceramics* (New Brunswick, NJ: Rutgers University Press, 2003), 159.

be porous. Ceramics are thus not only closely associated with bodily functions and engagements with the world, but they can be said to possess a transitive property, not only coenacting bodily performances with the body but themselves emerging and circulating as traces of the body. Many pipes are ceramic. But also: bricks are ceramic.

Second, although craft production itself constitutes only a minor part of any urban economy, economic geographers have recently called attention to the role of craft production in the post-Fordist city. In their discussion of this overlooked sector of the "Third Italy" (industrial districts in northern and central Italy dominated by small manufacturing firms), Bertacchini and Borrione write of the need to attend to "the revitalization of craft based and design-intensive sectors whose products carry a strong semiotic and aesthetic content." [18]   Though artisans are often strongly embedded in the cultural traditions of particular places, rather than being anachronistically out of place, craft production sits easily as a supplementary mode of flexible production alongside the consumption of mass-produced commodities financed through the deployment of nimble, footloose capital. The invisibilization of craft production in literatures on economic geography, as well as its marginalization in the art world, is inseparable from its status as feminized labor or, when performed by men, as "queer labor." The historian Allan Bérubé denotes work by men in the "decorative, designing, and self-expressive arts" as one such type of queer labor. [19]   Mathieu argues that the traditionally large number of gay and lesbian potters might be the result of parallels with craft's marginalization in the art world. That marginalization, Mathieu suggests, is because of the commonness of ceramics — its usefulness and touchability devalue it in relation to the precious and untouchable "uselessness" of purely visual art.

The work of Frederik Andersson and Will Martin indexes the potential of desire, desublimated, to organize care. Gay white migrants to the global city of London, both men are prolific and active on social media. They both produce vessel work, often replete with sexual imagery, that they market through Instagram, Etsy, and local craft markets — Andersson through his comic illustration, sometimes imprinted on his pots; and Martin through his decorative urns, installation work, and other forays into the register of fine art. Both men's work is emblematic of the way ceramics constitutes a form of infrastructure, a set of improvisations for how erotics of care might be visualized and circulate to index fragments and gestures of the queer urban.

Swedish-born illustrator and ceramicist Andersson was trained as an illustrator and is a restless and prolific producer

18 Enrico E. Bertacchini and Paola Borrione, "The Geography of the Italian Creative Economy: The Special Role of the Design and Craft-Based Industries," *Regional Studies* 47, no. 2 (2013), 135–47, here 136.

19 Allan Bérubé, *My Desire for History: Essays in Gay, Community, and Labor History* (Chapel Hill: University of North Carolina Press, 2011), 268.

of queer images, notorious for his anal imagery, in particular his depiction of rimming (oral-anal sex). **fig.1** His ceramic work is mostly in the "vessel tradition"—objects useful in the social reproduction of everyday life. Cups, plates, and bowls are tools deployed in the work of providing nourishment to loved ones,

fig.1 Fred Andersson, *Rimming Vases*, 2020, ceramic. Source: Fred Andersson

a form of hidden and unpaid yet socially indispensable labor that, as feminists have long argued, subtends and subsidizes the productive capacity of capitalism itself. [20] Like photographs, ceramics are what Divya Tolia-Kelly calls "image objects," things that circulate materially while they signify. [21] As Mathieu notes, the core experience of craft is centered on touch—the passage of objects from hand to hand, whether through direct sale or through the provision of food and drink—as opposed to visual art, which separates us from the world and is perceived only with the eye. But Andersson's bawdy vessels insistently call attention to themselves, doggedly depicting imagery of male buttocks and rimming to disrupt the complicit invisibilization of infrastructures of reproductive labor through the exuberant discursive inscription of queer motifs on hand-produced items.

For French proto-queer theorist Guy Hocquenghem, anality functions as a form of queer sociality because, while it is most private and in many ways constitutive of personhood, it cannot be owned and does not circulate discursively in the same way the phallus does. Drawing deeply on Gilles Deleuze and Félix Guattari, Hocquenghem's 1970s essays describe nonmonogamous gay sex cultures as a "pickup machine" in which "all encounters become possible" and "polyvocal desire is plugged in on a non-exclusive basis." [22] He offers the example of the "sexual communism" of the Turkish baths, where the anus recovers "its functions as a desiring bond and [is] collectively reinvested ... against a society which has reduced it to the state of a shameful little secret." [23] This is a project of rejecting sublimation by subverting the paranoia that is traditionally understood as its guardian.

The successful sublimation of homosexual desire channeled through the anus into productive social action and the genitalization of heterosexual desire in the properly oedipalized individual is a core tenet of psychoanalytic thought. [24] Sigmund Freud fully fleshes out his concept of the relation between homosexual desire, paranoia, and sublimation in *The Schreber Case*. [25]

[20] See Mariarosa Dalla Costa and Selma James, *The Power of Women and the Subversion of the Community* (Bristol: Falling Water Press, 1973), 5.

[21] Divya Tolia-Kelly, "Materializing Postcolonial Geographies: Examining the Textural Landscapes of Migration in the South Asian Home," *Geoforum* 35, no. 6 (2004), 675—88.

[22] Guy Hocquenghem, *Homosexual Desire* (Durham, NC: Duke University Press, 1993), 131.

[23] Hocquenghem, *Homosexual Desire*, 111.

[24] See Sándor Ferenczi, "Stimulation of the Anal Erotogenic Zone as a Precipitating Factor in Paranoia," in *Final Contributions to the Problems and Methods of Psycho-Analysis* (London: Karnac, 2002), 295—98, for a discussion of a man who withdraws from active participation in parish life after an operation to remove an anal fistula.

[25] Sigmund Freud, *The Schreber Case: Sigmund Freud*, trans. by Andrew Webber (New York: Penguin, 2003).

Schreber, a nineteenth-century German judge confined to a psychiatric hospital, wrote extensive memoirs in which, according to Freud, he reported experiencing instinctual libidinal homosexual longings. In Freud's reading, these desires were unacceptable to Schreber, who defended against them by attributing them to the active desire of an Other. According to Schreber, first his doctor (Flechsig) and then God wanted to castrate and then penetrate him. Freud uses the case to argue that not just Schreber but everybody has homosexual and heterosexual libidinal urges and that in proper subjects the homosexual urges are sublimated or repressed into the unconscious and channeled into other, socially acceptable outlets. All of Schreber's desires that might be about pleasure and receiving it are transformed into familial longing, an attempt at nonincestuous closeness with his deceased brother and distant, formidable father. **26**

26 I am grateful to conversations with Adam Gaubinger for these and other ideas.

Freud uses the case to argue that paranoia is a way of reacting to the homosexual wish fantasy: in this and all similar cases, paranoia is about homosexual desire and the fear that one can never quite repress and sublimate it enough into socially acceptable channels. This is all couched in language full of bursting and flows:

"People who have not fully released themselves from the stage of narcissism ... are open to the danger that a flood of libido which finds no other outlet may subject their social drives to sexualization and so reverse the sublimations that they have achieved in the course of their development." **27**

27 Freud, *Schreber Case*, 52.

Schreber illustrates how the terrifying failure to effectively sublimate homosexual desire leads to the failure of the narcissist's world in the form of a collapse into paranoia.

Hocquenghem, writing decades later, chafed against the homophobia embedded in Freud's notion of a properly oedipalized subject whose homosexual longings are appropriately channeled into productive social investments. Hocquenghem posits a new ontology of queer desire, one that resists and circumvents the imperatives of sublimation to celebrate the polyvalent possibilities of sexual and social realignment always foreclosed by the teleology of psychoanalysis. He writes,

"To fail one's sublimation is merely to conceive social relations in a different way. Possibly, when the anus recovers its desiring function and the plugging in of organs takes place subject to no rule or law, the group can then take its pleasure in an immediate relation where the sacrosanct difference between public and private, between the individual and the social, will be out of place." **28**

28 Hocquenghem, *Homosexual Desire*, 111.

The radical potential for homosexuality is its "group" or "annular mode," from the Latin word for "ring," which causes the "'social' of the phallic hierarchy ... to collapse." [29] Informed by his experiences in May 1968 in Paris, Hocquenghem sees the emergence of the radical gay movement at the same time as a wholly new form of the social that refuses any ontology of politics that excludes desire and that "desublimates everything it can by putting sex into everything." [30] These gay groupings are free to range across modes of sexual and political practice because they are predicated not on the repression of anal energy into civil society but on liberation from that repression. Nonmonogamy is not incidental here. This reformulation of the political infrastructure of desire allows us to reimagine the neoliberal city as one that is aspirationally post-oedipal; that is, not constructed according to heteropatriarchal logics of the family. This city is one in which sexual impulses, rather than being channeled through sublimation into the construction of "proper" infrastructures of reproductive futurity, proliferate through the creation of new modes of experiencing and inhabiting body parts in proliferating combinations. Thus we see how the enactment of multiple simultaneous forms of being-in-relation of publics and privates, and the ludic inscription of this anal order onto Andersson's ceramic objects, enacts the queering of orders of subjecthood and objecthood.

Andersson is keen to point out that his work is not "erotica" but "cute," a way of visualizing, circulating, and prompting discussions about queer sex without making it "horny talk." [31] Andersson's objects can thus sit on public view within private homes, viewed by owners and curious visitors alike, drawing attention to themselves through a recursive emphasis on the anal on and in clay. This ability to attain nuanced registers of the erotic is, he explains, the very nature of illustration. Andersson's simple line allows sex to be depicted explicitly but in ways that do not alienate casual viewers. Craft production in a deeply unequal global city rests on a compromise such that, despite any radical intentions of artisanal producers like Andersson, to make ends meet they need to sell their products at high prices to those who can afford them. Mechanizing production would lower prices, but that, for Anderson, is unthinkable. His provisional response to this contradiction is to spend a large fraction of his time donating "cute erotic" art to and volunteering for social service organizations that serve the most disadvantaged queers in London.

"Rather than speak for a community I'd rather offer my services for a community as a white gay/queer man. ... You have to sell hand-made ceramics for a certain price in London. A queer person that doesn't have a home wouldn't be able to buy

29 Hocquenghem, *Homosexual Desire*, 111.

30 Hocquenghem, *Homosexual Desire*, 138.

31 All direct quotes come from two interviews conducted by the author in London. The interview with Fred Andersson occurred on March 10, 2019, and with Will Martin on August 11, 2021.

it, but that's why I work with the Outside Project, an LGBT home-less shelter."

His practice is implicitly not radical or disruptive but an improvised response that takes place within the confines of capitalist urbanism.

If gay male discourse enables a theorization of urban space as a "thirstscape" where we can locate ourselves through on-going encounters with strangers, it might also enable new modes of misogyny through the invisibilization of women within narcissistic gay fields of vision. This points to the uneasy or even agonistic relation of multiple "queer" communities and identities to one another when premised on economies of desire: How do we articulate modes of accounting for—and caring for—those whom we do not desire? This inherent instability of the coalition of "queer" undermines any claims that formulations like Herbert Marcuse's famous world of Orphic Eros, a space of non-repressive sublimation, "where the life instincts would come to rest in fulfillment without repression," [32] are modes of utopia. Does the city emerge as a potential space of drowsy satisfied repose in which, as Marcuse has it, Eros and Thanatos converge through a desire to reintegrate the self with the rest of the natural world, or does it persist as a space of continuously multiplying yet unfulfilled desire that, as opposed to narratives of queer-as-excess, constitutes the urban as a space of lack, a space of "never enough"?

The work of South African-born Will Martin unsettles these seemingly binary choices. Martin works in a variety of media, including textiles and installations, but is perhaps best known for his series of ceramic chains. **fig. 2** These chains clearly index modes of infrastructure as ligaments that connect as they also close-off and shackle. They are also in a sense trickster objects that are both fragile and indestructible. Martin mentions that they are an example of "the contradictory way I use my materials. And then there's the BDSM component that chains inevitably invoke." The fragility of ceramics also calls forth a time element. As Mathieu writes about queer ceramics in general,

"In our world there has been a resurgence of funerary or ritualised objects in the wake of the AIDS crisis, which brought to the forefront once again the relationship between sex and death; Eros and Thanatos. These objects, like all other ceramic objects, will become, in the distant future, testament and witness to our time, when all other materials have been reabsorbed into oblivion. And if sexuality is necessary for the continuation of the organic world, then similarly ceramics' capacity for preservation functions as the memory of humankind." [33]

32 Herbert Marcuse, *Eros and Civilization: A Philosophical Inquiry into Freud* (Boston: Beacon Press, 1974), 146.

33 Mathieu, *Sex Pots*, 13.

As material assemblages that underpin sociality, the ceramic chains—future unlinked links and shards of links—perform an infrastructural queer time of horizontality in which past, present, and future are copresent. These ceramics are delicate, always on the verge of snapping, and yet they also promise to remain as and with our waste for eons to come. The sexuality of the objects does not hover as decoration on the surface but is suffused into the way the chains are hailed in moments of durational performance. As in *Midsommar*, discussed below, Martin makes chains available to be worn by event and performance participant-observers, linking them to circuits of mutual enjoyment, calling into question the divisions of self and other that always suffuse the politics of spectatorship.

In my conversations with Martin he indicated that, for him, pottery was "a way of ... sublimating my anxiety and my desires

which at the time were unacceptable" in the conservative white South Africa of his youth. He continues to make pottery as a way of managing anxiety—but, crucially, "making pottery itself is also quite anxiety inducing if you become financially reliant on it, and that for me was a bit of a killer." Precipitated by Britain's long lockdown in response to the 2020 to 2021 COVID-19 pandemic, Martin shifted his pottery production from a "fine art" register—for instance, his series of large funerary urns adorned with phalluses and linked by chains—to the vessel tradition focused on bowls and other tableware for which he can find a much bigger market. For Martin, making the functional ware was a "more down-to-earth way of functioning. It's less subject to the mania and depression of high stakes art, big shows, hoping someone will pick you up and look after you."

fig. 2 Will Martin, *Architrave*, 2016, ceramic installation, Charterhouse Square, London. Photograph: Will Martin

Regarding his current work, Martin's approach to pottery as a vessel of his own intentional sublimation has shifted:

"I'm trying to not sublimate at the moment, I'm trying to not dissociate. I'm trying to stay very present. With the wheel you have to be present. No chatting. If I'm not present and paying attention, this isn't going to go well. You have to perform

the movement or else it's not going to work. So it's the opposite of sublimating in a way."

For his current tableware work, he finds explicit use of representational stylistic elements to be unnecessary. fig.3 Martin, working on the wheel, notes that clay gives the artist an immediate feedback loop, as the clay responds immediately. The wheel is less forgiving than other methods of making ceramics. As Martin says,

"If you do something, it's there for the rest of the object's life. So it acts as almost a diagnostic tool for how I feel. It's just you and this very receptive material. The material itself is very prone to projection. It's also a great way of forming and communicating identity. People tell me who they are by how they treat the clay."

The objects themselves emerge as erotic infrastructure both through their circulation as craft commodities and through their enfolding into durational performance work that enacts an Orphic world.

In summer 2021, shortly after the United Kingdom relaxed the limits restricting social gatherings imposed at the height of the COVID-19 pandemic, allowing for outdoor meetings of up to thirty people, 34 Martin, along with his two domestic partners, organized and performed an immersive event called *Midsommar*. 35 The event, although inspired by the Swedish pagan tradition of celebrating the summer solstice, was heavily influenced by both classical mythology and the melancholic pastoral Englishness of films by Ismail Merchant and James Ivory, such as *A Room with a View*. Martin made a large set of tableware specifically for the event, including large numbers of white, textured serving bowls made in crank. In the afternoon, Martin hosted a picnic party on his lawn with twenty-five invited guests. fig.4 The second half of the event was styled as a sexy bacchanalian party organized around the fire pit at the bottom of the garden, which he had rewilded over the previous year. Guests were sent a mood board suggesting they come in cheesecloths or dress as Victorian gentlemen. Martin's porcelain chains were also available in the living room along with a dress-up rail, so guests who did not bring a costume could choose something.

Midsommar was a decidedly ambivalent work of art. Its air of self-regard and sense of seclusion from the urban hustle and bustle could be read as profoundly anti-urban, a hypercuratedness that ruled out moments of unexpected encounter with, much less hospitality toward, the stranger, ideals that, as Tim Dean forcefully argues, are at the very root of a queer ethics of alterity. 36 For the guests, *Midsommar* was likely a high-camp party. But for

fig.3 Will Martin, Queer Art Boot Fair, 2021.

34 On the lockdown timeline, see https://www.instituteforgovernment.org.uk/charts/uk-government-coronavirus-lockdowns (accessed April 24, 2022).

35 More information is available at https://www.williamjohnmartin.com/exhibitions/midsommar2021 (accessed April 24, 2022).

36 Tim Dean, *Unlimited Intimacy* (Chicago: University of Chicago Press, 2009), 176.

Martin it was an enveloping but nondidactic durational performance for which he and his partners built the structure, which guests then fleshed out through their own enjoyment. The table was laid in the garden and covered in twill, broadcloth, and lace. Vases filled with flowers from the garden flanked some of Martin's

earlier urns. Home-cooked food was served in Martin's bowls, and drinks were served in his porcelain cylinders. **fig.5** The event also functioned as a solo show for Martin's recent tableware pieces, all exhaustively documented with photographs, some of which now illustrate the website Martin uses to sell his work. In

fig.4 Will Martin, *Midsommar* (Early), immersive food event, June 26, 2021, Camberwell Grove, London. Photograph: Will Martin

the second half of the evening, guests drank wine, cavorted, and reclined in the wild grass of his nighttime garden. The relation to domesticated nature was thus key to the work: timed to the solstice, *Midsommar* involved guests reposing among flowers while they used and were adorned by clay objects.

The queerness of *Midsommar* emerges through its staging of an erotic relation to the world, in which libido is multiplied out, transfuses with work, and engages a sublime natural world, one not gazed at but inhabited. In the retelling, the piece could appear fey, camp, or even satirical, depending on the modulation of the narrative. But neither irony nor narrative was the driving motor of the event. An air of almost radical, even "tenderqueer" sincerity pervaded *Midsommar*, lending it a kind of power, an absorption of, as well as a transcendence of, camp. The essential quality of the work was a combination of bacchanalian excess crossed with Orphic stillness and repose with nature. The work was in no sense a parody but rather a kind of homage to Englishness on the part of an immigrant—a play with alterity that carefully abjured the seduction of judgment. The art of the event radiates out from Martin's sturdy, useful craft tableware, through the ephemeral erotic atmospheres of the event's curation, through to the surrounding urban natural landscape, which plays its role not only as an object of consumption but as an actant in the performance's assemblage. The queer space produced is intentionally ephemeral and notionally severed from the surrounding city landscape. In this aspirationally prefigurative setting, care is taken and care is passed around through clay objects, and it is inseparable from the pleasures taken from food, drink, bodies, and repose.

Geographers have grappled with the queer city in ways informed by a territorial ontology of space that owes much to modernist, functionalist understandings of cities. I argue for an understanding of the social that is premised not on repression of the erotic but its liberation, whereby social obligations of care are aligned with a whole field of erotic vision. This is premised on a desire "for," but it is also a desire "with": queer infrastructures enable moments of care-taking and world-making in which the exigencies of capitalist exchange are exchanged for forms of craft work that align logics of cuteness and beauty with an erotic enmeshing of subject and object, public and private, in an oceanic expanse of fullness.

Ceramics thus constitutes one mode of queer infrastructure. Craft production plays its role in the neoliberal city but exists only in ambivalent relation to post-Fordist regimes of accumulation in global cities like London. Lauren Berlant asks, "do we need a better structural imaginary to organize the complexities of stranger intimacy?" [37] Ceramics as queer infrastructure performs a kind of recuperation and redemption that allows us to rethink not only the humanism but the supposed posthumanism of the contemporary city. They are a means to undoing urban chaos and alienation, which are embedded within and not exter-

37 Lauren Berlant, "The Commons: Infrastructures for Troubling Times," *Environment and Planning D: Society and Space* 34, no. 3 (2016), 393–419, here 398.

fig. 5 Will Martin, *Midsommar* (Late), immersive food event, June 26, 2021, Camberwell Grove, London. Photograph: Patrick Smith

nal to post-Fordist cities. In a reiteration of the overwhelming flows of libido that can never be totally repressed, I also keep seeing the tumescence of these bodies and these pots, filled up and on the cusp of bursting. Ceramics possess a quality that indexes lines of power, surviving through visible fra-

gility, the threat of breakage, that appears every time a ceramic vessel is moved or used. Ceramics perform a queer infrastructure as craft that is improvised. By viewing, feeling, holding, passing around, serving food and drink in, and constituting community through queer ceramics, we improvisationally craft the erotic infrastructure that keeps the queer city going. In this sense we can also accept Andersson's and Martin's queer craft's complicity with and enfolding into practices of urban restructuring internationally. Eros is desublimated, but I do not read these works as utopian totems of sexual liberation, radical economic practice, or declarations of zones of autonomy. Their work orientates us to a new mode of thinking queer embeddedness within the rhythms of the city, in relation to but never outside capitalist modernity. It is a provisional response to the fragility of our refusals, because it congeals circuits of erotic care that sustain us as we gesture our way toward a less repressive sublimation.

Caregiving as Method
Anooradha Iyer Siddiqi, Can Bilsel, Ana Miljački, and Garnette Cadogan, with Javairia Shahid

"Caregiving as Method" is an articulation emerging from the intellectual preoccupations of those whose domesticities center on the care of others. We are scholars and people of color, women, LGBTQIA+ people, subjects of the postcolonial world, and, for most of our careers in academia, have identified what Fred Moten and Stefano Harvey call the "undercommons." [1] In 2021, Anooradha Iyer Siddiqi invited eleven colleagues to extend mutual concerns and ongoing conversations with one another by producing a proposal for a wider discussion through the platform of the Society of Architectural Historians (SAH) in the United States. With the support of the SAH, she organized a digital workshop in September 2021, convening this group of twelve scholars, who are situated in institutions in Singapore, India, the United Kingdom, and the United States and who hold direct professional and personal commitments to various parts of the Americas, Europe, Africa, and Asia, as well as broader ecofeminist political commitments to the world and many unwritten corners within it. [2] In spite of the problems and compromises that we have experienced in the academy's broad adoption of the medium of Zoom, including its suppression of Palestinian speech, enabling of the exploitation of workers involved in academic instruction, and flattening of the embodied experience of discourse, we maximized its capacity to fabricate simultaneity in order to converse with one another. [3] Across three sessions, we offered brief presentations and a roundtable discussion on the themes of care (presentations by Itohan Osayimwese, Kush Patel, and Anooradha Iyer Siddiqi, moderated by Garnette Cadogan), repair (presentations by Lilian Chee, Delia Wendel, and Jay Cephas, moderated by Ana Miljački), and method (presentations by Ikem Stanley Okoye, Peg Rawes, and Elis Mendoza, moderated by Can Bilsel). Such multiplicity and collaboration are inherent to the practice and methodology we wish to cultivate.

We opened each session by asking all attendees to write down the name of someone in their

Anooradha Iyer Siddiqi is Assistant Professor of Architecture at Barnard College, Columbia University.

Can Bilsel is Professor of Architecture and Art History at the University of San Diego.

Ana Miljački is an Assistant Professor of Architecture at Massachusetts Institute of Technology.

Garnette Cadogan is a Visiting Scholar at the Institute for Public Knowledge at New York University and editor-at-large of *Nonstop Metropolis: A New York City Atlas*.

Javairia Shahid is a doctoral candidate at Columbia University's Graduate School of Architecture, Planning and Preservation (GSAPP).

1 Stefano Harvey and Fred Moten, "The University and the Undercommons," *The Undercommons: Fugitive Planning and Black Study* (Brooklyn: Minor Compositions, 2013), 22–43.

2 *Caregiving as Method*, Society of Architectural Historians (SAH Connects) workshop, September 10, 17, 24, 2021, video archived at https://www.sah.org/conferences-and-programs/sah-connects/2021/caregiving-as-method (accessed February 28, 2022). In addition to the current text, versions of "Caregiving as Method" will be published in the online journal *Platform* and aired on the radio show and podcast *Conversations on Care*. The article(s) in *Platform* will contain an edited version of the discussion following each session, and *Conversations on Care* will focus on the audio material for each session, preceded by introductory discussions between the radio host, Ana Miljački, and the series organizer, Anooradha Iyer Siddiqi.

3 See Bill V. Mullen, "The Palestinian Exception in the Age of Zoom: A Bellwether for Academic Freedom," *American Association of University Professors Journal of Academic Freedom* 12 (2021), 1–17.

lives whom they wished to honor. Valorizing others by name, a feature of both recent radical and early modern scholarship, served as a productively contradictory starting point for our discussions. This practice was intended to extend our methodology of collaboration and collectivity across borders of time.

Our purpose is to open a discussion, both in architectural history and in our individual fields of scholarship, on the problematics and methods of critically merging our work as scholars and our work as carers. We perceive these two very special kinds of work as coexisting and intersecting, yet we are often made to hold them separate. Addressing the ways in which the act of caregiving informs and inflects methodological approaches to scholarship, we built a discussion around three themes to theorize architectural history and caregiving together. Among us, we care intimately and unrelentingly for elders, children, community members, relatives, and partners, while developing and teaching the history and theory of architecture. The twelve of us—collectively (in the workshop discussions) and uniquely (in our interventions presented below)—find that our work intersects in *caregiving as method*, a subsidiary of a broader theory about the overlaps of architecture, history, and power.

Our collaboration addresses issues of *caregiving*, yet we note feminist approaches to *care* and acknowledge intellectual debts to theorizations that make substantive openings for our work. [4] The questions raised in these theorizations—on labor and work, ecologies, taxonomies, and epistemologies of care, state-sanctioned versus autonomous care, and the ethics and science of care—lie squarely within our considerations. To that end, our focus is not merely on caregiving but on its methodological applications to histories of architecture, constructed environments, art, aesthetics, and sociospatial and ecological relations and inhabitations. Each of our interventions takes on a methodological issue, translating theory into praxis and vice versa.

As the nine presenters in the workshop discussed, our intent is to study the impact of domestic caregiving on our scholarly questions and orientations, as well as the shape of scholarly caregiving

4 As examples of starting points, a collaboration such as this owes intellectual debts to Christina Sharpe, Hiʻilei Julia Kawehipuaakahaopulani Hobart, and Tamara Kneese on radical care as praxis, to bell hooks and Audre Lourde on self-care and self-love, to Angela Davis and Silvia Federici on labor and housework, to Sarah Ahmed on affective economies, to Miriam Ticktin on state-imposed care regimes and a feminist commons, to Menna Agha on "the emotional as a placemaking regimen," to Maria Puig de la Bellacasa and Joan Tronto on ethics, ontologies, and sciences of care, to Donna Haraway and Elke Krasny on ecologies of care, to Virginia Held and Sara Ruddick for philosophical analyses of care, and to Alice Walker on an epistemology of sisters, mothers, and grandmothers. Christina Sharpe, "And to Survive," *Small Axe*, no. 57 (vol. 22, no. 3) (2018), 171–80; Hiʻilei Julia Kawehipuaakahaopulani Hobart and Tamara Kneese, "Radical Care: Survival Strategies for Uncertain Times," *Social Text*, no. 142 (vol. 38, no. 1) (2020), 1–16; bell hooks, *Feminism Is for Everybody: Passionate Politics* (Cambridge, MA: South End Press, 2000); Audre Lourde, *A Burst of Light* (Ithaca, NY: Firebrand Books, 1988); Angela Davis, "The Approaching Obsolescence of Housework: A Working-Class Perspective," in *Women, Race, and Class* (London: The Women's Press, 1981), 222–45; Silvia Federici, *Wages against Housework* (Bristol: Falling Wall Press, 1975); Sarah Ahmed, "Affective Economies," *Social Text*, no. 79 (vol. 22, no. 2) (2004), 117–39; Miriam Ticktin, *Casualties of Care: Immigration and the Politics of Humanitarianism in France* (Berkeley and Los Angeles: University of California Press, 2011); Miriam Ticktin, "Building a Feminist Commons in the Time of COVID-19," in "Complexities of Care and Caring," special issue, *Signs* 47, no. 1 (Autumn 2021), 37–46, http://signsjournal.org/covid/ticktin/ (accessed February 28, 2022); Menna Agha, "Emotional Capital and Other Ontologies of the Architect," *Architectural Histories* 8, no. 1 (2020), 23; Maria Puig de la Bellacasa, *Matters of Care: Speculative Ethics in More than Human Worlds* (Minneapolis: University of Minnesota Press, 2017); Joan Tronto, *Moral Boundaries: A Political Argument for an Ethic of Care* (London: Routledge, 1993); Donna J. Haraway, "Making Kin: Anthropocene, Capitalocene, Plantationocene, Chthulucene," in *Staying with the Trouble: Making Kin in the Chthulucene* (Durham, NC: Duke University Press, 2016), 99–103; Elke Krasny, "Radicalizing Care: Feminist Futures for Living with an Infected Planet," in Elke Kransy et al., eds., *Radicalizing Care: Feminist and Queer Activism in Curating* (Berlin: Sternberg Press, 2021), 28–37; Virginia Held, *The Ethics of Care: Personal, Political, and Global* (New York: Oxford University Press, 2006); Sara Ruddick, *Maternal Thinking: Toward a Politics of Peace* (1989), 2nd ed. (Boston: Beacon Press, 1995); and Alice Walker, "In Search of Our Mothers' Gardens" (1972), in *Within the Circle: An Anthology of African-American Literary Criticism from the Harlem Renaissance to the Present*, ed. Angelyn Mitchell (Durham, NC: Duke University Press, 1994), 401–409.

and intellectual society writ large within the domestic spaces of a pandemic. As we noted in our prompt,

"We begin by asking how caregiving intersects with social constructs of identity, and how these constructs shape our research questions, understandings of evidence, approaches to authorship, and the format and language of research products. We examine the visibility and invisibility of labor in history writing, considering how to develop an ethos of mentorship and collaboration in order to make intellectual production more horizontal — indeed, how to build networks and entanglement with others in our work. We turn to interrogations specific to the pandemic and an imagined post-pandemic world, thinking about how caregiving during this time has impacted or changed our scholarship and the historical understanding of our topics and subjects of interest, for example, articulating which voices we now give space to and why. Methodologically, we identify to what extent caregiving in our scholarship is a biographical enterprise and to what extent it concerns other (scholarly) subjects. We attempt to theorize how methodologies that have emerged in our own particularistic experiences sit in relation to other pressing issues in architecture or architectural history." [5]

As a means to propose that architectural historical work is fundamentally enriched by empathy and entanglement with the care of others and that the process of profound domestic caregiving is not only germane but pivotal in bringing forward theory, we used the tactic of posing questions that, for us, have not been part of a discursive field and, moreover, have rarely been encouraged. In the workshop, we discussed, largely in terms of our individual experiences, how theory is generated. [6] We believe that audience members and readers should inhabit these questions and layer their own experiences upon those we offered. As a critical starting point, we proposed the specific intertwining of two critical terms, *caregiving* and *method*, so as to extend and give form to understandings of histories and futures, and we proposed the analytic of "caregiving as method" to produce a value shift, naming an intertwined praxis of domestic and scholarly caregiving from which theory might spring.

Our workshop was animated by a collective desire to "support careers driven by forces other than generally recognized forms of achievement, while also examining the fine grain of collaboration and care that inform scholarship"; to "drive cultural change in our discipline and support academics living under various signs of difference, who are caregiving within a variety of modes of kinship"; and to make space "to consider how scholarly and domestic caregiving together find a way to extend into social

5 Jay Cephas, Lilian Chee, Elis Mendoza, Ikem Stanley Okoye, Itohan Osayimwese, Kush Patel, Peg Rawes, Anooradha Iyer Siddiqi, and Delia Wendel, "Caregiving as Method," Society of Architectural Historians (SAH Connects), 2021, https://www.sah.org/conferences-and-programs/sah-connects/2021/caregiving-as-method (accessed February 28, 2022).

6 Jay Cephas, Lilian Chee, Elis Mendoza, Ikem Stanley Okoye, Itohan Osayimwese, Kush Patel, Peg Rawes, Anooradha Iyer Siddiqi, and Delia Wendel, "Caregiving as Method," edited by Kush Patel and Delia Wendel and prepared by Javairia Shahid, *Platform*.

worlds that restrict or oppress," attending to "profound domestic caregiving in contexts in which it is seen as normative and others in which it is seen as non-normative" — naming, in particular, "BIPOC parents nursing or homeschooling in a pandemic, immigrants caring for elders at home or elsewhere, queer and trans communities producing care structures within or outside national law, and scholars subjugating individual interest to mutual aid." [7] We carried out this practice via a politics of representation, thoughtfully assembling ourselves as people crystallizing certain symbolic and embodied positions in the academy. We leaned on multivocalities, requesting interventions from each presenter in the form of word and image and reflections from moderators, who themselves brought freight to the discourse. We limited the time on Zoom to three one-hour discussions, each separated by one week during which participants could reflect. We tried to bring love into the room: for each other, for our work, for the audience, and for our cherished ones, who inadvertently occasioned this conversation. Ultimately, we hope this conversation and its spirit will extend into many communities and ecosystems of thought.

Caregiving as method hinges on the three thematic frameworks of "care," "repair," and "method," which we enfolded in a discursive arc. In bringing these themes to their fullest fruition, we benefited from the participation of Cadogan, Miljački, and Bilsel, each assigned a thematic panel, each cross-referencing all the panels, and each helping to build over time, as Bilsel noted, "a new conversation about agency, vulnerability, and the anguish of writing." [8] Each term carries different burdens in the different parts of the world and institutions into which we seek to intervene. Nevertheless, each concept focuses on a problem related to "caregiving as method" that illuminates its thorny and vibrant potential.

On care, Cadogan gathered the provocations that Osayimwese, Patel, and Siddiqi presented on the conceptual frames of vernacular and community engagement. He located these framings in architectural discourse and pedagogy in North American contexts, questioning, for example, the conceptual limitations of categories such as "vernacular architecture" and the manifestation of the design-build studio and its products. He also opened onto repair and method. He confounded expectations by conflating a discussion of the preventative possibilities of care with the redressive capacities of repair. Articulating what might be described as "community-engaged history," he asked what methods community engagement requires of historians and how these delineate practices of care. In response, he reflected on time as a conceptual through-line in the consideration of care:

7 Cephas et al., "Caregiving as Method" (2021).

8 The following paragraphs draw from unpublished writings and spoken interventions by Garnette Cadogan, Ana Miljački, and Can Bilsel.

"We think of care as a reparative act, as a way of countering neglect. In your discussion, care is not merely care about space. So often when we think of care, we think of space, of infrastructure — whether a physical or social infrastructure. But in your work there is also the understanding of care as embrace. What does it mean to think of care as a way of putting others closer to you? What does it mean to do so in a way that you not only inhabit time more intimately, but inhabit time more repetitively, such that repair emerges from that embrace? There is the idea of shared space in your discussions, but also a way of sharing time and a way of inhabiting time differently, more intimately. How are you seeing and thinking of care as an embrace and how are you thinking of time differently? In architecture, we speak of care as a kind of labor. Instead, what does it mean to think of care in terms of time, as something other than just the measure of labor?" 9

On repair, in the second session, Miljački took up these very questions, underscoring *affective labor*, *intimate historiography*, and *critical closeness* as three key terms for review:

"Though they may do so differently, in different ratios perhaps, they each contribute to a triad of epistemological, political, and personal forms of repair. All require what Wendel has called 'emotional labor,' but also specific narrative choices. She spoke of time lapses in her story, an intimate history that foregrounds individuals affected by trauma, and by places shaped by loss and activism. Chee's story is a collection of intimate micro-ethnographies, whose very writing is validating for those it involves, producing a reversal resulting in 'observant participation.' Cephas' 'critical closeness' implicates the historian in the writing in a way that may indeed transform both." 10

In addition to attempting to inscribe a lexicon culled from the dialogue, Miljački catalogued the labor performed by images and visual languages in each provocation. She remarked that Chee's work brought into view and acknowledged affective and transient domestic labor through formal drawings and grids of seeming programmatic permanence. For Wendel and Cephas, the presence and absence of images, respectively, had provoked criticism from previous audiences, forcing each author to absorb reproval even while electing to include or exclude an image precisely to return or repair the humanity and citizenship of those pictured. Within conventional academic discourse, the presence or absence of certain images offers audiences a formal and low-stakes means to take issue with work whose high moral content prevents its critical discussion; the presence or absence of certain images, which may skirt or suggest the obscene, can also provoke outrage. Neither option made the "establishment" comfortable.

9 Garnette Cadogan, "Caregiving as Method: Care," Society of Architectural Historians (SAH Connects), 2021, https://www.sah.org/conferences-and-programs/sah-connects/2021/caregiving-as-method (accessed February 28, 2022).

10 Ana Miljački, "Caregiving as Method: Repair," unpublished notes, 2020.

Miljački drew upon her embodied, autobiographical connection to the interventions to raise the notion of the emotional labor of memory. She reminded us that in studies of the transition from socialism to capitalism and in modern East European histories of the Second World (especially Yugoslavia), historian Tanja Petrović proposes a method of affective history that involves the labor of memory. [11] With regard to this historical and geographical context, Miljački writes,

11 Tanja Petrović, "Towards an Affective History of Yugoslavia," *Filozofija i društvo* 27, no. 3, (January 2016), 504—20, here 506.

"Affective history invites a specific kind of embodied knowledge of socialism to play a role in its historical description. This is intended to combat, and possibly repair, the overwhelming Cold War, Western, neoliberal narrative of that history, but also, and especially in Yugoslavian studies, it is directed at a kind of validation of the experience of socialism and of the Yugoslavian project, and thereby also at the repair of that project. In writing about this, Tanja Petrović emphasizes the way that (for various reasons) negative memories of the socialist experience have had greater impact on the production of historical narratives than the positive experiences of the same." [12]

12 Miljački, "Caregiving as Method."

On method, in the third session, Bilsel built the sinews between this condition of embodied knowledge and its specific historiographic orientations by discussing vulnerability. "We have reflected on vulnerability," he reminded us, "beyond the masculinist notions of helplessness and victimhood, challenging the paternal assumption that vulnerability requires protection, refuge, humanitarian aid, or forensic analysis to administer 'justice.'" [13] Vulnerability appeared in many forms in our talks; for example, the researcher putting herself at risk to share the lives of those she is writing about. (A photograph with Siddiqi in the United Nations Dadaab refugee camps powerfully captures this.) To be able to write is to be admitted to a "sovereign" domestic space. The interlocutor is acknowledged as the architect of her space, which also offers a narrative. Caregiving places the subject somewhere between "acting and suffering," beyond the conventional historical and ethnographic models of research. [14] Caregiving, in both the literal and metaphoric sense, offers a new way of looking at domestic spaces. We discussed invisible labor and the anguish inflicted on others in domestic spaces, as well as in academic settings, where we participate in defining the conditions of employment and the lives of others. Then, there is the anguish of writing about someone, a space most writers are intimately familiar with. The effect of the image goes beyond the evidentiary nature of Western art-historical analysis: the images we see—and the images that are hidden from us—offer something else, perhaps mourning and catharsis. One more thought:

13 Can Bilsel, "Caregiving as Method: Method," unpublished notes, 2021.

14 See Zeynep Gambetti, "Risking Oneself and One's Identity: Agonism Revisited," in Judith Butler, Zeynep Gambetti, and Leticia Sabsay, eds., *Vulnerability in Resistance* (Durham, NC: Duke University Press, 2016), 28—51.

caregiving is timely but is not confined by topicality. The projects that are shared here are the signposts of multigenerational and decades-long commitments to acknowledging what Ikem Okoye calls, after Elisabeth Grosz, "the possibility of a different inhabitation." 15 We believe there is also reason for optimism about the future of African, Indigenous, and diasporic experiences: a new approach that does not reify architecture in the spatial fixity of "buildings to be preserved" but one that cherishes *relations* across archipelagos of the desert and sea. 16

Bilsel found intimate, embodied, and tactical spaces in the individual and collective interventions by Okoye, Rawes, and Mendoza. Examining two sides of the contemporary in Okoye's mapping of the rarefied "biennale art" and the diasporic vernacular (which sometimes sit side by side in the same city), Bilsel recalled how, according to Okoye, contemporary art and an African "transnationality" may be produced and represented, asking whether we need distinctions between larger public works and "whimsical, diminutive work," such as that of Sokari Douglas Camp, whose work Okoye was forced to rethink when he became a parent. In examining Rawes's work (applying her earlier critiques of the biopolitics of mapping to her writing about the artist Tom Corby's daily "affect-data" in the artwork *Blood and Bones*), Bilsel returned to questions of time, to how the daily registry of "affect" co-opts medical data into a tactical practice that unfolds time as precious, limited, and boundless for both the person living with disease and the caregiver. 17 In response to Mendoza's desire to build a "community of care and solidarity" and interrogate the enforced "separation of academic work and praxis," Bilsel observed that cooperative work and solidarity are often erased from architectural histories and replaced by a history of authors, and how we might counter this erasure by building methodological foundations of care, for example, acknowledging Fred Cuny's coworkers Pedro Guiza and Jinx Parker, as well as rescuing Cuny himself, from his own hagiography.

The themes of vernacular architecture and community solidarity raised in the first session returned, like a poetics that cannot be denied, in the rhythms of the third session. Questions of intimacies, affect, and visual rhetoric in historiography echoed across the discussions, as did the technicalities and precisions of caregiving as method, both as the measure of the relation between historian and subject and between the collective historical project and its objects. These are the echoes and traces that we hope this adventurous experiment sets into motion — or rather, registers and extends. The following texts compile the provocations presented in the workshop, preserving the order of

15 Ikem Stanley Okoye, "Elusive Things: Materialities and Spatialities in the Vicinity of Nigér" (lecture, Aga Khan Program for Islamic Architecture at the Massachusetts Institute of Technology, Cambridge, MA, November 12, 2020).

16 See Édouard Glissant, *Poetics of Relation* (Ann Arbor: University of Michigan Press, 1997); and Bilsel, "Caregiving as Method."

17 See Rawes's text in this issue. Also of relevance is Peg Rawes, "Biopolitical Ecological Poetics," in Peg Rawes, Timothy Matthews, and Stephen Loo, eds., *Poetic Biopolitics: Political and Ethical Practices in the Arts* (London: I.B. Tauris, 2016), 11–23.

presentation of the three sessions; the ensuing discussions and their interpretations will appear in forthcoming publications. We hope that in engaging them, the reader is spurred to formulate her own interventions, to design her own methods, and to interpolate caregiving into all the scholarly attentions she may be privileged to demonstrate. This is only one step, we hope, of many.

Caregiving in the New England Triple-Decker
Itohan Osayimwese

In December 2012, my father, who could no longer find his keys and was forgetting to turn off the stove, was diagnosed with Alzheimer's disease. Since my siblings and I all lived hundreds of miles away and since my parents had relocated permanently to the United States only in 1997 and had not found a support network in the southeastern Pennsylvania town where they lived, I invited my parents to live with me. I envisioned a duplex in which I would live on one side and they on the other. The idea was that by living in such close proximity, I could provide emotional and hands-on support to my parents.

This article focuses on one instance of African-Caribbean immigrant caregiving and academic life in the United States. Caring as living with elderly family members is a social practice that continues to sustain many African and Caribbean societies. Comments from friends and colleagues highlight the unusualness of this practice in the context of the demographics of academia in the United States. But,

if care is "an activity of relationship, of seeing and responding to need," and if an "ethic of care" places care at the center of life, then it is imperative that we give credit to those who work to create an intellectual space where we can have a conversation about a topic that would, to many scholars, seem unworthy of intellectual investigation. [18] One principle of caregiving as method is for caregivers—especially those of us (people of color, women, immigrants) who are conditioned by society not to do so—to claim credit for our work even as we bring out of the shadows those who walked before and alongside us. [19]

Living with my parents has led me down a path of discovery. Little did I know that Providence, Rhode Island, and the wider New England region has a long history of multifamily housing—the double-decker and triple-decker. [20] **fig.1** Built from wood,

Itohan Osayimwese is Associate Professor of the History of Art and Architecture and affiliate faculty in Africana Studies, Urban Studies, and the Center for Latin American and Caribbean Studies at Brown University, Providence, Rhode Island.

fig.1 A triple-decker apartment building, 1959–1963, Boston, MA. Photograph: unknown. Source: Northeastern University Libraries, Archives and Special Collections, Box 75, Folder 2922, A003688, http://hdl.handle.net/2047/d20156360

18 See Ester Conesa, "How Are Academic Lives Sustained? Gender and the Ethics of Care in the Neoliberal Accelerated Academy," *LSE Impact Blog*, March 27, 2018, http://blogs.lse.ac.uk/impactofsocialsciences/2018/03/27/how-are-academic-lives-sustained-gender-and-the-ethics-of-care-in-the-neoliberal-accelerated-academy/ (accessed February 3, 2022); Karyn Miller, "The Ethics of Care and Academic Motherhood amid COVID-19," *Gender Work Organ* 28 (2021), 260–65, https://doi.org/10.1111/gwao.12547; and Joan Tronto, *Moral Boundaries: A Political Argument for an Ethic of Care* (New York: Routledge, 1993).

19 See https://www.citeblackwomencollective.org/ (accessed February 3, 2022).

20 With three main floors and an attic, the triple-decker typically has three or four apartments, while the double-decker has two or three apartments (on two main floors and attic). Despite differences in size, the triple-decker and double-decker belong to the same building type. "Triple-decker" continues to be used to describe both types.

these houses have an identical apartment on each floor: a large porch out front and, on either side of a hall, two to four bedrooms, a parlor, living room, bathroom, and kitchen. From 1880 to 1930, sixteen thousand triple-deckers, housing about 192,000 people, were built in Boston. [21] As late as 1972, triple-deckers housed one-third of the population in Worcester, Massachusetts. [22] But double-deckers and triple-deckers also became symbols of debates about national identity and the future of the United States. They had been built as housing for European immigrant workers in New England's industrial belt. Rather than renting, however, these immigrants soon started to buy these houses: they would live in one apartment and rent out the others to pay the mortgage. Their aspirational activities brought about a predictable political reaction: by the 1910s, anti-immigrant feeling had morphed into anti-triple-decker feeling. In Providence, city leaders spoke of "the triple-decker menace," and reformers in Boston called it a "weed" in need of eradication. [23] Cities across New England imposed zoning ordinances to limit the construction of triple-deckers and slow the upward mobility of immigrants. Triple-deckers deteriorated but experienced a renaissance in the 1980s as housing demand grew and prices skyrocketed.

As I looked around for a duplex, the Providence double-decker appeared as a possible solution. My realtor tried to dissuade me by saying, "Portuguese families often live there." I would later find out that "Portuguese" referred to the tens of thousands of Cabo Verdeans and Azoreans who have migrated to New England since the eighteenth century. [24] By the twentieth century, this housing type had lost its previous association with Irish and French immigrants and acquired a new reputation as the type typically occupied by immigrants from Cabo Verde, the Dominican Republic, Vietnam, and other non-European nations. [25] These "new" immigrants and their triple-decker lives became the latest target of anti-immigrant and, often, anti-Black rhetoric. [26]

But the double-decker's separate front doors and shared back stair met my need for private but conjoined space. Unlike other examples of urban multifamily housing in the Western world, the double-decker masquerades as a single-family house in its gable-roofed massing even as its internal layout meets the bourgeois middle-class ideal of domestic privacy for each family living in separate apartments. [27] Full of contradiction, the double-decker also prioritizes community through its shared back stair and multiple porches that function as a visual extension of public space. As my father's health deteriorated, the double-decker made more and more sense: I sat with my father on the porch, found solace in gardening with my mother, popped into my parent's apartment for

21 See "The Rise, Fall and Rebirth of the Triple Decker," New England Historical Society, last updated in 2021, https://www.new englandhistoricalsociety. com/rise-fall-rebirth-new-england-triple-decker/ (accessed February 21, 2022). The only major texts on the triple-decker as a housing form are Kingston William Heath, *The Patina of Place: The Cultural Weathering of a New England Industrial Landscape* (Knoxville: University of Tennessee Press, 2016); and Kingston William Heath, "Housing the Worker: The Anatomy of the New Bedford, Massachusetts, Three-Decker," *Perspectives in Vernacular Architecture* 10 (2005), 47—59.

22 "The Rise, Fall and Rebirth."

23 "The Rise, Fall and Rebirth," Providence Chamber of Commerce; "Housing Conditions in Providence," *Providence Magazine*, February 1917, 79—96; and James C. O'Connell, *The Hub's Metropolis: Greater Boston's Development from Railroad Suburbs to Smart Growth* (Cambridge, MA: MIT Press, 2013), 84.

24 See Waltraud Berger Coli and Richard A. Lobban, *Cape Verdeans in Rhode Island: A Brief History* (Providence: Rhode Island Heritage Commission, 1990), 7.

25 See Marc Levitt, *Triple Decker: A New England Love Story* (film, forthcoming).

26 Though perceived as such in the twentieth century, Cabo Verdeans were, in fact, not new immigrants to the United States.

27 On the bourgeois ideal of domesticity in U.S. architecture, see Gwendolyn Wright, *Moralism and the Model Home: Domestic Architecture and Cultural Conflict in Chicago, 1873—1913* (Chicago: University of Chicago Press, 1985).

a quick check-in before falling into my own bed. While he was able to walk unaided, the compact, one-level layout of the apartment eased his movement around space. As his illness worsened, we converted one of the bedrooms into a sick room, avoiding hospitalization for as long as possible and minimizing the disorientation that many Alzheimer's patients suffer when placed in unfamiliar environments such as memory care facilities. The double-decker was as functional and socially sustainable in 2018 as it was in 1890. As an academic with an immigrant background, peripatetic obligations, and no other family within a two-hundred-mile radius, my double-decker became a mini universe of care.

It did not always work. I often felt that I was falling short of providing enough care due to the demands of being an untenured college faculty member. But even with the severe time constraints I faced, the double-decker, through its design, encouraged a praxis of care. It also reoriented my scholarly practice. After leaving home for college at age seventeen, living with my parents in my forties provided an opportunity to reencounter their lived experience as knowledge. From a batik textile hanging on my parents' wall that led to an article in *African Arts* about my aunt, Ifueko Osayimwese Omigie, who was a batik artist and likely the only female member of the Zaria Art Society in 1950s Nigeria, to an essay on homemaking and gardening among West Indian women immigrants in 1970s Nigeria, from a counterhistory of Maxwell Fry and Jane Drew's University of Ibadan campus based on the memories of generations of West African faculty families, to a book on migration and remittance properties as the primary route to full emancipation for African-descended people in the Anglo-Caribbean, caring for my parents in the double-decker led to new questions and methods. As Saidiya Hartman said, "the autobiographical example" is "about trying to look at historical and social process and one's own formation as a window onto social and historical processes." **28** So I offer another principle for caregiving as method: *write what you know not because you want to reify the sign of difference under which you may live but because you will do less harm and may even do the work of repair.*

Kinship as Keyword
Kush Patel

"Every evening, Madhuben sits on the otla and goes over her grandchildren's homework, asking them to talk about their day lessons. She makes sure they follow time, participate in the arts, remain curious in school, and eat lunch from their tiffin boxes. She doesn't read or write." **29**

28 Conversation between Saidiya Hartman and Patricia Saunders, cited in Christina Sharpe, *In the Wake: On Blackness and Being* (Durham, NC: Duke University Press, 2016), 8.

Kush Patel is a faculty member in, and Head of Studies for, the Postgraduate Arts Program in Technology and Change at the Srishti Manipal Institute of Art, Design, and Technology, Manipal Academy of Higher Education, in Bengaluru, India.

29 Kush Patel, Twitter, July 19, 2018, 6:28 AM, https://twitter.com/ kshpatel/status/ 1016267821276250112 (accessed March 3, 2022). *Otla* is the Gujarati term for a raised platform typically in stone that serves as a threshold between the street and the house interior.

"For years, Leelaba has blessed me with utmost love and care. At 80 years old, she still sits up when I visit her, holding my hand tightly as we talk, and asking her grandchild to sit with us as I share my university experiences with them. She doesn't read or write either." [30]

"My mum continues to share with me the brilliance and care of her mum and other women in the family. Her affirmations, critical insights, and self-discipline are life-giving. She couldn't pursue higher education, but her everyday feminism informs my world view." [31]

I posted this thread of tweets during my visit to India in the summer of 2018. I was preparing to travel back to Michigan, when I found myself reflecting on connections that I had seen my mother nurture throughout my growing-up years. Madhuben and Leelaba were chosen family across historically persistent class and caste divides. A sister to my mother, a caregiver to my maternal grandmother, and a friend to me, Madhuben saw education as the only means to dignity in society. As mutual carers through sickness and copresence, Ba (as I affectionately called Leelaba) and my paternal grandparents modeled a form of friendship that affirmed collective well-being. Together, these experiences constituted the starting points of my notes on chosen kinship at the 2021 Society of Architectural Historians (SAH) Connects virtual workshop "Caregiving as Method," [32] where I recounted one of my last meetings with Madhuben, who passed just days after the conclusion of the three-part series, on the morning of September 29, 2021, in her home village — and beside her grandchildren.

bell hooks's *Talking Back: Thinking Feminist, Thinking Black* was one of the first texts that explained to me my own lived difficulty with the limits of academic language in bringing us — "the members of oppressed and/or exploited groups as well as those radical visionaries who may have race, class, and sex privilege" [33] — closer to kin and communities. Language as discourse and material praxis separates classes but also holds the potential to counter hegemonies and oppressive boundaries of how we know and with whom we come to know the world. Such a praxis of *knowing with* acknowledges the centrality of one's background and makes visible the connection of scholarship to deliberate kinships.

For several years, as part of my public scholarship practice in architecture and the digital humanities (DH), I have been involved in framing care-centered pedagogies that ask what it means to learn across differences of "class and education" while honoring long-traveled solidarities. [34] To critically reflect on the meaning of the word *kinship* in such a framing is to begin by

30 Kush Patel, Twitter, July 19, 2018, 6:29 AM.

31 Kush Patel, Twitter, July 19, 2018, 6:40 AM.

32 "Caregiving as Method" was organized by Anooradha Iyer Siddiqi and hosted by the SAH in three online sessions, September 10, 17, and 24, 2021. For details, see https://www.sah.org/conferences-and-programs/sah-connects/2021/caregiving-as-method (accessed March 3, 2022).

33 bell hooks, *Talking Back: Thinking Feminist, Thinking Black* (Boston: South End Press, 1989), 81.

34 bell hooks, *Talking Back*, 12.

naming the "Savarna merit" that constituted my access to education in India and the United States and that continues to afford me a comparatively safe space for queer life in the academy. "Savarna" is a marker of caste dominance and mobility that is sustained by Hindu social structures both in India and among members of the South Asian diaspora. Naming this location of power and privilege is essential for me, because, as bell hooks asks, "how can we organize to challenge and change a system that cannot be named?" 35 Following bell hooks, and learning from my mother's revisioning of community networks, to center care in scholarship is to practice a vocabulary that helps us analyze the dominance of cis-hetero patriarchy and its intersections with caste in knowledge mobilization—a vocabulary that may allow us to queer kinship against its endogamic histories. In short, if kinship has meant a structured, affective, and generational articulation of casteist patriarchy and cis-heteronormativity, what might change as we build its relationship with knowing in the world differently?

Figure 2 shows a photograph taken in 2019 by undergraduate student researcher Kalyani Menon in the fishing village of Madhipuram, located south of Trivandrum in Vizhinjam, Kerala. 36 fig. 2 It features her classmates Neethi Mary Regi, Raania Mohammed, Aysha Ansari, and Rizwa Kallada, as well as our community interlocutors, who asked not to be identified to protect themselves amid tensions with vested political power interests in the region. "We are safe," read Kalyani's

text message to our messenger group. The studio community was out in the field, working and braving the sudden weather change from warm to brutally stormy. Text messages kept us together despite our dispersal along the mighty Arabian Sea coast and amid rains and the flooding that followed. The "we" in Kalyani's message, however, was not just a reporting back of individual well-being but rather an accounting of a way of *being with* individuals in a complex landscape. That my students and I were outsiders in an environment with a limited communications infrastructure was apparent. That we were simultaneously also modeling reciprocity across this digital and social divide required ongoing translation. For us—the local fisherfolk and studio participants—the study of community infrastructures made fragile by settler colonial technologies was also a study of how to structure the ownership of research and knowledge around language. Following bell hooks, "it is important that we know who we are speaking to, who we most want to hear us, who we most long to move, motivate, and touch with our

35 bell hooks, *The Will to Change: Men, Masculinity, and Love* (New York: Atria Books, 2014), 25.

36 This undergraduate urban humanities studio for the 2019 semester nine pre-thesis cohort at the Avani Institute of Design, Calicut, was entitled, "Cities for Whom? Caring for Infrastructural Lives in Vizhinjam, Kerala." My co-instructors in this studio were Nimisha Hakkim and Mithun P. Basil. Situated within the communities of Madhipuram and Kottapuram in Vizhinjam, the studio made visible the otherwise palpable infrastructures of access, equity, waste, economy, and climate change involving the local fisherfolk's lived realities. Vizhinjam is a port community located toward the south of Trivandrum with a history of growth and displacement since the 1960s. Today, the livelihoods of these fisherfolk face new uncertainties from the construction of another project: the International Transshipment Terminal, currently being built near the villages toward the south. See Kush Patel, "Queer Disclosures, Queer Refusals: Notes on Survival Praxis in Architecture and Academia," in Kush Patel and Soumini Raja, eds., *Gender and Academic Leadership in Architecture in India: Research Symposium Proceedings* (Calicut: Avani Institute of Design, 2021), 119—29, here 125.

fig. 2 Neethi Mary Regi, Raania Mohammed, Aysha Ansari, and Rizwa Kallada, and community participants in the fishing village of Madhipuram, Kerala. 2019. Photographer: Kalyani Menon words." 37 How might we bring this lived politics into a methodological view?

37 bell hooks, *Talking Back*, 78.

My research and teaching remain structured around a shared interest in analyzing socially just infrastructures—understood as relational embodiments of a place inscribing minoritized histories and as scaffolds of community-engaged knowledge creation in and with the digital. This approach has enabled me to move the historical and theoretical analysis of architecture, space, and the city from critique to praxis, as well as to learn collaboratively, coalitionally, and pedagogically not just in analog, physical space but in digital environments and organizing. As cofounder of the Pedagogy of the Digitally Oppressed Collective, 38 for example, I work within cross-disciplinary DH frameworks to reconceptualize how we might approach the ethics of creating stories and constructing archives through computer-based platforms in distinct community contexts. With Kalyani, Neethi, Raania, Aysha, Rizwa, and other student members of the studio, we positioned our firsthand recordings of the place, including testimonies, oral histories, and digital photographs, as *terra communis*, not *terra nullius*; as sovereignty, kinship, and collective, not frontier land or empty land to be charted. Specifically, we located this work in discussions of intimacy, or the microspatial histories of intimate care and conflictual repair tied simultaneously to individual self and collective struggles of everyday survival. The photograph I share in this brief article serves both as an embodiment and a translation of this care work. Thus, how I access my sources and material finds, how I see them as narrative and community data, and how I use digital tools to imagine the possibility of archiving and documenting on community terms together represent an epistemological process to inquire not just into the relationship between the researcher and researched but also to explore the implication of self in knowledge-making.

38 With Ashley Caranto Morford and Arun Jacob, I cofounded Pedagogy of the Digitally Oppressed, a digital humanities collective that is committed to rethinking the boundaries and possibilities of un-, re-, and co-learning digital research and pedagogy along deliberate queer, feminist, and anticolonial lines. Our partnership is a result of our respective and interconnected place-based public scholarship careers in India and territories that are colonially called Michigan, Pennsylvania, and Ontario, with ongoing involvement with networks within, across, and beyond these regions. Paulo Freire's writings on the *Pedagogy of the Oppressed* (1967–1978) are foundational to the naming and structuring of this collective. See Paulo Freire, *Pedagogy of the Oppressed*, trans. Myra Bergman Ramos (New York: Herder & Herder, 1970).

Scholarship as Mutual Aid
Anooradha Iyer Siddiqi

A photograph taken near Dadaab, Kenya, in the United Nations High Commissioner for Refugees' Dagaheley camp, shows me showing a group of children a photograph of my four-year-old son on a small digital camera. fig.3 "Waa magaciisa? [What is his name?]," they ask in Somali. "Sahil," I reply. They recognize the name; it is close to that of one of their friends. The photograph was taken in 2011 in the vicinity of these children's homes. It was taken with the permission of their families, who are standing just outside the frame. I share it here because the children are now grown and cannot be recognized. I will not share their names.

People have been living in the refugee camps at Dadaab since 1991. I had the privilege of visiting them as part of my doctoral research at New York University and as a member of a team of researchers working for the Women's Refugee Commission on a report studying the connections between gender-based violence and livelihoods in the camps. This research and advocacy organization based in the United States is affiliated with the International Rescue Committee, the humanitarian nongovernmental organization implementing services in the camps that facilitated the visit of our team, which included me, an Indian-born US citizen, and my colleague Bethany Young, a Jamaican citizen and student at Columbia University, who took the photograph. The children are among the third generation of people raised in the Dadaab refugee camps, although they are members of more recently displaced communities. Some were born in southern Somalia and traveled to Dadaab with their parents as a means of coping with the social breakdown and militarization that made living at home untenable. While that armed conflict is often narrated as internal to Somalia, it is directly related to US militarism in East Africa, the actions and inactions of the United Nations, and the geopolitics of the security state apparatus in which the government of Kenya participates. These forces refuse to allow young people, such as those who surrounded me and my son in this photograph, the emancipatory possibilities of being aspirational, caring people and instead consign them to a subjecthood of humanitarian need, confinement, and settlement.

In this short contribution, I discuss the impacts of caregiving upon scholarship; in particular, how *scholarly conceptualization* may grow out of extreme forms of domestic caregiving. My scholarship examines a refugee camp as a heritage architecture, not only a humanitarian one, and takes migration as an epistemic problem, not only a sociopolitical one. [39] I worked in several refugee camps to make an archive of architectures of forced migration, ultimately focusing on the object lessons offered by Dadaab and the many concept histories that converge within it. While I do not compare my experience to that of people living in the camps, I acknowledge that in doing this research I assumed personal, existential, and financial risk. Over the course of twelve years, I have talked to approximately three hundred people living or working in Dadaab or connected to it, most of them women. As an architectural historian, I asked people about design, construction, craft, landscape, ecology, settlement, urbanism, and territory. As a mother, I asked them how they made their homes. Where did they get food, water, milk? The aid agencies distributed foodstuffs and even utensils for cooking but

[39] Anooradha Iyer Siddiqi, *Architecture of Migration: The Dadaab Refugee Camps and Humanitarian Settlement* (Durham, NC: Duke University Press, forthcoming 2023).

not fuel. Who, if anyone, cared for the children when their caregivers traveled to find kindling? When they foraged for firewood outside the camps, putting themselves at risk of sexual violence and hyena attacks, did caregivers have any choice but to take their children with them?

Hearing women discuss their lives and livelihoods was perhaps possible only because I was asking questions about their labor, work methods, and how they built things. I was a woman talking mostly to women about gender, politics, homemaking, and camp-making. I was also a mother talking to mothers whose

sons had been abducted and conscripted into armies and who had fled home for the safety of all the others they needed to care for. I was forced to come to terms with the asymmetries in my scholarship, precisely concerning the relative safety and security of my own child, who I nevertheless ached for during our separation.

fig. 3 Children in Dagaheley. United Nations High Commissioner for Refugees' Dagaheley camp, 2011. Photograph: Elletra Legovini. Archive of Anooradha Iyer Siddiqi

These experiences and my orientations led to writing a history of significant architectures created by people who were mothers and forced migrants. My commitment, including assuming risk in spite of my own responsibilities as a primary caregiver, grew out of a political solidarity with the migrations and urgencies of my interlocutors. However, the empathies and comprehensions of what I was seeing and studying stemmed from my role as a primary domestic caregiver during all the years of my research — from my first day of PhD coursework to the day I submitted a book manuscript to a publisher — with all the demands and desperations the work of caregiving produces in any situation.

This double work of scholar-caregiver added nuance to my theorizations. Understanding how a refugee camp was built, by whom, and under what historical conditions gave way to questions of how, in emergencies, homes are recovered or constructed and, similarly, how, in migration, histories are recovered or constructed. I started to see how personal an archive can be, how it can be a life force for a child or a family fleeing from harm. On a day when the census was being taken by humanitarian workers in Dagaheley camp, journalist and refugee Musa Adan Mahmud discussed with me the camp's spatial arrangement and assignment of plots. **fig. 4** They embodied the refugee census that was predicated upon them, impacting political consolidations and representative voting for leadership and policies in the camp. For Mahmud, neither the census nor the spatial layout of the camp was an abstraction,

fig.4 Musa. United Nations High Commissioner for Refugees' Dagaheley camp, 2011. Photograph: Anooradha Iyer Siddiqi. Archive of Anooradha Iyer Siddiqi

nor did any dwelling operate merely as shelter. Each element of the built environment acted as a conceptual archive of the lives lived in Dadaab, in turn, becoming monuments to the futurities of the children who surrounded us, playing, as we talked—racing, spinning, chasing, fighting, and laughing.

People in emergencies are forced to live *out of time* and also to live *with time* in unsettling ways. Their experiences of presents, pasts, and futures become inextricably and unrelentingly entangled. Even those of us in arenas of privilege have experienced the unruliness of timespace after March 2020, when the daily markers of work and school evaporated. The experience is amplified when time is tethered to a responsibility for the life of another. Time becomes pregnant. Caregiving becomes an extreme experience of time, embodied and urgent. A response to this extreme condition that emerges organically is the straightforward act of mutual aid, a form of ethics that we do not often associate with scholarship.

I have been thinking about an ethic of scholarly caregiving and the forms of mutual aid that scholarship can provide. People displaced in emergencies need food and water and the architectures that provide them, but as they shelter they also need the intangible horizon beyond. They need the assurance that histories and narratives can remain intact in their custodianship and that the people under their care can hear, value, and build futures from them. Thus, studying an architecture of emergency, of migration, has the epistemic power to construct a scaffold for futures. As I have explained elsewhere, I have practiced an ethic of scholarly caregiving by trying to write with people, literally and metaphorically, toward a common future. **40** I aim to build an epistemic scaffold together with others. I have begun to comprehend this practice as a form of accountability, sometimes to people I will never meet again, which is, in part an acknowledgment of a position of producing scholarship within the US academy and thus of benefiting from various forms of oppressive power. However, I have come to regard this accountability—which is at the base of forms of mutual aid in scholarship—as a competency to be valued and a value to be cherished. Such accountability demonstrates that scholarly work is mutually indebted; it conditions relations between the scholar and the subjects and objects of scholarship as they co-constitute methods:

40 Anooradha Iyer Siddiqi, "Writing With: Togethering, Difference, and Feminist Architectural Histories of Migration," in "Structural Instability," ed. Daniel A. Barber, Eduardo Rega, *e-flux Architecture*, July 2018, https://www.e-flux.com/architecture/structural-instability/208707/writing-with/ (accessed Aug. 22, 2022) all constructing an ethics of research aimed toward reparation and restitution as forms of knowledge and understanding.

This thinking ultimately stems from my concern with the embodiments and entanglements that carers inhabit. In the simple act of revisiting a photograph of my child every day, sometimes in the company of other people's children, I began to understand how caregiving acts as a germ for scholarly empathy, imagination, and collaboration—with figures in the present and the past. Caregiving, both laborious and life-giving, impacts not only what and why we study but how we decide to understand, feel, and narrate. By contributing to the construction of an ethic in this way, scholarly caregiving creates epistemic power through a scholarly practice of mutual aid and, from that foundation, scaffolds futures.

Insinuating the Invisible
Lilian Chee

"What interests the historian of everyday life is the *invisible.*" 41

Cecil Asong is a thirty-nine-year-old woman from the small township of Zarraga (population 27,000) in the Province of Iloilo in the Philippines. She has two teenage daughters—the younger, in secondary school, is still doing home-based learning, and the elder has just begun her tertiary education. The girls have no internet access at home. They make do by sharing the service with a neighbor. Cecil's husband is a farmer of a smallholding. He grows vegetables, and they have two pigs. Cecil's mother-in-law stays close to help with the girls. They are a close-knit family. Cecil is intelligent, resourceful, tenacious, and reliable. She is good with children. I know all this because she has been living with my family in Singapore for the last eight years as our domestic helper. Without her labor I would not be able to write this brief statement about caregiving and the significance of "repair" in an academic context. With my adult asthma risks and the family choosing not to go out so as to minimize my chances of falling seriously ill during the pandemic, she has also been staying at home with us since March 2020. We owe her a huge debt of care.

I begin with a brief biography of the foreign domestic worker, an essential component of affective care work in Singapore. On arrival in Singapore, these women are trained to assimilate and adapt to local conditions. The list of words in Figure 5 is an excerpt from a vocabulary sheet given to them by their local agents. fig.5 They are encouraged to learn local dialects and languages, practice social etiquette, intuit instructions, and anticipate needs. The high wages are enticing enough for them to leave behind their own children, spouses, previous lives, and histories. Subsequently, they live within an impasse, 42 with a contracted

Lilian Chee is Associate Professor in the Department of Architecture, National University of Singapore.

41 Paul Leuilliot, preface to Guy Thuillier, *Pour une histoire du quotidien au XIXe siècle en Nivernais* (Paris: Mouton, 1977), xi–xii, cited in Michel de Certeau, Luce Giard, and Pierre Mayol, *The Practice of Everyday Life*, Vol. 2, *Living and Cooking* (Minneapolis: University of Minnesota Press, 1998), 3.

42 Lauren Berlant, *Cruel Optimism* (Durham, NC: Duke University Press Books, 2011).

sense of personal space and sociality. We, in turn, know little of their lives, loves, dreams, and desires.

The active import of foreign domestic workers to Singapore began when local women were encouraged to join the manufacturing workforce in the 1970s. [43] In 1978, the Foreign

fig. 5 Vocabulary sheet for foreign domestic workers. Source: Anthea Phua, "How to Live with Another" (Master's thesis, National University of Singapore, 2021)

SALAM / UCAPAN

BAHASA INDONESIA	BAHASA INGGRIS	BACAAN MANDARIN	BAHASA KANTONESE	BAHASA HOKKIAN	BAHASA MANDARIN
Apa Kabar	How are You	Ni Hau	Nei Hou	Li Ho	您好
Maaf	Sorry	Tue Pu Jhi / Pau Chien	To Em Ji	To Em Ju Phai She	對不起 抱歉
Permisi/Terima Kasih	Excuse Me	Ching Wen	Em Koi	Chia Meng	請問、
Sampai Jumpa ...	See You	Cai Cien	Coi Kin	Cai Kien	再見
Selamat	Congratulation	Kong Si	Kung Hei	Kiong Hi	恭喜
Selamat Datang	Welcome	Huan Ying	Fun Ying	Fan Ying	歡迎
Selamat Jalan	Goodbye	Man Cou / Cai Cien	Man Man Hang	Man Man Kia	慢走 再見
Selamat Makan	Have Nice Meal	Jing Man Yong	Jing man-man sik	Chin Jai Ciak	請隨意
Selamat Malam	Good Evening	Wan An	Man On	Mi Si Ca	晚安
Selamat Pagi	Good Morning	Cau An	Cou San	Dhau Ca	早安
Selamat Siang	Good Afternoon	U An	Em On	E Po	午安
Selamat Tahun Baru	Happy New Year	Sin Nen Cin Pu	Sen Nin Failok	Sin Ni Quelok	新年進步
Selamat Tidur	Good Night	Wan An	Co Dao	Ai Gun .	晚安
Selamat Ulang Tahun	Happy Birthday	Sen Re Kwai Lok	Sang Yat Failok	Sin Lik, Que-lok .	生日快樂
Silahkan	Please	Ching	Jing	Jia.	請
Tak Apa - apa	Nevermind	Mei Kuan Si/ Pu Yau Ching	Mo Man dai	Bo Wa Kin	沒關係/不要緊
Terima Kasih	Thank You	Sie Sie	To Chie	To Sia	謝謝
Terima Kasih Kembali	You Are Well Come	Pu Ghe Jhi/ Pu Kan Tang	Em Sai Hak He	Mien Ghe Ghi	不客氣

Chinese words maid must know:
Mop the floor 拖地 (ma di); Sweep the floor 扫地 (sao di); Cooking 煮饭 (cu fan); Fold Clothes 折衣服 (ze yi fu); Iron Clothes 烫衣服 (tang yi fu); Shower/ Bathe 冲凉 (cong liang); Sleep 睡觉 (shui jiao)

Wash clothes 洗衣 (si yi); Washing Machine 洗衣机 (si yi ji); Wash dishes 洗碗 (si wan); Wash hands 洗手 (si shou)

Cut fruits 切水果 (cie shui guo); Eat 吃饭 (ci fan); Water 水 (shui); Salt 盐 (yan); Sugar 糖 (tang)

Keep 收 (shou); Push 推 (tui); Pull 拉 (la); Open door 开门 (kai men); Close door 关门 (guan men); Lock the door 锁门 (suo men); Open windows 开窗 (kai chuang); Close windows 关窗 (guan chuang)

Living Room 客厅 (ke ting); Dining Room 饭厅 (fan ting); Bed Room 房间 (fang jian); Table 桌子 (zuo zi); Bed 床 (chuang); Chair 椅子 (yi zi); Tissue 纸巾 (zi jin); Wet Tissue 湿纸巾 (shi zi jin)

Morning 早上 (zao shang); Afternoon 下午 (xia wu); Night 晚上 (wan shang)

Go upstairs 上楼 (sang lou); Go downstairs 下楼 (xia lou)

Number:
1. It 6. La 11. Cai tiem
2. di 7. Ci 12. Kau tiem sai
3. sa 8. Pui
4. si 9. kou
5. go 10. Cap

Teochew Words:
Learn, o; Car, pue; Chop sticks, Te; Bowl, Wa; spoon, teng ci; Fork, Huang si; Light, trang; shower, chang e; up stairs, lau teng; Down stairs, lau e; Jors sticks, #10; Chairs, i; Table, sheng teng; Door, mung; windows, teng mung; Go shop, khe tiang; At Home, Na lai; Go out, chu te; orange, a kam ka; Pray, Pai pe kong

TEOCHEW WORDS:
fish : He; Vegetable : Cai; Apple : Bangkue; Orange : kam; Fruits : si kue; chicken : kue; Duck : AK; pork : Te bak; Go toilet : be ca ... pe; Pass urine : pang sio; Pass motion : pang sai; Eat Rice : Cea peng; Eat porridge : moi; Morning : cha ki; Afternoon : e bua; Night : mi kua; off the light : kue tiang; on the light : kui hang; first Floor : li lau; Third Floor : jia lau; second floor : ... lau; Wash cloth : soe sa; Mop the floor : ...; Iron the cloth : ut sa; ground floor : lau e; Drink water : lim cai; shower : cang ek

Domestic Worker Scheme was introduced with five thousand women enrolled from overseas. [44] In 2020, despite travel restrictions, 247,400 foreign women—mostly from neighboring Southeast Asian countries, including Indonesia, the Philippines, and Myanmar—worked as domestic helpers in Singapore. [45]

The reality is that the Singaporean "family unit" is increasingly incomplete without a domestic helper. Housing 82 percent of the resident population, the Housing and Development Board's incessant research into occupancy configurations (nuclear family, extended family, aging householders, and singles, although marriage remains a precondition for subsidized private housing) has far-reaching outcomes. Yet, these women do not figure as residents in the official statistics. Sleeping on roll-up mattresses, pull-out or foldable beds in shared bedrooms, kitchens, living rooms, and illegally in windowless bomb shelters, they are still accommodated tenuously, consistent with their moniker, "transient foreign worker." [46]

In *How to Live Together*, Roland Barthes states that reciprocity, such as feelings of attachment or friendship, can exist only within the same social rank and class. [47] I am painfully aware that my need for paid help at home both sustains Cecil's family *and* curtails her freedom. No matter how long a helper stays with the family, or even when she becomes co-opted as a beloved member, an unbridgeable gulf remains, cut deep by profound differences in education, class, and racial discrimination.

43 See Lee Kuan Yew School of Public Policy, "Foreign Domestic Workers in Singapore: Social and Historical Perspectives" (2016), National University of Singapore, https://lkyspp.nus.edu.sg/docs/default-source/case-studies/fdws_in_singapore.pdf?sfvrsn=2ac5960b_2 (accessed February 12, 2022).

44 See Theresa W. Devasahayam, "Placement and/or Protection? Singapore's Labour Policies and Practices for Temporary Women Migrant Workers," *Journal of the Asia Pacific Economy* 15, no. 1 (2010), 45–58, https://doi.org/10.1080/13547860903488229.

45 Yufeng Kok, "Businesses, Families Would Have Been Severely Hit if Singapore Had Closed Borders to Migrant Workers: MOM," *Straits Times*, May 18, 2021.

46 In older public housing, the ground floor covered open space (called "void decks") that had amenities such as benches, tables, and the area around the (now defunct) public phone. These were occupied by domestic workers. For a discourse on the void deck, see Lilian Chee, "Keeping Cats, Hoarding Things: Domestic Situations in the Public Spaces of the Singaporean Housing Block," *Journal of Architecture* 22, no. 6 (2017), 1041–65, https://doi.org/10.1080/13602365.2017.1362024.

47 Roland Barthes, *How to Live Together: Novelistic Simulations of Some Everyday Spaces*, trans. Kate Briggs (New York: Columbia University Press, 2012), 89.

Perpetuating a colonial legacy of "servants," the figure of the domestic helper is not new. British expatriate families had live-in local servants. Subsequently, wealthier Chinese families employed poorer families as domestic help.

The repair work in this specific instance first involves recognition and inclusion—that is, naming the persons we rely on and making space for them reciprocally in the knowledges we create. Action can be taken in how I, as an academic, designer, mother, and employer, choose to talk about and to include Cecil and her fellow workers in the stories I tell, the classes I teach, the design projects I supervise, and the research I conduct. **48** **fig.6** Second, repair can be sustained at the level of embodied and lived knowledge creation. The insertion of the domestic helper into architectural scholarship requires tactical intervention and invention. I borrow from Michel de Certeau and Luce Giard, who argue that the study of the everyday ordinary (for this is where we find the missing helper) is a "practical science of the singular," emphasizing particularity and concreteness of situations over abstractions made from research tools ill-suited to capture the "inventive proliferations" of everyday domestic life. **49** In defining the tactical (as opposed to "the strategic"), de Certeau gives the French example of *la perruque*. *La perruque* is when the worker steals time in the course of their work by improvising with leftovers to create something that cannot be economically or financially quantified. **50** De Certeau's "economy of the gift" and "ethics of tenacity" are insightful. **51** I interpret these as the creative clearing of domestic time and space for the mutual exchange of talents and, with that, the beginnings of solidarity.

Cecil and I have a shared interest in plants. Planting edible crops between ornamental plants in our small, walled, urban

garden has yielded surprising harvests of basil leaves, limes, and water spinach. Between house chores, she teaches me how to mend broken branches and rejuvenate orchids. Working together in our jungle-garden has nurtured friendship and healing. Through cooking, we discover shared ingredients, cooking methods, and necessary improvisations for heirloom recipes. Cooking revives family stories—hers and mine. She creates, mends, and makes at a domestic scale. Her sustainability is actionable, grounded,

48 See Anthea Phua, *How to Live with Another* (2021), http://www.presidentsmedals.com/Entry-56191 (accessed February 12, 2022). See also Lilian Chee and Silvia Federici, "We need forms of reproduction that do not separate us from each other," in "Contemporary Feminist Spatial Practice," special issue, *Arch+* 246 (February 2022), 66–75.

49 De Certeau, Giard, and Mayol, *The Practice of Everyday Life*, Vol 2, 256.

50 Michel de Certeau, *The Practice of Everyday Life*, Vol. 1 (Berkeley and Los Angeles: University of California Press, 1988), 25–26.

51 De Certeau, *The Practice of Everyday Life*, Vol. 1, 26.

fig.6 Cecil and George harvesting herbs in the back garden during the covid pandemic. Photograph: Lilian Chee, 2020 and real. She influences us. While it may not be the sort of transgression that de Certeau intended, these micro-tactics upend household routines and social hierarchies because they are creative, generative, and generous.

This version of *la perruque* changes the worker and her employer. At the same time, this discourse must also insinuate itself into wider public practice—it must change the way we think about design, transform the making of policy, become intrinsic to our pedagogy, and figure in our writing. Caring for the stranger without draws one closer to one's own past. Perhaps this is the most significant threshold that we need to mentally overcome before reparation can begin, for everyone.

Unruly Sites of Repair: Rwanda, 1994—2019
Delia Duong Ba Wendel

Delia Duong Ba Wendel is Assistant Professor of Urban Studies and International Development at the Massachusetts Institute of Technology.

I am an architectural historian and cultural geographer who explores the spatialization of peacebuilding in relation to unresolved histories of harm and the legacies of uneven redress. I work primarily in Rwanda, where I have been reflecting on the unruly nature of repair after the 1994 genocide. *Repair* implies efforts to mend or compensate for harms that result from crimes and a range of wrongs not necessarily recognized by law, including psychosocial injuries, nonprosecutable forms of state terror, and structural oppression. Repair is both an individual matter and a fundamentally social dilemma concerned with issues of redress for whole groups of people. Forms of repair range from material payments and redistributive policies to truth-telling and forms of recognition, mutual aid, and the restoration of relationships. Repair is no easy task; it is unruly. Nonetheless, individuals and communities seek repair to fulfill the possibility to endure; to feed bodies in need of some measure of acknowledgment of wrongs, restitution, and perhaps healing. Endeavoring to repair recognizes both the impossibility and necessity of that task.

A memorial can be a potent act of communal repair. Memorials also resist notions of repair as inevitable, immediately accessible, or achieved through techno-scientific acts of reconstruction. Rwanda's genocide memorials are distinct sites: they conserve places of killing and victims' remains in attempts to materialize collective memory of Tutsi survival and erasure. Among them, the Murambi Genocide Memorial is prominent for its display of mummified genocide victims at the massacre site. Attempting to understand the ethical and political motivations behind the conservation of genocide victims and sites compels engagement with the views and experiences of individuals who did that memory work. Doing so has led me to an intimate historiography of repair. [52]

52 My approach to writing what I call "reparative histories" (Delia Duong Ba Wendel, *Rwanda's Genocide History: Between Justice and Sovereignty* (Durham, NC: Duke University Press, forthcoming 2023)) is informed by the work of Yvette Abrahams, Ariella Azoulay, Catherine Hall, Saidiya Hartman, and Toni Morrison.

On April 21, 1994, state-sponsored militants attacked the Murambi Technical School and killed an estimated 35,000 people who had sought refuge at the complex. [53] The next day, local authorities disposed of the evidence, throwing bodies into newly dug mass graves. The following year, an iterative process of exhumation, conservation, memorialization, and reburial was initiated by a local community group and, later, by the Genocide Memorial Commission. The commission was convened and funded by the postgenocide governing regime. At Murambi, its charge was to conserve victims' remains and the weapons and place of massacre and to make that genocide evidence available to view, creating a memorial site that was at once commemorative and a justice-seeking corrective. Work was led on-site by a Rwandan archaeologist, Dr. Célestin Kanimba Misago, and a Chilean United Nations human rights worker, Mario Ibarra. The commission's work was complicated by the divergent aims of the new regime, whose interest in genocide memorials was as much about justice as about securing national sovereignty and quieting dissent. [54]

Two photographs taken by Ibarra near Murambi engage what it was like to conserve evidence of the genocide in 1996. fig. 7 a, b In one, a woman's arms gently encircle a child who watches an infant playing with the grass at their feet. Blankets to keep the pair warm are close in case comfort is needed. The woman is resting and looking off to the distance, where another woman sits partially out of frame. She holds a baby to her chest, nestled in a blanket on her lap. In a second photograph, the camera centers on a multitude of hands suspended over a sheet of plastic that tenuously holds soapy water. They rub human skulls to wash the dirt and remaining bits of hair, blood, and flesh from genocide victims found in a mass grave. Several groups are at work conserving hundreds of bones and skulls, some for display at the Murambi Memorial and others for burial in consecrated graves. Photographs of the "backstage" work of conservation and mothering challenge a reading of those memorials solely as commemorative monuments, inviting questions about the politics and emotional labor of repair.

The majority of conservation workers at Murambi were young women whose children accompanied them as they did their work. Most survived the genocide yet lost their family members. Vestine featured in numerous photographs of Murambi conservation work in 1996. When I spoke with her in 2018, she described what it was like to conserve bodies and bones. The conservation of killing sites was gruesome, difficult, and emotional. She said that she and other genocide survivors were still sad and grieving. The stiff, withered bodies were inordinately heavy and smelled

53 The estimated number of individuals killed at the Murambi massacre on April 21, 1994, varies according to the account. In 1996, the Genocide Memorial Commission estimated that 35,000–40,000 people were killed at the site, based on the 20,154 dead bodies found in area mass graves and witness testimonies. See Genocide Memorial Commission, *Rapport Preliminaire d'Identification des Sites du Génocide et Des Massacres d'Avril-Juillet 1994 au Rwanda* (Kigali: MINESUPRES, Feb 1996), 55. By contrast, subsequent African Rights and government reports identify 50,000 dead at the site. See African Rights, *Murambi: "Go. If You Die, Perhaps I Will Live"* (Kigali: African Rights, 2007), 134, https://francegenocidetutsi.org/MurambiGikongoroAfrRights.pdf (accessed March 13, 2022).

54 Research on the government control of genocide memorials is exhaustive, represented partially by the following: Jennie E. Burnet, *Genocide Lives in Us: Women, Memory, and Silence in Rwanda* (Madison: University of Wisconsin Press, 2012); Hélène Dumas and Rémi Korman, "Espaces de la mémoire du génocide des Tutsis au Rwanda: Mémoriaux et Lieux de Mémoire," *Afrique contemporaine* 2, no. 238 (2011), 11–27; Nigel Eltringham, "Bodies of Evidence: Remembering the Rwandan Genocide at Murambi," in Nigel Eltringham and Pam Maclean, eds., *Remembering Genocide* (London: Routledge, 2014), 200–218; Timothy Longman, *Memory and Justice in Post-genocide Rwanda* (New York: Cambridge University Press, 2017); Olivier Nyirubugara, *Complexities and Dangers of Remembering and Forgetting in Rwanda* (Leiden: Sidestone Press, 2013); and Claudine Vidal, "La commémoration du génocide au Rwanda: Violence symbolique, mémorisation forcée et histoire officielle," *Cahiers d'études Africaines* 3, no. 175 (2004), 575–92.

fig. 7 a, b Residents living near Murambi, Rwanda, employed by the Genocide Memorial Commission, care for their children and clean the bones of genocide victims found in area mass graves, 1996. Photograph: Mario Ibarra, personal archive, Chile

Caregiving as Method

of decay. Yet, Vestine cleaned the bodies of the dead to bring her kin some measure of dignity. She continues to care for them today, returning to the school buildings every day for the last three decades to clean the grounds and the bodies in one of the classrooms. This despite being laid off for a time by the memorial managers, and the recurring migraines and high blood pressure that doctors explain as trauma-related. She did the work despite all this because the job provided her and her two surviving children with some income, and, as she said, "they were our people."

These efforts of repair are oriented to what I call an ethics of non-erasure, which holds that the very representation of genocidal crimes helps to counter the intended obliteration of a people. Acts of recognition train the averted gaze back to that which it seeks to evade and tells otherwise ignored or hidden truths. This is a form of memory justice, one that bears witness to erasure. In Rwanda, the views of those involved in early genocide memory conservation demonstrate that it was not exclusively government directed. The conservation of bodies, bones, and massacre sites developed from local initiatives motivated at least in part, as Vestine helps to highlight, by care for those killed. As unruly sites of repair, genocide memorials refuse closure. The sites are simultaneously state symbols of power and hold contested memories, providing windows onto marginalized remembrance.

What might architectural historiography learn from unruly sites of repair — as a matter of epistemology, method, and subject of focus — that it could then use to reckon with its own historical omissions and the dispossession, marginalization, and oppression enacted through built environments? Considered as a method for writing history, Vestine's approach to repair — that is, her caregiving — might be described as one that intervenes directly in the violence of historiographical omission by seeking to recognize lives lost and by recalibrating the ways in which genocide histories are narrated. Architectural historians attentive to those dynamics participate in parallel acts of repair, activating both a politics of recognition and forms of scholarly care. The latter emerge from a radical seeing and listening that refuses to turn away, that is attentive to Vestine's agency and struggle.

In my research in Rwanda, I am undoubtedly an outsider. My privilege as a foreigner with the ability to travel and ask questions and my disadvantages as a foreigner who has none of the knowledge and expertise possessed by Rwandans were raised by nearly everyone I spoke with. I sought to balance my outsider status in the country by gaining Kinyarwanda language proficiency and, where local dialects challenged my understanding, by partnering with a Rwandan translator (who prefers not to be identified).

Though certainly more familiar with the culture and language than I, they, too, were a relative outsider to the communities we visited, for they did not grow up in those places. I describe our collaboration as one animated by questions about interpretation, un/ease, what was narrated, and what was possibly left unsaid. Without their humanity and insight this work would have been both less joyous and less meaningful. Forging some measure of intimacy with individuals and images in the course of writing this history has produced a body language of welled up feeling that always catches me by surprise. I hear continuities of the past in the passion, heartbreak, resolute determination, and resignation to larger forces in those moments when photographs were explained or experiences relived. I endeavor to see and hear despite my own substantial distance from the experiences relayed.

My research has also confronted another, unexpected outside: an aversion, particularly within forums related to architecture and architectural history, to engage with images that document genocide massacres and memory work. The most extreme of such reactions occurred in 2019 in a remote conference hosted by a European university. Halfway into my presentation, the panel moderator turned off my presentation screen, removing my slides from the audience's view. At another conference, in a panel on architectural histories of conflict, a senior professor expressed significant unease with the images I showed. Audience members at both conferences challenged my intent in relation to the triggering effects they experienced. I had been most concerned with describing the traumatic experiences and memory activism of those represented in the photographs. Images of violence are never easy to receive and are furthermore overlaid with issues of vantage and power that can reproduce pain and harm. However, I present my research frequently within African studies conferences and seminars and in those settings have never confronted refusals to engage.

Declaring the visual and spatial evidence of violence as outside the purview of architecture and its history has significant consequences for those seeking to confront the damage done to marginalized communities by design and planning. Prevalent abstractions of violence typically refer to dispossession as reform policies and to acts of enclosure as modernization. Such abstractions rarely allow for causal relationships between policies and the loss of life and other forms of violence, and they render damaged homes and the destruction of civic space as if they were mere symbols of war. My hope is that an intimate, reparative history of genocide memory work will help to inform the design and planning fields struggling to come to terms with the violence they have perpetrated and reproduced. A reparative historiography resists abstraction. It engages both repair and care as method to represent unruly sites of memory and the complex personhood of individuals. In doing so, a reparative historiography foregrounds people and places that are erased and misrecognized, enabling discussions around topics otherwise wrapped in silence. Writing an architectural history from Rwanda's genocide memorials in this way requires that I confront, and not seek to resolve, the justice, politics, and trauma of memory work. It begs the intimacy that grows from attempted, close understanding, and a learning from — a transposition of — efforts of repair in the world to reparative representations of the past.

A Critical Closeness
Jay Cephas

Jay Cephas is Assistant Professor in the History and Theory of Architecture at Princeton University.

55 See Belgin Turan Özkaya, "Visuality and Architectural History," in Dana Arnold, Elvan Altan Ergut, and Belgin Turan Özkaya, eds., Rethinking Architectural Historiography (New York: Routledge, 2006), 183—99.

56 Claire Zimmerman, "The Monster Magnified: Architectural Photography as Visual Hyperbole," Perspecta 40 (2008), 136—47, here 136.

57 Nana Last, "Thomas Struth: From Image to Archive to Matrix," Praxis: Journal of Writing and Building 7 (2005), 78—87, here 78.

58 Mark Wigley, "Unleashing the Archive," Future Anterior: Journal of Historic Preservation, History, Theory, and Criticism 2, no. 2 (Winter 2005), 10—15, here 11.

Research in architectural history has long relied on visuality as both an object and mechanism of historical analysis. [55] Photographs in particular have served as important visual evidence of architectural production, and they have in turn positioned the architectural image as a "critical collaborator" in producing an architectural subject that consists not just of buildings but also of "perceptions, opinions, effects, spatial constructs, utopian realities, [and] subsequent histories." [56] The architectural image makes its way into presentations and texts as evidence of the condition under study with the image itself as demonstrating "specific knowledge about a subject." [57] Conspicuously missing from the architectural subject and its archive is the human subject. If the archive "exists outside of time" in its effort to preserve historical documents, [58] then what happens to the researcher who enters this timeless space?

The primacy of the image in the production and dissemination of architectural research is without question. However, I would like to put it into question, not with the aim of removing images as a primary source of analysis but for the purpose of understanding a formative relationship between the central role of visual evidence in architectural research, the relative absence of human bodies in that visual evidence, and how the discipline of architectural history conceives of the relationship between the architectural historian and the work of architectural history.

My research engages with the fact of laboring bodies as spaces of social production, and through various projects I have encountered a difficult tension between the visioning of architectural production required by the field of architectural history and the often messy and difficult entanglement of bodies, buildings, and practices that constitute my subject of inquiry. One such example arose when I had been deep in the archives of the

Ford Motor Company, sifting through the records of the industrial hospital located within the Ford River Rouge automobile factory just outside Detroit. Housed within what was widely believed to be the largest factory in the world at the time in the 1920s, the Ford factory hospital saw thousands of cases per month — of workers with grave and disturbing injuries. At one point, I was focused on just the records from the department of ophthalmology, which detailed the hundreds of workers it saw *each week* with severe eye injuries — burns, lacerations, ulcers, contusions, and infections, among others. Some of these workers were as young as sixteen years old. Almost all of them were recent migrants, from rural Eastern Europe and from the rural southern United States. The hospital fixed them up, then discharged them — from the hospital and also from their jobs and livelihoods, only to be replaced by other workers out of the thousands waiting for employment and eager to risk severe bodily injury or even death in exchange for a living wage.

fig. 8 This space intentionally kept blank

Reading through the details of mangled bodies, some deceased, and seeing the images of severe burns and eyes lacerated and pierced was difficult. Also difficult was the expectation that I, as a researcher, was not to acknowledged this difficulty or even feel emotionally affected by the conditions faced by the subjects of my research. So it was with great relief that I engaged in discussion with my office mate at the time, Delia Wendel, about these research challenges. I told her about the difficulty I was having reading through these records and seeing these images, and she told me about the difficulty she was having with her own research in contending with the evidence of the genocide in Rwanda following the 1994 civil war. What we experienced as researchers and readers of these archives cannot compare to the conditions that the subjects of our research actually lived through and experienced. But that was a part of the conversation as well. A sort of emotional restoration emerged from these conversations, and I began to question the methodological gaze of the scholar and the expected distance between the researcher and the subjects of the research.

Around the same time, I gave a conference talk on a different research project that took a related but divergent approach to understanding spaces of embodiment. In this project, I examined the spatial performance of hunger strikes by analyzing how bodies served as the site of public discourse when dissidents were forcibly removed from the public square. The hunger strikers in question – who were in India resisting British colonization in the 1930s and in Northern Ireland advocating independence in the 1970s – were imprisoned and thus removed from public view, which meant that the condition of their deteriorating, starving bodies was not viewed directly by the public. However, the discourse prompted by their embodied political action created a new public square, one sited within their absent bodies. To exemplify this bodily absence, my presentation slides consisted of blank images, just pure white pages that I scrolled through as I read my paper. fig.8 The blank slides represented the bodily absence of the hunger strikers in the public discourse they generated about their respective conditions. I also abstained from using images of the hunger strikers because I had become increasingly frustrated with how bodies – especially Black and Brown bodies – appeared in academic presentations as illustrations accompanying intellectual ideas. Simply put, I refused to serve up Brown bodies for visual consumption or as tools to support my argument. Following my presentation, I received significant and intense criticism for not showing images. In fact, the ensuing discussion centered entirely on my decision to not show images, with no response to the actual work I presented. A point that came up repeatedly was of critical distance. Audience members sensed that I was uncomfortable with images of the hunger strikers and assumed it was because I was "too close" to the subject of my research. And they were correct. I was deeply emotionally affected by the images of starving, emaciated bodies, and my emotions about these bodies entered into my research and shaped my analysis.

Critical distance posits that to be true to both the subjects and intentions of research we must be removed from them to some degree. This removal can range from observing and understanding the conditions under study independent from oneself to isolating the subject and conditions of research entirely. Critical distance is typically presented as a way to ensure the validity of research – that the research is not simply a rendering of one's own opinion but emerges from a thorough and rigorous process that yields relevant insights. Critical distance has typically protected against undertaking research "close" to the researcher in any personal way, instead arguing that the intellectual objectivity necessary for analysis can be attained only if the researcher can approach the work as a condition unfamiliar to them in some way. In archival research, such critical distance arguably allows for a presumed objectivity that can allow for documents and artifacts to be read purely within their own historical context and for that context to not be confused with the conditions within which the researcher finds themself. While notions of critical distance often emphasize the distance between the researcher and the subject, ultimately it is the "critical" part that is important here more so than the "distance" — that criticality means always having a questioning and analytical eye toward the subject matter.

Instead of enacting a critical distance, what would it mean to be critically close? To normalize the study of things physically close — such as the places in which we have lived — and things emotionally close — such as the stories of our ancestors? To embrace the subjects of our research with care and criticality? To treat the archive as not an arrest of time but as a continuously unfolding present? A critical closeness would emphasize self-reflexivity on methods and approaches as a means to not only allow ourselves to be emotionally affected by the subjects of our research but also to understand and analyze how that affective engagement can shape the framework for analysis. Notions of what I call "critical closeness" are not new. In the early 2000s, Loïc Wacquant urged ethnographers to shift away from participant observation in favor of what he called an "observant participation" that would locate the researcher as part of the social scene under study. Wacquant came to this position when he began training at a local boxing gym while doing a sociological study of Black Chicagoans, which led to a personal transformation that shifted his research project into an ethnography of boxing. [59] This immersive approach to research drew from 1960s critiques of the white gaze in sociological research and from 1970s feminist critiques of geography, such as Gloria Anzaldúa's *Borderlands*, that embraced embodied experience as a method of analysis. [60]

A critical closeness would not only allow for an intimate connection to archival material but also recognize the emotional labor of research and allow that affect to enter into and shape one's research method. Recent scholarship on urban repair and maintenance emphasizes ties between the care of place and the care of community. [61] Critical closeness as a mode of integrating the practices of everyday care into research could similarly build ties between expressions of care and compassion for the subjects of research and expressions of care of self and community. Such a "politics of care" pushes beyond the sequestering of affect into the private sphere of the home to instead allow emotional engagement to be present in the public life of research: in the lab, the office, the conference, and the archive.

I am interested in the potential of critical closeness as both an intellectual method and a reparative exercise for and within architectural history. As a method, it might mean recognizing one's own experiential framework and how multiple, intersecting identities shape analysis, understanding that the acknowledgment

59 Loïc Wacquant, *Body and Soul: Notebooks of an Apprentice Boxer* (New York: Oxford University Press, 2004).

60 Gloria Anzaldua, *Borderlands/ La Frontera: The New Mestiza* (San Francisco: Aunt Lute Books, 2007).

61 See Tom Hall and Robin James Smith, "Care and Repair and the Politics of Urban Kindness," *Sociology* 49, no. 1 (February 2015), 3–18, here 3.

of one's subject position(s) can allow for richer interpretations while contributing to both a disciplinary and an individual repair. As a reparative exercise, it might challenge the role of presumed objectivity in architectural history analysis to instead question the subjectivities involved. I cannot help but wonder whether the relative lack of human subjects in the primary evidence of architectural research—the image—contributes to an emphasis on a critical distancing between the researcher and the subject of research. Are we analytically treating the bodies of human subjects just as we treat the bodies of architectural subjects, as mere evidence of the work of research and as objects of analysis for the architectural-historical gaze? If, as Shannon Mattern suggests, "to study maintenance is itself an act of maintenance," then perhaps being critically close to research can similarly stand as a form of self and disciplinary care. [62]

62 Shannon Mattern, "Maintenance and Care," *Places Journal*, November 2018, https://doi.org/10.22269/181120.

Caregiving, Scholar-Parenting, and Small Works
Ikem Stanley Okoye

Ikem Stanley Okoye is Associate Professor in the Department of Art History, University of Delaware.

The 1988 catalog of Nigerian-born Afro-British sculptor Sokari Douglas Camp's first exhibition under the auspices of the British Arts Council, *Echoes of Kalabari*, has on its back cover a photograph of the artist reclining in a hammock, clearly an expectant mother. I cannot recall whether baby had arrived by the time I visited (or was a toddler already), but the pregnant photograph came to help me, much later, make sense of what at the time were rarely exhibited artworks distributed across the modern house shared with her husband—white, English architect Alan Camp. [63] Diminutive, whimsical objects, they appeared playful, decorative, not demanding any particular contemplation. I did not photograph them, but the work titled *Family*, dated 1990, may have been one such work. fig.9 About 12 inches high and 14 inches long, it shows a woman walking, three shopping bags in hand, pushing a stroller while occupied with a protesting baby even as she grasps her four- or five-year-old, who calmly walks beside her. A familiar childcare scene in the urban universe of a London where help with such tasks is usually forsaken because it is unaffordable. *Family* is in marked contrast to some of the public work Camp was producing at the time, such as *Rosie and Vi* (1990), in which life-size adult figures stand together at a London market, and even larger work, such as *"I accuse the oil companies of practicing genocide against the Ogoni people"* (2007), which is too large to be contained within the ordinary room heights of most museums.

63 The artist had given me access and free range to her house sometime in 1994.

The small works were not maquettes for Camp's larger works, I presume, because they were carefully placed around the house in ways that suggested intimacy and significance for the artist, as they were visible only to close friends who might come to dinner. I wondered at the time, *Was she hiding these works?* Why? Why were they not in the few exhibitions she was lucky enough to show in?

In my subsequent writing on Camp, I did not mention these works, nor did I raise the questions they brought up. Instead, I favored her more public works. This outcome was partly because of an event held at the Haus der Kulturen der Welt in Berlin before I began writing about the artist. Simon Njami and Okwui Enwezor were cospeakers. I presented Camp's more public work and distinctly recall Enwezor casually if playfully dismissing it. 64 There was something harsh about the dismissal, because few UK-based Black women artists were allowed any reputation whatsoever; moreover, in this period Camp was hardly attended to by the fledgling Black art scene in London. 65 I suspected that Camp's quiet likely had more to do with the consuming demands of childrearing and caregiving than with either the failure of her work or her unproductiveness as such, but I had no way to speak to this.

As an untenured assistant professor, I later published critiques of Camp's life-size work from the late 1980s in chapter contributions to two anthologies (edited by Nkiru Nzegwu), considering them foundational for insights into the meaning of her work. 66 Yet, the memory of the diminutive work I had seen in her home continued to haunt me. Enwezor's comment, and

Camp's retreat into what turned out to be a momentary invisibility did, however, start to make sense to me a few years later, by which time I was myself already a few years into the work of caregiving. Encountering difficulties juggling the impossible demands of care and career, I noticed I was experimenting with a new strategy. I started producing small, playful, polemical work as a kind of guerilla tactics for survival. I produced about fourteen such works over the next decade, distributed across an unlikely disciplinary range, from contemporary African American art to critiques of modern African literature, a tactic that seemed the only ground of possibility for continuing an increasingly precarious scholarly career — since I was intent on a full and present experience of parenting. 67 Now recognizing this move as a methodic tactic

64 Enwezor was still relatively fresh from the 2nd Johannesburg Biennale, and I was still enjoying the afterglow of curating a small London exhibition of Japanese architect Takamitsu Azuma. See *Tageszeitung*, July 4, 1997.

65 She was hardly alone in this: the same befell other artists who have since become well known such as Keith Piper, Lubaina Himid, and Mona Hatoum, who once exhibited only in community-run, financially precarious, small, privately owned borough-funded spaces in Brixton and Finsbury Park.

66 See Nkiru Nzegwu, ed., *Contemporary Textures: Multidimensionality in Nigerian Art* (Binghamton, NY: University International Society for the Study of Africa, 1999); and Nkiru Nzegwu, ed., *Issues in Contemporary African Art* (Binghamton, NY: University International Society for the Study of Africa, 1998).

fig. 9 Sokari Douglas Camp, *Family*, 1990, welded steel, 33 × 35.6 × 15.2 cm. Private collection. Image source: Invaluable LLC

67 In my case, childrearing (bottle feeding, baths, nappy changing, bedtime storytelling, school runs, nanny management, cookery, "floor time," worrying, anxiety, after-school activities and clubs, PTA meetings, et cetera, et cetera), albeit in that role as a cisgendered male father operating within a heteronormative immigrant household.

68 Barbara Kutis, *Artist-Parents in Contemporary Art: Gender, Identity, and Domesticity* (New York: Routledge, 2020).

69 I have published several short essays (none addressing the topic of the present article) that are polemical, whimsical, and future-imagining. See Stanley Ikem Okyoe, "Tribe and Art History," *Art Bulletin* 77, no. 4 (December 1996), 610–5; and Stanley Ikem Okyoe, "Linger or Flee? Pieter Aertsen, 'Iguegha Uhe,' Michel Leiris," in Mariët Westermann, ed., *Anthropologies of Art* (New Haven: Yale University Press, 2005), 59–88.

70 I produced such work for publication, aware it was far less strategic for an early career academic. In humanities academia, sustained studies unfurling a significant object, after one's doctoral dissertation, is the only sure bet for work security (tenure). This valuation structure is not necessarily maintained in other academic fields.

71 These ranged from a peripheral landscape design for a beer garden in Abuja, Nigeria, to producing a credible building proposal for a company's headquarters in Boston, Massachusetts—the sole purpose of which was to secure a parcel of land from the state for a Black business (the project was limited because the client understood it was not likely ever to be built).

72 Together, these arrangements meant I was allowed to continue modeling the space of a "dad at work," while also allowing the children to play safely. I could start and stop work easily because small projects can be disrupted and re-engaged quickly.

different from but related to what Barbara Kutis, writing about artists such as Elżbieta Jabłońska, describes as artist-parents, **68** caregiving as a Black scholar-parent led me not just to make new kinds of work to meet skeptical professional demands but produced a richer critique of Camp's overlooked whimsy. **69** Which brings me back to those diminutive works.

It has dawned on me that the small whimsical works I saw scattered through the house were in fact the artist's own version of continuing to make art while fully caring for her newborn. By making art that incorporated or depicted "childish" themes, or in some way invoked or commented on caregiving, Camp was not working in the manner of, say, Kutis's subjects (e.g., Jabłońska or Guy Ben-Ner), whose art (typically performative) incorporates the actual presence of the child and its care needs. Rather, the subjects of Camp's works of this period operate within the headspace required of a caregiver who is trying to remain in practice—in her case, it seems, the work is either a comment on the overburdened mother (*Family*, 1990) or, more typically, seeks to engage and experience the light, the awe, the world through the eyes of a child, to revisit the "childish" wonder and magic that progressively gets erased and replaced as the pessimism of adulthood inevitably sets in. Her success as an artist today—bestriding serious themes, from Sigmund Freud to racism to environmental struggles to political repression in the Niger Delta, while remaining accessible to ordinary British people—is likely a product of a sensibility developed through imagining and making those small private works while a caregiver.

As I grappled with my increasingly complex caregiving obligations, a personal dilemma drove some of my intellectual curiosity about how Camp worked. If in the late 1980s I had lived between architecture as both a practice and an intellectual inquiry, twelve years later I had in addition become caregiver to two small children in a situation sometimes requiring me to be the sole caregiver for forty-eight-hour periods or even, atypically, for weeks at a time. I revalued Camp's small works and their distribution across the intimacy of her home as much as my memory allowed—recognizing, in part, that her approach suggested new possibilities for my situation. I begin to place value on the briefer but more condensed work that I, too, was already producing with some hesitancy. **70** I became more insistent on not giving up architecture as a practice and started soliciting clients for small-scale projects. **71** I engaged such projects, moreover, while working from the small basement of my home that doubled as a creche. **72**

Inadvertently, these experiences led to me revalue my own work and recognize that small works can be all-consuming, difficult, challenging, and fulfilling. They are not inferior. My experience has also led to an awareness and connection to other kinds of architecture and spaces, including that of the Niger Delta to which Camp's work often turns, but often extended across West Africa, drawn to the traditional tiny buildings. My research proposals also came to speak, with ease, of

"diminutive architecture," recognizing that such architecture was often more significant than the large buildings in the same locales. Small architecture and the intimate spaces that constructed their legibility held a special meaning for African societies, and I have since tried to understand not only the care involved in producing them but the social mechanisms that produce their value. fig.10 I took to them questions such as, *Can one know whether this is a building or a sculpture?* If buildings can be tiny and inhabited by small sculptures that are themselves regarded as actual beings, or if the very same societies resist attempts to describe or become attuned to both of them, then the scale of the world is suddenly opened to questioning and to the radical instability that can still produce change.

fig.10 Robert Sutherland Rattray, *Whitewashing the Molded Walls of a Model Building— Crate and Bucket,* ca. 1921–1932. Photograph: courtesy Pitt Rivers Museum, University of Oxford

Dex Stories: Living-with, Working-with, Vulnerability
Peg Rawes

From the scale of the home to the city, inequalities of care have become even more entrenched in recent years. They have been embedded into everyday corporeality. The Coronavirus pandemic has led to the rapid national and international redesign of soft and hard architectures of life. The result has been new hospitals and vaccine technologies — but also unequal access to core treatments and failures in the supply of oxygen, together with the repurposing of existing drugs. One example of the latter is Dexamethasone, a cheap corticosteroid with anti-inflammatory properties used in blood cancer treatment. Today it is being employed to assist the ventilation of COVID-19 patients. An immunosuppressant, "Dex" has long been used to augment chemotherapy drugs. But it produces unpleasant side effects, including increased blood pressure, appetite and weight gain, nausea, insomnia, and fierce mood swings.

Peg Rawes is Professor in Architecture and Philosophy at the Bartlett School of Architecture, UCL, London.

I have been "living with" Dex for the past ten years. I am not a medic or pharmacologist and do not take it myself. Instead, it has been one of my domestic "agental relations" in caregiving since Tom Corby, the artist I live with, was diagnosed with multiple myeloma, a form of blood cancer. Judith Butler describes "living with" as "a relation to a field of objects, forces, and passions that

73 Judith Butler, "Rethinking Vulnerability and Resistance," in Judith Butler, Zeynep Gambetti, and Leticia Sabsay, eds., *Vulnerability in Resistance* (Durham, NC: Duke University Press, 2016), 12–27, here 25.

74 Gillian Howie, "How to Think about Death: Living with Dying," in Victoria Browne and Daniel Whistler, eds., *On the Feminist Philosophy of Gillian Howie: Materialism and Mortality* (London: Bloomsbury Academic Press, 2016), 131–44.

fig. 11 *Dexamethasone*, May 2015. From Tom Corby, *Blood and Bones: Metastasising Culture*, University College Hospital, London, 2019

impinge or affect us in some way." [73] These lived experiences could also be understood as living with a proximity to vulnerability. In "How to Think about Death: Living with Dying" (2012), the philosopher Gillian Howie examines life-limiting illness, arguing that bringing critical thinking to such life stories demystifies ignorance and discrimination of the vulnerable and can simultaneously affirm the singularity and collective agency of those who live such lives. [74]

Corby's art practice examines the environmental and expressive intersections of bodies, environments, climates, and their data. Within this practice, Corby's research project and exhibition *Blood and Bones: Metastasising Culture* (2013–2019) charts his body's affective, psychological, and physiological "data" during six years of oncology treatment, which included a

stem-cell transplant and extended periods of self-isolation akin to COVID-19 shielding. Using diary entries, graphic visualizations, photography, and drawings, Corby shows the physical, temporal, and emotional experiences of "living with" the illness and the impact of lengthy treatments. These include the ongoing presence of Dexamethasone, used to treat the cancer in combination with chemotherapy and immunomodulatory drugs and to enhance their efficacy. **fig. 11** Two graphs show the daily rise and fall of Corby's immune system and blood platelet production during a treatment known as "PAD," a combination of three drugs, Bortezomib, Doxorubicin, and Dexamethasone, which preceded a stem-cell transplant and, during this period of treatment from 2012 to 2013, required him to self-isolate for six months. **figs. 12 and 13** Three drawings of chemotherapy infusions prior to the stem-cell treatment are shown. **figs. 14–16**

Corby's artful expressions of "living with" dis-ease now resonate afresh with our present-day architectures of vulnerability and care in the pandemic. Returning to look at Corby's visualizations of cancer treatment in light of the daily corporeal architectures of COVID-19, which have been streamed into our homes via public health briefings since spring 2020, reveals new multiscalar experiences of the dis-ease of living with life-limiting illness. While the topic of life-limiting illness may be too painful for many of us to dwell upon, the pandemic has brought our vulnerabilities sharply into focus and shown the extent to which our bodies and our relationships are composed of social, environmental, and biopolitical understandings of ourselves. Most immediately, the images preview the experience of self-isolation by those who have been classed as "vulnerable" during the COVID-19 pandemic. Second, they show the dis-ease of living with a life-limiting illness and the pharmaceutical impact of the drugs on the self and his body. In addition, Corby highlights the biopolitical nature of "life" in which the artist's body is not only a producer of data or information — a record of contemporary National Health Service healthcare provision in the United Kingdom and its close interaction with the pharmaceutical industry — but also a deeply personal record of his experiences. In this respect, *Blood and Bones* provides us with the potential to learn from vulnerability and to also understand the management of health and of illness on an individual basis and through an advanced Western healthcare system (now also highly vulnerable to extractive corporate interests).

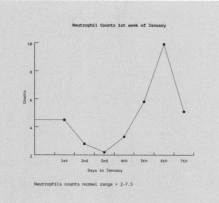

fig. 12 *Neutrophil counts*, first week of January 2013. From Tom Corby, *Blood and Bones: Metastasising Culture*, University College Hospital, London, 2019

Howie's thinking about living with life-limiting illnesses, or alongside someone with such a diagnosis, resonates powerfully here with its attention to experience that comes from vulnerability. She recognizes how feelings of self-grief that such a diagnosis produces can lead to mental and physical time and space becoming finite in distressing, fearful, and isolating ways. For some, however, the trauma of a diagnosis not only makes work but can also be put to work. If an individual can live

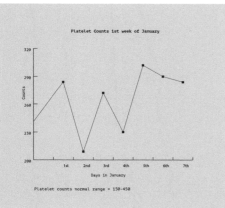

fig. 13 *Platelet counts*, first week of January 2013. From Tom Corby, *Blood and Bones: Metastasising Culture*, University College Hospital, London, 2019

through (bear) these intense states of alienation, at other times dis-ease may enable engagement in one's own and others' worlds: of self, work, family, community, friendship, politics, and poetics. Time is lived differently: not "having time" means that powers of self-determination are intensified. [75] And, for those of us who give care, this may also require learning to create "holding" relations rather than relations of touch, especially when the dis-ease is too painful for the individual who is ill.

Corby's, Howie's, and Butler's examinations of vulnerability therefore help show us how caregiving can be an artful — rather than governmental — practice. While they each address specific lived experiences of vulnerability, together they offer important understandings of care that extend into our interpersonal, social, professional, and community relations more broadly.

75 Peg Rawes, "Unusual Alliances?," *Radical Philosophy* 2, no. 2 (2018), 122–4.

figs. 14–16 *Drip*, 2013; *Inject*, 2013; *Hand and cannula*, 2013. From Tom Corby, *Blood and Bones: Metastising Culture*, University College Hospital, London, 2019
→ p. 118, 121, and 122

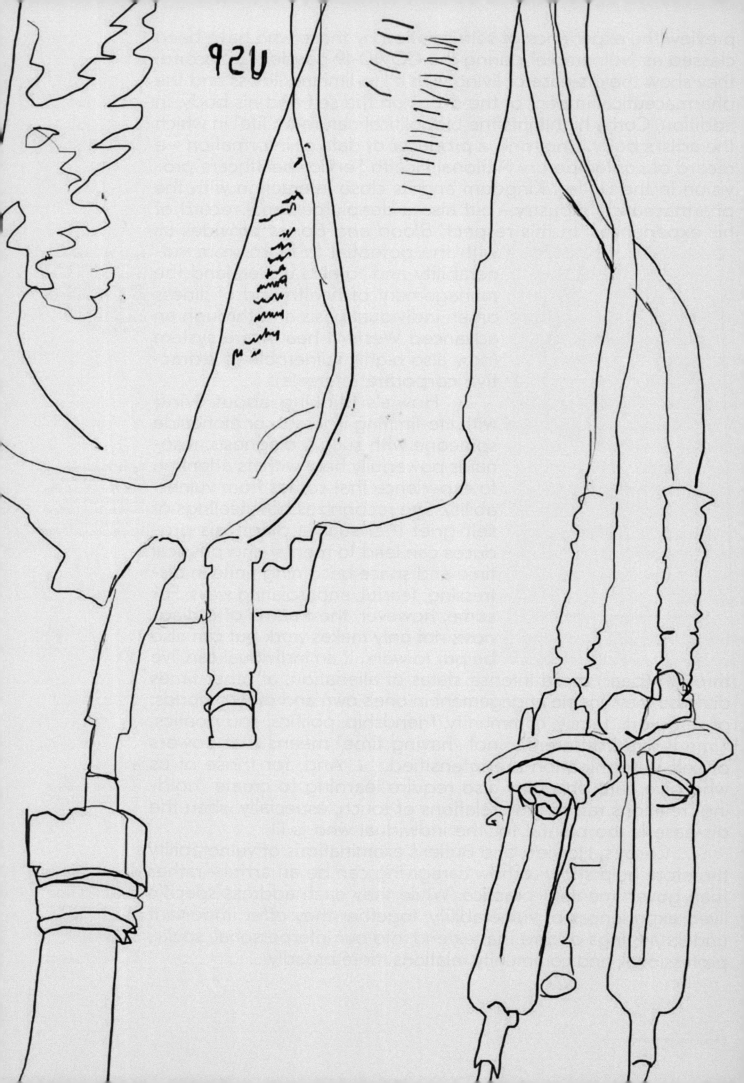

Tracing Humanitarian Work: Caring about the Gaps in Documenting Knowledge Production
Elis Mendoza

For a long time, I consciously separated my academic job from my praxis as if the two were incompatible. On the one hand, I had been repeatedly told that scholars who are activists are not taken seriously. On the other hand, I had been repeatedly advised to "package" my work into attractive maps, sections, and 3D models that could be exhibited in biennials so that my work would become a visible part of my scholarship. Wishing to avoid extractivist practices, I have refused to do the latter; however, I still aim to find a way to bridge both sides of my work and thus convey my research as part of a communal effort in the search for justice using the tools of history and design.

Elis Mendoza is a doctoral candidate in the History and Theory of Architecture, Princeton School of Architecture Master's Degree Program in Critical, Curatorial and Conceptual Practices in Architecture.

What would happen if we dropped the assumption that ideas are generated by a brilliant but solitary mind and instead recognized that knowledge is created through our relationships, experiences, and communities? If we wrote about groups, communities, and collaborators instead of valorizing single figures who are already in a position of power, perhaps we could start thinking about our own scholarly production in terms of collaboration. This mindset would allow us to create healthier and more collaborative relationships with our peers — relationships based not on hierarchies or competition but on generosity. What kinds of histories would this produce?

For the past few years, I have been writing a history of the first generation of designers to be influenced by countercultural architectural experiments on housing and the development agenda of the 1970s. [76] At first, my project centered on Fred Cuny, a Texas urban planner who became an influential disaster and humanitarian specialist after founding Intertect, a consulting company. By any metric Cuny is a fascinating historical character, a sensible choice through which to study the humanitarian system at large. He acquired a reputation for having a vast knowledge of disasters, working on every significant emergency from 1968 to 1995 by consulting with the main voluntary agencies (now referred to as nongovernmental organizations, or NGOs) active in the humanitarian system of the period. Intertect was admired for its capacity to intervene in multiple missions simultaneously. As an agency, it developed training courses and operational handbooks for international aid practitioners that have been fundamental in developing disaster response guides. Nonetheless, I struggled to portray Cuny in ways that did not simply mimic the hagiographies through which humanitarians who have died in the field are usually canonized. So I set out to assess his work

[76] This research is part of my dissertation, "From Refuge to Shelter: Frederick Cuny's Humanitarian Architecture as Deferred Utopia."

through a critical lens, attempting to distinguish institutional narratives from political strategies and personal choices.

This research shifted in meaning after the COVID-19 pandemic threw many of us into invisibility, and we found ourselves spending even more of our time in caregiving, inside and outside academia. This forced isolation, however, also made us reach out virtually and inspired discussions of the deeper meaning of our scholarship and our responsibilities in building a different post-pandemic world. After the forced hiatus imposed by closed daycare centers and archives, I began revisiting my research through a new perspective, looking for the voices that had been forgotten or effaced in the archives I had already consulted. Even before this, when I had written about the people who worked with Cuny, I noticed myself describing their interactions as encounters rather than moments of collaboration. These encounters, as I portrayed them in my writing, were often asymmetric, even extractive — a pattern that persisted even when all the actors involved were different.

Where were all those actors in supporting roles who enabled characters like Cuny to have such an expansive practice? Cuny advocated leaving the decision-making processes during an emergency to those who were under distress, as they were the ones who understood their own needs better than anyone else. He believed in the horizontal transmission of knowledge and the use of local technologies. How then to explain the protagonistic inclination of someone known as an advocate for communal agency? Cuny was attempting to subvert the largely bureaucratic systems that he criticized as being the main obstacle in effectively solving crises. Dealing with paperwork, hierarchies, and realpolitik was a burden that did not need to be shared with collaborators. Conversely, this often meant their names did not always end up in the institutional archives. Intertect archives are erratic, and the names of some collaborators are traceable as authors and coauthors of Intertect's reports. However, some names have not received the due they should, especially those of local collaborators and women in supporting roles.

In following the thread of collaborators, I found the work of Pedro Guitz, a trainer of *extensionistas*, local farmers who travel through small communities to teach agricultural practices that will yield better crops and preserve the land. Guitz worked on a development project with World Neighbors in Guatemala before the 1976 earthquake. **fig. 17** In analyzing the causes of the structural failure of houses in the San Martin region, Cuny noticed Guitz's house had survived. According to Ian Davis, Guitz had reconstructed his house a few years earlier by applying structural

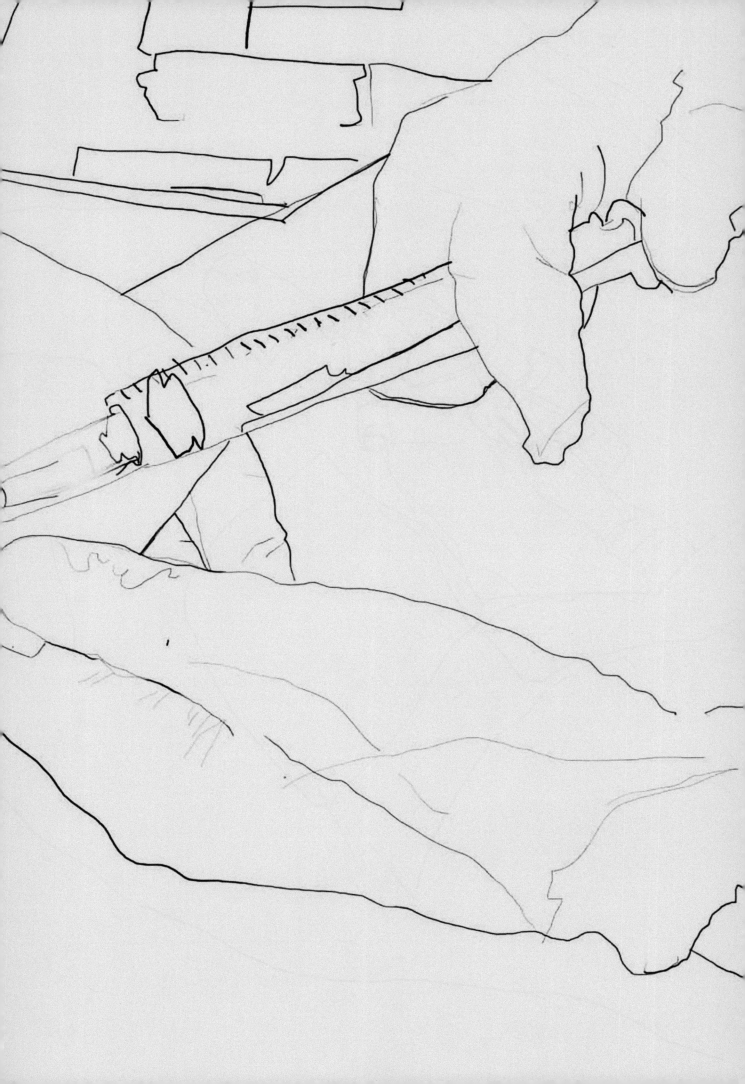

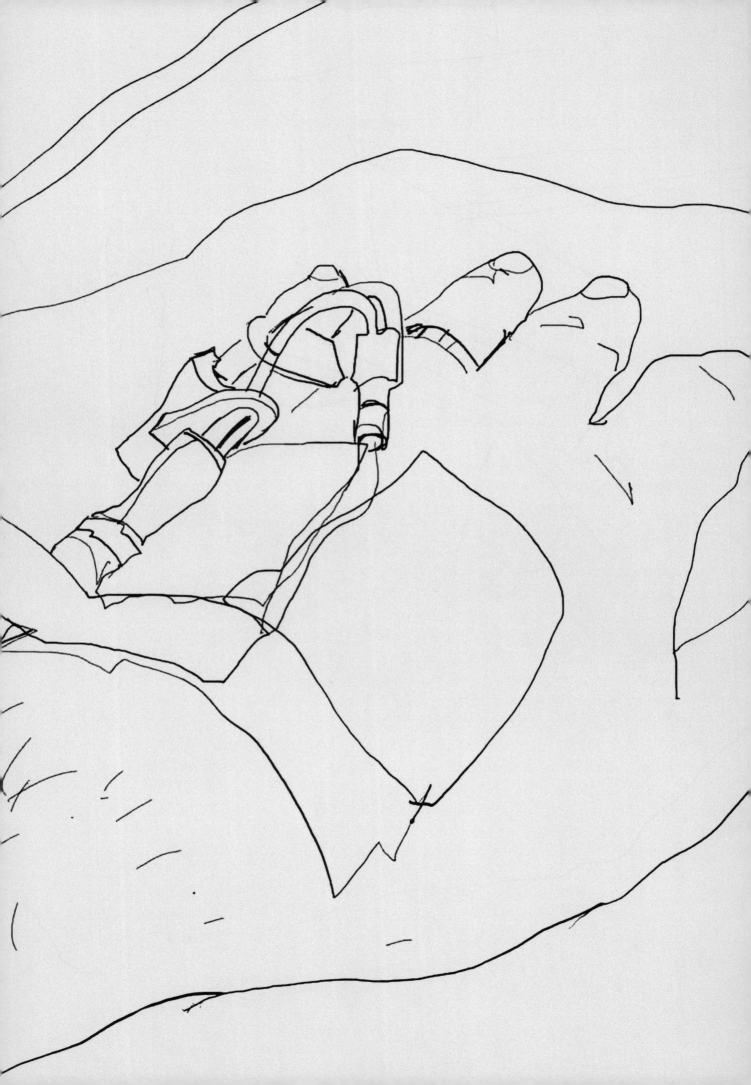

principles he had learned during research in his local library. 77 As part of Oxfam and World Neighbor's Kuchuba'l program, Guitz worked with Cuny in developing new building strategies. Invited to continue his work coordinating the model house program throughout the country, he visited nearly fifty sites, training people in small villages to salvage materials and reuse them to produce structurally sound houses. He worked with Cuny, World Neighbors, and Oxfam to develop comics that acted as building manuals, and together they built a series of model houses throughout Guatemala. The houses were conceived as living examples of

diverse building strategies but quickly turned into meeting points where Indigenous groups could discuss ideas of land tenure and *campesinos* rights. Using the strategies he developed with these foreign institutions, Guitz often travelled by himself to instruct people in other villages that fell outside the areas covered by the aid programs that had hired him. He would also train new aid workers freshly arrived in Guatemala as part of relief projects. After the civil war started a few years later, many of the *extensionistas* and locals he had trained as part of the Kuchuba'l program disappeared. 78

Another important name is Jean Parker, who appears in several documents as a manager, a secretary, and the main contact at Intertect. Historians and humanitarian practitioners have often described Cuny's agency as a one-man show in which, although other specialists were hired on a per project basis, everything stemmed from Cuny's genius and his celebrated capacity to elicit information. Parker, however, was much more than the titles given in the documentary record might suggest. In my interviews with Cuny's close collaborators, she was described as "the other half of Intertect." 79 Parker was Cuny's secretary, yes; she also oversaw the celebrated Intertect information center and coordinated most of the agency's missions from offices in Dallas. 80 She also made sure that Cuny was healthy, ate well, had a place to stay, and stayed connected with his son. These types of care labor are rarely recognized and assigned space in institutional archives, and therefore rarely make their way into academic writings that give archives a central role.

Since I began to pay increased attention to marginal notes and the desires and concerns of refugees, migrants, and women, the polyphony of their voices has substantiated my research and writing. Humanitarian history is not the only one to canonize and

77 Ian Davis and David Alexander, *Recovery from Disaster* (London: Routledge, 2015), 241–2, https://doi.org/10.4324/9781315679808.

fig. 17 Pedro Guitz training *extensionistas* for Oxfam's Kuchuba'l project. Guatemala November—December 1976. Photograph: Peter Stalker for Oxfam. Oxford Bodleian Libraries, MS Oxfam COM/5/2/2/2/58 Folder 1

78 Paul Thompson, phone interview by the author, February 19, 2020.

79 Paul Thompson, phone interview by the author, February 19, 2020; and Volker Hartkopf, phone interview by author, February 22, 2019.

80 After Cuny's death, Parker founded Parker and Associates, an agency specializing in international disaster mitigation.

aggrandize male figures and use them as anchors in its construction; architectural history knows this method all too well.

The exercise in self-reflection brought about by the COVID-19 pandemic simultaneously made me reassess my professional career. For the past seven years, I have run a parallel research practice using the tools of architecture and my training as a historian to work with segregated and Indigenous communities on legal cases involving human rights violations. My work has led me to get deeply involved with the communities I serve. I have worked with victims of sexual violence during war, mothers searching for their disappeared children who have become forensic experts by necessity, and victims of state violence — all of them women, forming a community of care and solidarity.

My practice has been strongly delineated by my work in the Sepur Zarco case in Guatemala, where survivors of sexual and domestic abuse during the civil war took their case to the Court for Vulnerable Victims after more than thirty years. The legal strategy, designed by Mujeres Transformando el Mundo, a feminist NGO, taught me the importance of establishing close, horizontal relationships with those at the center of the claims and the specialists working on the case. Through this lens I can situate my work as providing a tool that can aid survivors in revealing and giving shape to information that would otherwise remain hidden to the naked eye. I have assisted in crafting the narratives and visualizing the evidence presented in human rights courts in Guatemala and Mexico.

My desire is to find ways to translate to academia the spirit of horizontal work and generosity I have seen while working with those pursuing justice for human rights violations. I hope that the isolation we have been through and our need for community will, in time, translate to a more inclusive way of practicing scholarship.

Microcosmic Design:
Glass Envelopes and Otherworldly Entanglements
Natasha Baranow

With each striding step or brush of the hand, we unknowingly traverse entire worlds too small to notice. All around us, assemblages of tiny beings coalesce, taking shape as rocks of planetary complexity or puddles as murky as primordial seas. Despite, or perhaps thanks to, their unassuming contiguity with daily life, miniature spaces recede to the periphery of happenings more often noticed at the "meso scales of human perception." [1] These innumerable space-times, or microcosmos, occur at the limits of human sense-ability and at scales in which the body can never fit but the imagination is readily projected.

Natasha Baranow is a researcher at the Center for Rural Studies at the University of Vermont.

The terrarium — a miniature, sealed garden — is one site through which individuals actively seek out and cultivate such small

realms. **fig.1** The following article engages with this horticultural pastime by closely examining the practices of contemporary terrarium design and discussing the challenges of propagating a dynamic autonomy within miniature hermetic structures. Drawing from interviews with professional terrarium builders, analyses of internet forum discussions, and my own terrarium care experiences, this study traces the ways that little worlds actualize, endure, and dissipate within glass orbs. Moreover, it finds that encounters with such spaces are dictated by small-scale "response-abilities" and "sense-abilities" that can manifest through the affective experiences of anxiety, longing, or wonder.

1 Robert Frodeman, "Nanotechnology: The Visible and the Invisible," *Science as Culture* 15, no. 4 (2006), 383—89, here 385.

fig.1 Flask terrarium from above. Photograph: Natasha Baranow, 2020, Vermont

Ultimately, I propose that terrarium construction and maintenance can be understood as a process of *microcosmic design*: a blend of miniature infrastructuring, iterative experimentation, and prolonged forms of care that sustain otherwise tenuous forms of existence. Rather than reducing the terrarium to the "bits of matter" that constitute our familiar three-dimensional environment, [2] we will see how these worlds arise performatively from conditions sustained by dynamic infrastructures and more-than-human labor. That is, human beings do not create small worlds but have learned to carefully design and cultivate the circumstances from which these space-times may or may not emerge. And the terrarium, as both observational tool and world-unto-itself, becomes an experimental device for encountering novel configurations of the small-scale and the spectral, affording moments in which to slow down, sense, and speculate.

2 Alfred North Whitehead, *Modes of Thought* (New York: Macmillan, 1938), 179.

Potted Histories

Terrarium technologies were initially developed during the Victorian era and quickly incorporated into the biocolonial efforts of British imperialism before going on to stimulate the rise of contemporary horticultural industries. 3 But though the terrarium has shaped the global distribution of plants, irrevocably altering the earth's biosphere, its origins are modest at best — emerging out of an encounter between a man and a glass bottle. fig. 2 Indeed, the invention of the terrarium is generally attributed to a doctor and gentleman horticulturalist, Nathaniel Bagshaw Ward, who discovered and publicized the device in the nineteenth century. 4

In 1829, during attempts to cultivate fragile plants within the smog of East London, Ward stumbled upon a curious phenomenon. Having placed a moth's chrysalis within a glass bottle to observe its metamorphosis, he noticed that the very plants he had struggled to keep alive in his back garden had willingly taken root within the sealed ecosystem. 5 Ferns and mosses unexpectedly thrived, shielded by the walls of the glass vessel and surrounded by a "moist atmosphere free from soot or other extraneous particles." 6 Ward quickly disseminated his findings and began to construct variations of this glass jar, filling every windowsill and the roof of his home with glazed cases of every dimension. 7 After several years of experimentation and collaboration with prominent botanists, the Wardian case was placed on ships bound for the colonies in the 1830s. 8 Whereas previous attempts to transplant seeds and seedlings between continents had proved unsuccessful, with specimens arriving shriveled and lifeless, Ward's sealed glass boxes provided a solution for sustaining delicate vegetation across oceans. fig. 3

With the aid of these cases, vast networks of people, plants, and practices began to shift. By the mid-nineteenth century, the British Empire and other European powers had uprooted and transported tea, coffee, bananas, and rubber from their origins across the global tropics. An invisible catalyst for the age of the plantation, 9 terrariums facilitated the establishment of sprawling monocultures and extensive collections of specimens at botanic gardens. 10

3 As devices meant to enhance plant resilience, glass cases have been entwined within the geometries of power and geographies of the state since their inception. For general histories, see Jim Endersby, *Imperial Nature: Joseph Hooker and the Practices of Victorian Science* (Chicago: University of Chicago Press, 2008); Stuart McCook, "'Squares of Tropic Summer:' The Wardian Case, Victorian Horticulture, and the Logistics of Global Plant Transfers, 1770–1910," in Patrick Manning and Daniel Rood, eds., *Global Scientific Practice in an Age of Revolutions, 1750–1850* (Pittsburgh: University of Pittsburgh Press, 2016), 199–215; and Sten Pultz Moslund, "Postcolonial Aesthetics and the Politics of the Sensible," in *Literature's Sensuous Geographies* (New York: Palgrave Macmillan, 2015), 45–57. Also see Donal P. McCracken, *Gardens of Empire: Botanical Institutions of the Victorian British Empire* (London: Leicester University Press, 1997).

4 The terrarium was first documented by Scottish scientist A.A. Maconochie in 1825, but the early examples were named after Ward. David Elliston Allen, *The Victorian Fern Craze: A History of Pteridomania* (London: Hutchinson, 1969), 9.

5 See Margaret Flanders Darby, "Unnatural History: Ward's Glass Cases," *Victorian Literature and Culture* 35, no. 2 (2007), 635–47.

6 Nathaniel Bagshaw Ward, *On the Growth of Plants in Closely Glazed Cases*, 2nd ed. (London: Samuel Bentley and Co., 1852), 37.

7 See David R. Hershey, "Doctor Ward's Accidental Terrarium," *American Biology Teacher* 58, no. 5 (1996), 276–81.

8 Jen Maylack, "How a Glass Terrarium Changed the World," *The Atlantic*, November 12, 2017.

9 Or the "Plantationocene." See Donna Haraway, "Anthropocene, Capitalocene, Plantationocene, Chthulucene: Making Kin," *Environmental Humanities* 6, no. 1 (2015), 159–65.

10 Katja Neves, *Postnormal Conservation: Botanic Gardens and the Reordering of Biodiversity Governance* (New York: SUNY Press, 2019).

By compressing space and time, the small worlds of the terrarium brought about change on planetary scales while distilling plants, and indeed entire archipelagos, [11] into a terrain that is miniature, manageable, and knowable. At the same time, the transport and opening of the terrarium, like Pandora's box, [12] amplified worldly complexities through novel encounters, spawning innumerable uncertain futures. Other plants and organisms accompanied these voyages: stowaways that accelerated the extensive propagation of lively networks deemed weed, pest, or disease. [13] Beyond their role as tools of colonial enterprise, terrariums also became desirable ornaments on Victorian windowsills and thus objects of conspicuous consumption. [14] Encompassing pockets of clean air within the heavy fog of industrial London, Wardian cases were not only a symbol of wealth and imperialist nationalism but a visible reminder to Victorians of the atmospheric "contact and contagion" resulting from urban manufacturing practices. [15]

Despite the historical and political significance of this technology, scholars have not often examined the contemporary implications of bounded plant life, such as within the shopping mall, greenhouse, or terrarium. Exceptions include the work of Rob Bartram and Sarah Shobrook deconstructing Biosphere II—the largest sealed ecological system in the world—as a simulacrum of nature perfected, or an "eco-utopia." [16] More recently, Natasha Myers examined plants under the glass canopy of Singapore's Cloud Forest Conservatories in the Gardens by the Bay, a building she describes as "infrastructure for end-of-time botanical tourism." [17] Through her ethnographic work, she outlines how garden boundaries, whether composed of glass, wood, or ceramics, enact and sustain their own kinds of biopolitics and visions of the future. Although gardens are often crafted as "space[s] of seclusion set apart from the world," [18] she argues that they can also become sites in which to confront a world marred by extractive capitalism and design different arrangements of life. Debbora Battaglia pulls us into the aeroponic portals of some of these futures—a geodesic greenhouse in the center of a Disneyworld theme park and a zucchini planter on the

11 And family units. See, for example, Anna Tsing, "Unruly Edges: Mushrooms as Companion Species: For Donna Haraway," *Environmental Humanities* 1, no. 1 (2012), 141—54.

12 See Bruno Latour, *Pandora's Hope: Essays on the Reality of Science Studies* (Cambridge, MA: Harvard University Press, 1999).

13 See Alfred W. Crosby, *Ecological Imperialism: The Biological Expansion of Europe, 900—1900*, 2nd ed. (Cambridge, UK: Cambridge University Press, 2004); and Luke Keogh, "The Wardian Case: How a Simple Box Moved the Plant Kingdom," *Arnoldia* 74, no. 4 (2017), 1—12.

14 See Lindsay Wells, "Close Encounters of the Wardian Kind: Terrariums and Pollution in the Victorian Parlor," *Victorian Studies* 60, no. 2 (2018), 158—70.

15 Jesse Oak Taylor, *The Sky of Our Manufacture: The London Fog in British Fiction from Dickens to Woolf* (Charlottesville: University of Virginia Press, 2016), 24.

16 Rob Bartram and Sarah Shobrook, "Endless/End-Less Natures: Environmental Futures at the Fin de Millennium," *Annals of the Association of American Geographers* 90, no. 2 (2000), 370—80, here 373.

fig. 2 Flask terrarium. Photograph: Natasha Baranow, 2022, Vermont

17 Natasha Myers, "From Edenic Apocalypse to Gardens against Eden, Plants and People in and after the Anthropocene," in Kregg Hetherington, ed., *Infrastructure, Environment, and Life in the Anthropocene* (Durham, NC: Duke University Press, 2019), 115—48, here 118.

18 Erin Despard and Monika Kim Gagnon, "Gardens," *Public* 41 (2010), quoted in Myers, "From Edenic Apocalypse."

International Space Station—to emphasize plants' "storied matter" and the "interbeing ethics" that remain suspended in the hedgerows of plant-people relations. [19] And as a counter to NASA's orderly ozone gardens, in which lichen are grown for the sole purpose of measuring air quality, Jennifer Gabrys offers the speculative bioindicator garden—characterized not by taxonomic order but by lichen-as-microcosm—to renegotiate the lines between species, community, and world. [20] In the artistic sphere, glass sculptures by artists such as Hans Haacke, Olafur Eliasson, and Tomás Saraceno serve as technologies to accentuate circumambient elements so

19 Debbora Battaglia, "Aeroponic Gardens and Their Magic: Plants/Persons/Ethics in Suspension," *History and Anthropology* 28, no. 3 (2017), 263–92, here 278.

20 Jennifer Gabrys, "Sensing Lichens: From Ecological Microcosms to Environmental Subjects," *Third Text* 32, no. 2–3 (2018), 350–67.

fig. 3 Wardian case. Shirley Hibberd, *Rustic Adornments for Homes of Taste*, rev. ed. (London: Groombridge and Sons, 1895)

often overlooked: water, light, and air. Underlying these practices, both scholarly and artistic, is not only a desire to distinguish how worlds precipitate as shapes and forces but also an attempt to apprehend what lies beyond our ability to perceive.

Bounded worlds, as these individuals demonstrate, need not be taken at face value. Instead, they are sites imbued with an onto-political charge, sustained by the life within and around them. Terrariums are one garden-like enclosure in which these worldmaking encounters perhaps occur, stimulating what María Puig de la Bellacasa identifies as a feminist *alterbiopolitics* or, more simply, a politics of care. [21] Through her speculative investigations, Puig de la Bellacasa extends the typically anthropocentric idea of care to the more-than-human alliances of soil food-webs in permaculture practices. Drawing on this work in her own studies of contemporary English farming practices, Anna Krzywoszynska

21 María Puig de la Bellacasa, *Matters of Care: Speculative Ethics in More than Human Worlds* (Minneapolis: University of Minnesota Press, 2017).

approaches soils as a relational materiality whereby human beings and living biota coassemble soils through ongoing networks of care. [22] Here, *care* refers to an ethical orientation toward ensuring the well-being of other entities, as well as a recognition of the interdependence of all biological life. Within the sealed environment of the terrarium, linkages of care shift from a broader world to the smaller scale: relationships are severed and rewoven, and existence is reimagined. Following these lines of thought, I do not approach terrariums as inert, ornamental objects on a windowsill, wholly controlled by godlike caretakers. Instead, I conceptualize these small ecosystems as "other worlds that occasionally graze" our own [23] — space-times that in their day-to-day unfoldings mostly withdraw from human beings.

Isolation

The research for this project emerged out of unfamiliar and experimentally generative conditions. In March 2020, as a large percentage of the global population sheltered within their homes due to a pandemic, bodily coincidence within space and time was no longer feasible. In semi- or complete isolation, people experienced profound uncertainty against a media background of viral infections, job losses, police brutality, and political insecurity. At the same time, households also began to turn inward and tend to small worlds: erecting a balcony garden, updating a blog, or painting a nursery. My own project was thus tethered, theoretically and methodologically, to these kinds of everyday enclosure.

Nonrepresentational methodologies, developed to attend to the intangible or insensible aspects of ordinary life, [24] are part of the suite of approaches through which I apprehended microcosmic realities, caretakers, and inhabitants. Using sensory-focused ethnographic techniques, [25] I attempted to defamiliarize, to amplify, to "draw difference out," and to make the miniature palpable when physically visiting research sites was out of the question. [26] Specific methods were chosen for how they attend to the perceptible and imperceptible, while also preserving tensions and inconsistencies in the research process that surfaced along the way. [27]

Data collection and analysis were primarily conducted from my home in Vermont, a small, rural state in the northeastern United States. Over the course of several weeks during the summer of 2020, I employed a varied set of socially distanced qualitative methods to begin to immerse myself within the worlds of hobby terrariums. These techniques included remote interviews with people involved in the construction and maintenance of miniature worlds, including professional terrarium builders, artists, and dedicated hobbyists. Remote conversations with these individuals were

22 Anna Krzywoszynska, "Caring for Soil Life in the Anthropocene: The Role of Attentiveness in More-than-Human Ethics," *Transactions of the Institute of British Geographers* 44, no. 4 (2019), 661–75; and Anna Krzywoszynska, "Nonhuman Labor and the Making of Resources," *Environmental Humanities* 12, no. 1 (2020), 227–49.

23 Kathryn Yusoff, "Insensible Worlds: Postrelational Ethics, Indeterminacy and the (K)nots of Relating," *Environment and Planning D: Society and Space* 31, no. 2 (2013), 208–26, here 216.

24 See Nigel Thrift, *Non-representational Theory: Space, Politics, Affect* (New York: Routledge, 2007); and Phillip Vannini, ed., *Non-representational Methodologies: Re-envisioning Research* (New York: Routledge, 2015).

25 See Sarah Pink, *Doing Sensory Ethnography* (London: SAGE, 2009); and Paul Stoller, *Sensuous Scholarship* (Philadelphia: University of Pennsylvania Press, 1997).

26 See Derek McCormack, "Devices for Doing Atmospheric Things," in Vannini, *Non-Representational Methodologies*, 89–111, here 94.

27 See Stephanie Springgay and Sarah E. Truman, "On the Need for Methods beyond Proceduralism: Speculative Middles, (In)Tensions, and Response-Ability in Research," *Qualitative Inquiry* 24, no. 3 (2018), 203–14.

supplemented with virtual ethnography conducted in multiple online social media forums dedicated to hobby terrariums.

I also undertook autoethnography, taking notes as I learned to build and care for several enclosures of my own. Starting with a mason jar and mosses from the backyard, I quickly began to test combinations of vessels, plants, stones, and other objects. By early July 2020, I found myself caring for six terrariums of various dimensions, the smallest being the size of a thimble and the largest the size of a basketball. Over the course of the project, I spent time reflecting on and recording in-depth notes about the design, build, and maintenance phases of each terrarium: from selecting a nameless plant at the gardening store to pouring charcoal through a plastic funnel. These physical activities, written notes, and transforming structures became places of ongoing experimentation in vulnerability, indeterminacy, and ethics: of making live and letting die.

fig. 4 Front cover of *Terrarium*, Scott Russell Sanders Tor 1985

Under the Dome

Like a spaceship, the terrarium requires carefully designed, pre-built support systems that maintain the necessary surrounds for existence. **fig. 4** Design processes often begin with schematic abstraction: a sketch or list intended to capture some ethereal residue of the *not here* or *not yet*. Prior to crafting my first terrarium, I found myself drafting crude diagrams and lists of components, over and over again, in anticipation of the build process. Effortlessly blending and layering various materials, more seasoned terrarium builders participate in an iterative set of practices, whereby small quantities of matter are arranged to generate a microcosm meant to endure for weeks, months, or years. In this way, terrarium construction can be understood as a means of gathering and withholding heterogeneous elements to generate circumstances "felt in forms of life as the possibility of a world." [28]

Abstraction and design are tied to the ways that environments and worlds are generated through sets of protective infrastructures. Infrastructure, though a contested concept, [29] can be roughly understood as the extensive assemblages of materials, technologies, imaginaries, and practices that enable "the possibility of exchange over space." [30] As Arturo Escobar writes, producing "auspicious conditions for collective life projects demands the creation of supportive environments through appropriate 'infrastructuring,'" through which design and materiality are inextricably entwined. [31] In his own work, Escobar refers to infrastructures of the mostly human variety. But these designed life-projects can also be understood within the context of more-than-human material structures, such as living breakwaters made

28 Derek McCormack, "The Circumstances of Post-phenomenological Life Worlds," *Transactions of the Institute of British Geographers* 42, no. 1 (2017), 2–13, here 7.

29 See Hetherington, *Infrastructure, Environment, and Life in the Anthropocene.*

30 Brian Larkin, "The Politics and Poetics of Infrastructure," *Annual Review of Anthropology* 42, no. 1 (2013), 327–43, here 327. See also Casper Bruun Jensen, "Experimenting with Political Materials: Environmental Infrastructures and Ontological Transformations," *Distinktion: Journal of Social Theory* 16, no. 1 (2015), 17–30.

31 Arturo Escobar, *Designs for the Pluriverse: Radical Interdependence, Autonomy, and the Making of Worlds* (Durham, NC: Duke University Press, 2018), 162.

of oysters and techno-gardens. [32] Though materially distinct from one another, what links these design practices is a process of abstraction: a form of substantive engagement informed by environments and actualized in physical form through drafting, scenario building, and prototyping, or what might be called "technomaterial world-diagrams." [33]

Like a greenhouse, the closed terrarium is sustained first and foremost by a transparent outer capsule. These hollow structures—ordered online or pulled out of the kitchen cabinet—range from high-tech containers, such as the programmed aquarium tank, to more modest vessels, such as the jam jar. Fishbowls, glass jugs, clear-lidded plastic bins, or the traditional cloche can also be used, though one should be wary of any small openings or sharp angles that could overly impede accessibility to the space during construction or maintenance. For plants that prefer high levels of humidity and warmth, a cork or lid blocks the primary entrance point, serving to limit the encroachment of external, climatic forces. [34] **fig. 5 a, b**

Growing plants also require illumination. Too little sun and the plants inside will wither; glass or plastic enclosures must be amply translucent. Too much sun, however, and the structure will overheat. While differing architecturally from one another, then, the primary mechanism of these technologies remains the same: to trap precise levels of light, heat, and moisture, thereby generating a habitable milieu for the organisms within. In this way, glass structures become outer protective infrastructures for their inhabitants, just as layers of the earth's atmosphere enfold and sustain varied ecologies. The glass shell, or "enveloping membrane," [35] serves to insulate the entities within, while permitting a degree of acceptable exposure to essential outer-worldly conditions.

After selecting a vessel and site, one can begin to incorporate the structural materials that will constitute the nutrient base for vegetation and microfauna. A layer of larger stones is first spread across the bottom, acting as a catchment reservoir for excess water. Fine mesh is placed on top of this bumpy surface to inhibit contamination from soil and plant roots. At this point, activated charcoal is distributed as a fine layer, meant to filter downward-seeping water by chemically binding to any impurities and the byproducts of decay. Finally, a high-quality potting soil, often made up of fluffy materials, such as coconut coir, and a small amount of distilled water are sprinkled within. These strata later meld with plants' roots to distribute and refine elemental currents of water and air, thus becoming the "pipes, cables, and roads" [36] —or inner infrastructures—of the terrarium.

[32] See Stefanie Wakefield and Bruce Braun, "Oystertecture: Infrastructure, Profanation, and the Sacred Figure of the Human," in Hetherington, *Infrastructure, Environment, and Life in the Anthropocene*, 193—215; Battaglia, "Aeroponic Gardens and Their Magic"; and Natasha Myers, "From the Anthropocene to the Planthroposcene: Designing Gardens for Plant/People Involution," *History and Anthropology* 28, no. 3 (2017), 297—301.

[33] Alberto Corsín Jiménez, "Introduction: The Prototype: More than Many and Less than One," *Journal of Cultural Economy* 7, no. 4 (2014), 381—98, here 387.

[34] Open-faced terrariums are better suited to plants found in arid ecosystems, such as cacti and succulents.

[35] Derek McCormack, *Atmospheric Things: On the Allure of Elemental Envelopment* (Durham, NC: Duke University Press, 2018), 29.

[36] Thrift, *Non-representational Theory*, 163.

But for this system to work, less is usually more. By design, many terrarium builders avoid "clutter," partaking in a selective reduction and choosing only essential substances to fabricate these small ecologies. Constructing the exterior and interior of terrarium structures is as much about separating as it is about combining. Vessels should be liquid-tight to prevent inward or outward leakage. Substrata are held meticulously apart to avoid accidental alchemies as they strip contaminants from water and air. Some terrarium enthusiasts advocate the sterilization of inner components—baking soil in the oven and wiping surfaces with diluted bleach—to destroy any fugitive seeds or microbes. And upon sealing the cork, frigid air and "pests" are blocked from entry. Like composting and other gardening activities, [37] then, terrarium-building is about cultivating certain forms of togetherness while eschewing most others. Excessive entities and processes from surrounding worlds—frost, beavers, smog, powdery mildew, climate change, gnats, anxiety—are temporarily kept out. Still, despite builders' best efforts, some of these things begin to creep inward nevertheless.

Consequently, the terrarium's glass envelope is characterized by a set of exclusionary tactics through which particular objects are intentionally or unintentionally left out. Escobar calls this a type of "operational closure," whereby a designed system is defined by the various relations that demarcate and maintain its independence from other beings. [38] Though this might seem bleak, the separation is not a negative feature; without this boundary, the terrarium would simply disintegrate into the surrounding environment. Immersion within this "togetherness" of the atmospheric envelope thus becomes an essential condition for the living entities that constitute the small world.

Upon fine-tuning levels of light and moisture, water vapor should ascend and condense on the glass, engendering a foggy microclimate and descending as a soft rain. Glass walls both facilitate this circulatory system and become the "elemental tool" with which builders begin to apprehend it. [39] Scrolling through images of terrariums on online forums makes apparent how fog and light often enshroud these spaces, making them awkward to view and photograph. With my own structures, I would often find my vision obscured by a patch of water droplets and fleecy "organo-slime" clinging to the glass. Drifting in continual flux, organic and inorganic substances co-perform what might be considered weather-worlds, [40] withdrawing from the viewer or gripping the contours of the vessel's inner surface as glimmering dew. And at every incoming moment, circumstances may shift, and connections between events and entities are retied: a cork is tugged out, an untimely dusk falls, a structure tumbles

fig. 5 a, b Wardian case. Edward William Cooke, engraving, in Nathaniel Bagshaw Ward, *On the Growth of Plants in Closely Glazed Cases*, 2nd ed. (London: John Van Voorst, 1852), 21

37 See Sebastian Abrahamsson and Filippo Bertoni, "Compost Politics: Experimenting with Togetherness in Vermicomposting," *Environmental Humanities* 4, no. 1 (2014), 125—48; and Franklin Ginn, "Sticky Lives: Slugs, Detachment and More-than-Human Ethics in the Garden," *Transactions of the Institute of British Geographers* 39, no. 4 (2014), 532—44.

38 Escobar, *Designs for the Pluriverse*, 171.

39 Craig Martin, "Fog-Bound: Aerial Space and the Elemental Entanglements of Body-with-World," *Environment and Planning D: Society and Space* 29, no. 3 (2011), 454—68, here 465.

40 See Tim Ingold, "Footprints through the Weather-World: Walking, Breathing, Knowing," *Journal of the Royal Anthropological Institute* 16, no. 1 (2010), S121—S139; and Tim Ingold, *Being Alive: Essays on Movement, Knowledge and Description* (London: Routledge, 2011).

to the ground and shatters. Small atmospheres contract and swell, contingent on the changing conditions in which they are located and the extrusion of other worlds. In this way, infrastructural or geometric matters of shape and scale are augmented by "topological concerns." 41 Matter itself is revised as a series of multidimensional queries regarding the ongoing reconfiguration of worldly boundaries.

41 Karen Barad, *Meeting the Universe Halfway: Quantum Physics and the Entanglement of Matter and Meaning* (Durham, NC: Duke University Press, 2007), 244.

Though terrarium spaces may be small and initially somewhat simple to construct, their involute ecologies are not easily sustained over time. Many things can go wrong for the first-time builder: from stagnation or desiccation to mysterious blight and overgrown flora. Attempting to dodge some of these hurdles, amateurs like myself gather in online message boards to trade strategies and receive advice from more senior authorities. Many posts from forum-goers contain pictures of ailing vegetation and a plea for help: Why are my plants brown and crispy? Can you identify these little round bugs? In one internet forum, one builder encourages a fellow "newbie" by responding, "It's not as easy as it looks. I made several closed bottle moss terrariums at the start of the stay-at-home order, and three of the six are still healthy. The others quickly wilted away." 42 Nonetheless, these types of assurances do not do much to quell the panic that ensues when infrastructures themselves decline, particularly when unfamiliar or unknown bodies—insects, fungi, and bored cats—seemingly breach the glass envelope, finding their way into the enclosure. More often than not, these entities were there to begin with, waiting for the right moment to crop up.

42 Anonymous forum poster, June 26, 2020. Anonymity is maintained in all interviews in compliance with Central University Research Ethics Committee (Oxford) guidelines.

On small scales, then, worldly precarity is amplified. Over the course of a few days or weeks, terrarium builders can watch a vibrant ecosphere suddenly collapse. Initial unravelings are not always obvious. Once these infrastructures are established and left to burgeon, the symptoms of ecological deterioration can be difficult to perceive. Even when one feels the pressure to intervene, uncertainty can hold the builder back: altering the enclosure in a meaningful way comes with its own risks. As one online hobbyist astutely suggests, "It is far more difficult to negotiate micro changes in a small environment than it is in larger ones." 43 Sometimes processes of becoming flow in unwelcome directions, not always manifesting as discrete worlds but as tenuous spaces highly dependent on human care. Even for professionals, terrarium construction can be hit or miss:

43 Anonymous forum poster, August 1, 2020.

"Not all of them make it. What I try to do is—when I make them—I'll keep them for two to three months [prior to sale]. So, I think about them as 'being in the cooker.' And I watch them, I see how they're doing. And I just check on them. I open the

lid for a second, I poke around and smell ... I'm trying to be very mindful that if somebody buys something, they're getting something that's gonna last." [44]

Sharply attuned to the fragility of these ecosystems, professional builders develop their own careful routines intended to ward off bioecological snags. And, as implied by the builder above, the practices of circumspection that characterize the human-terrarium interface are underscored by a sense of responsibility, resulting in vigilant scrutiny. As feminist scholars have explored, forms of attentiveness are often tied to notions of care and everyday labor, whereby care is defined as "everything that we do to maintain, continue and repair" worlds. [45] Mending terrarium worlds can thus be understood within this framework of care, whereby sensory inputs, particularly sight, touch, and smell, guide specific responses from human caretakers.

Though maintenance tasks might vary significantly from person to person, they all rely on forms of bodily attentiveness: a process of "checking in." A slimy leaf might be extracted to discourage larger-scale decomposition. Distilled water might be spritzed on dry soils. An enclosure might be repositioned several times, rotated across each window of the house before finding its anchor point. Familiar glitches—wrinkled plants, mysterious molds, or bizarre aromas—become moments at which infrastructural repairs take place, sparking the opportunity for systemic changes, as "even ordinary failure opens up the potential for new organizations of life." [46] Failure, though perhaps not wholeheartedly embraced, is what builders anticipate, forcing them to attune to signs of malfunction and respond proactively to mitigate nascent concerns. As Escobar and Terry Winograd and Fernando Flores have written, these types of "breakdowns" can provide avenues for imaginative solutions. [47] At the same time, however, infrastructural breakdowns present the possibility of inadvertently fortifying a faulty system.

But human beings are not the only workers maintaining the terrarium. Just as in any other soil-based ecosystem, the terrarium environment is performed and sustained by ongoing forms of invisible, microbiotic labor. [48] Not only do these elusive organisms work to cycle atmospheric media on a miniature scale; they also actively reconfigure the surrounding material sphere. Bioactive *clean-up crews*—an affectionate term I often encountered online—enmesh themselves within organic waste, making otherwise inaccessible minerals available to others via metabolic processes. In my own terrariums, I would habitually observe fleeting patches of fungus: fuzz on detrital leaves or wispy mushrooms on driftwood. For days at a time, I tracked the

44 "Sarah" (pseudonym), a US-based professional terrarium builder, phone interview by author, June 31, 2020.

45 Puig de la Bellacasa, *Matters of Care*, 3. See also Joan Tronto and Berenice Fisher, "Toward a Feminist Theory of Caring," in Emily K. Abel and Margaret K. Nelson, eds., *Circles of Care: Work and Identity in Women's Lives* (Albany: SUNY Press, 1990), 36–54.

46 Lauren Berlant, "The Commons: Infrastructures for Troubling Times*," *Environment and Planning D: Society and Space* 34, no. 3 (2016), 393–419, here 393.

47 For more on this, see Escobar, *Designs for the Pluriverse*; and Terry Winograd and Fernando Flores, *Understanding Computers and Cognition: A New Foundation for Design* (Norwood, NJ: Ablex, 1986).

48 See Krzywoszynska, "Nonhuman Labor and the Making of Resources."

movements of ghostly springtails, tiny insect-like hexapods that would leave wobbly trails in the dew on their way to nibble a patch of mold. These beings, serving as "indicators" of ecological health, [49] negotiate the line between decomposition and re-composition, ensuring that rot results in renewal and vice versa. In this way, decay processes give way to world-building, whereby the unfolding of particular substances constitutes the novel re-formation of matter. [50] Moment by moment, the terrarium space is actively altered through myriad happenings, becoming a slightly different bodily arrangement than it was before.

Ancient relationships between molecule, microorganism, and macroorganism have arisen over millennia, emerging from entities' responsiveness and obligation toward others' variegated needs. Acts of care and labor are thus extended beyond the human and can be understood as animate beings' long-term commitments toward one another. But unlike agricultural soils or the petri dish, terrarium biomes are not shaped day-to-day within the context of human-microbe symbiosis; for the most part, they are left alone by their bipedal caretakers. Nor do terrarium worlds emerge solely from the synergies of lively microbiota. Inorganic beings also participate in and exceed these biological networks, affording essential nourishment. Vibrating particles, "a society of separate molecules in violent agitation," [51] join the "ranks" of "tiny laborers" [52] that partake in the rhythms of worldly inhalation and exhalation; both transformed and transforming in turn. In this way, small worlds exude not only the reticulation of nonlife and life but "the irrelevance of their separation." [53] Chemical ecologies of lively and nonlively beings cohere as loosely connected, inter-being choreographies of breath, entanglement, and care.

In this sense, prolonged care practices require an enduring trust in unknowable entities and an awareness that worldly happenings are sometimes beyond any individual's control. Like many maintenance processes, terrarium care compels difficult choices regarding whether to "uncork" and intervene in a system meant to thrive on its own. Elena, a terrarium expert based in London, writes about her urban-dwelling customers: "Everyone is super anxious about killing them, and we usually say that *over-care* [results in] usual deaths." [54] Anxiety—stemming from the Latin *angō*, meaning "to draw together" and "to choke"—is an apt descriptor within this context. Terrarium design, after all, is a process of drawing together, of assembling. Read another way, it can also be a process of asphyxiation of living beings, literally and figuratively. When knots of obligation become too tight, practices of upkeep can fall by the wayside or shift focus toward other modes of existence. Ironically, they can also pressure builders into overly hurried

49 Gabrys, "Sensing Lichens."

50 See Tim Edensor, "Waste Matter: The Debris of Industrial Ruins and the Disordering of the Material World," *Journal of Material Culture* 10, no. 3 (2005), 311–32; and Caitlin DeSilvey, *Curated Decay: Heritage beyond Saving* (Minneapolis: University of Minnesota Press, 2017).

51 Alfred North Whitehead, *Process and Reality: An Essay in Cosmology*, ed. David Ray Griffin and Donald W. Sherburne (New York: Free Press, 1978), 78.

52 Laura U. Marks, *Touch: Sensuous Theory and Multisensory Media* (Minneapolis: University of Minnesota Press, 2002), xxii.

53 Elizabeth A. Povinelli, *Geontologies: A Requiem to Late Liberalism* (Durham, NC: Duke University Press, 2016), 42.

54 "Elena" (pseudonym), a UK-based professional terrarium builder, email interview by author, June 24, 2020; emphasis added.

or unhelpful interventions. In this context, to conceptualize care in purely idealized or optimistic terms is naive. As Puig de la Bellacasa reminds us, engagements with care are often onto-politically ambivalent, riddled with these kinds of tensions: tied to feelings of affection just as often as feelings of apathy or disgust. [55]

When faced with the beginnings and ends of small worlds, practices of "letting go" become a necessary component of their care. As one builder told me, "It can be disheartening to see something you've put time and faith into die, but accepting that it's just part of the process is important." [56] On the one hand, then, "letting go" is a form of acceptance of the ways that worlds manifest and persist of their own discretion. On the other hand, it can be a form of "turning away," a mode of disentanglement from an intolerable relation [57] and thus a form of care toward oneself. In attending to the more-than-sensible, perhaps this means accommodating not only an ontology of relations but also one of detachment or absence. [58] In these ways, care underlies the insensible and unpredictable configurations of (in)organic labor that mediate small realms, becoming both an ethical matter and a matter that complicates ethics.

Small Worlds

Microcosmic space-times, in their very smallness, can be strange to encounter. One cannot walk, swim, or fly to get "there." Often, one must crouch low and squint one's eyes. Mostly, one must stop and concentrate. Like other miniature objects, terrariums require the viewer to get *close* to apprehend them. [59] At the same time, however, close contact against the glass only emphasizes the gulf between one's body and the world within. Thomas Doyle—an artist who constructs miniature environments struck by mysterious calamities—describes this same phenomenon with his encapsulated works: "because everybody wants to touch them and there's always nose prints and fingerprints all over the glass … I find that when I see miniature work, it does something to me where there's a sense of longing, an aching." [60] Encounters with glass envelopes are accompanied by an abrupt yearning to bridge the distance that remains between body and world, a feeling accentuated by a sensuous allure: "Small objects become tactile universes that have a visceral pull." [61]

In staring at the terrarium, then, one is tempted to access the space imaginatively, tumbling down rabbit holes of reverie. Perhaps this is what compels some individuals to construct tiny scenes within their terrarium enclosures, arranging scaled-down versions of everyday objects—such as cars, sheep, and graves—to serve as bridges or anchor points between worlds. **fig.6** In this

55 Puig de la Bellacasa, "Soil Times," *Matters of Care*, 169–216, here 147.

56 "Brian" (pseudonym), a UK-based professional terrarium builder, email interview by author, July 2, 2020.

57 Povinelli, *Geontologies*, 18.

58 See Ginn, "Sticky Lives"; and John Wylie, "Landscape, Absence and the Geographies of Love," *Transactions of the Institute of British Geographers* 34, no. 3 (2009), 275–89.

59 See Suzanne *Ramljak, "Intimate Matters," in M. Anna Fariello and Paula Owen, eds., *Objects and Meaning: New Perspectives on Art and Craft* (New York: Scarecrow Press, 2005), 186–97.

60 Thomas Doyle, phone interview by author, July 3, 2020.

61 Marks, *Touch*, 11.

fig.6 Front cover of *Terrariums & Miniature Gardens*, Kathryn Arthurs, 1973

fig.7 A terrarium as a retro-futuristic vision of a habitable bubble on an inhospitable planet. Knobby cacti fill the space within, enigmatic as to whether they themselves are the interstellar travelers. Andy O'Brien, *Out-world Dome*, 1983, glass terrarium with plants. Private collection, London

62 See Petra Tjitske Kalshoven, "The World Unwraps from Tiny Bags: Measuring Landscapes in Minia-ture," *Ethnos* 78, no. 3 (2013), 352–79.

63 Doreen Massey, *For Space* (London: SAGE, 2005), 140–43.

sense, miniatures offer a way of making sense of something mysterious or unknown, by having "a wonder." Builders with a penchant for the supernatural might assemble sequences of fairies, dinosaurs, gnomes, aliens, or toadstools, drawing upon familiar themes from science fiction and fantasy. Unlike other miniature hobbies, such as military simulation and model railroading, [62] terrarium scenographies are much less reliant on precise mensu-ration, however. They are not typically intended to replicate pre-existing realities. Instead they often deviate toward a "thrown-togetherness," in Doreen Massey's sense of the term, [63] playing with materials, time, and scale in ways that are imaginative and sometimes playfully absurd. In our inability to fully experience them, small worlds blur the line between real and unreal.

Yet to wonder also means to ponder or doubt. And as abstractions, terrariums allow us to contemplate a troubling status quo while prompting us to speculate about the future. Multiple builders with whom I communicated referenced environmental issues—such as climate change—as something brought to the fore during the construction and caretaking process. As these builders explained, interactions with small worlds can prompt a broader worldly consciousness by rendering large-scale phenomena more intimate and apprehensible—more *real*. Yet climate change is not the only worldly event dissected and reconfigured by terrarium hobbyists. Some individuals have crafted cogent commentaries on COVID-19 or modern militarism within their enclosures—broad-casting political missives by integrating their practice with social media. These types of scenes have included, for instance, masked figurines encased within several spheres of protective glass or a corroding toy warplane overtaken by verdancy.

64 See Donna Haraway, *Staying with the Trouble: Making Kin in the Chthulucene* (Durham, NC: Duke University Press, 2016); and Manuel Tironi and Israel Rodríguez-Giralt, "Healing, Knowing, Enduring: Care and Politics in Damaged Worlds," *Sociological Review* 65, no. 2 (2017), 89–109.

65 Patrick Jacobs, email interview by author, July 9, 2020.

66 Isabelle Stengers, "A Constructivist Reading of *Process and Reality*," *Theory, Culture and Society* 25, no. 4 (July 2008), 91–110, here 96.

67 Whitehead, *Process and Reality*, 256.

Through this kind of politico-aesthetic practice, small worlds help us "stay with the trouble" of contemporary issues, where-by care is used as a set of grammars to problematize the break-down of worldly infrastructures, sociopolitical or otherwise. [64] But more than this, as artist Patrick Jacobs tells me, working with small worlds "provides relief from the constraints of what we consider normal." [65] Terrariums thus hold the potential to prototype alter-nate scenographies or visions of the future, articulating matters of concern through a small but powerful spatiotemporal syntax. **fig.7** Microcosmic design becomes a process through which to draw out "empirically felt variations" [66] across worlds and attend to mat-ters of common interest to envisage new configurations of reality. In this way, worlds under glass become real unreals, or "tales that perhaps might be told about particular actualities." [67]

In their fragility, however, terrariums can appear uncon-vincing in their ability to endure, sometimes obliging builders to

68 Whitehead, *Process and Reality*, 338.

69 Annemarie Mol, *The Logic of Care: Health and the Problem of Patient Choice* (New York: Routledge, 2008), 93.

70 See Anna Tsing et al., eds., *Arts of Living on a Damaged Planet: Ghosts of the Anthropocene* (Minneapolis: University of Minnesota Press, 2017); and Marisol de la Cadena and Mario Blaser, eds., *A World of Many Worlds* (Durham, NC: Duke University Press, 2018).

71 Marisol de la Cadena, *Earth Beings* (Durham, NC: Duke University Press, 2015), 276. See also, Ben Anderson and John Wylie, "On Geography and Materiality," *Environment and Planning A: Economy and Space* 41, no. 2 (2009), 318–35.

72 Isabelle Stengers, "Introductory Notes on an Ecology of Practices," *Cultural Studies Review* 11, no. 1 (2005), 183–96, here 185.

Acknowledgements
I express my gratitude to Derek McCormack, my graduate advisor at the University of Oxford, and to the research participants who made this study possible.

intervene experimentally within parameters of near-total uncertainty. Instances of terrarium balance or stability are only ever fleeting: "permanence can be snatched only out of flux." **68** Mindful of their unruly trajectories, maintaining these ecologies teaches us to "give up dreams of perfection or control, but [to] keep on trying." **69** Caring for otherworldly beings necessitates not only a response-ability in the present moment but also space for beings to breathe and grow—even when they have yet to take shape.

Within the context of more totalizing notions of "world," including the Anthropocene, **70** microcosmic design can be appreciated as a world-building project that emphasizes practical activities while hinting that alternate, extraordinary arrangements of life are possible. These designs are speculative in that they gesture toward what has been left out or even toward "all that (dis)appears beyond" the ontological limits of our known worlds. **71** But looking back at how terrariums were embroiled in colonial violence—histories that are often left out of terrarium guides and online forum discussions—we see that design as "a tool is never neutral." **72** Garden boundaries and glass envelopes remind us that the political a/effects of world-building activities, even at the small scale, ripple through spaces and times. Because such design techniques are sensitive to the ways that bodies and environments relate and coproduce one another, they are well placed to explore how untold realities are performed, sustained, and extinguished. Perhaps future scholarly research-creation might examine other expressions of these little spaces, whether in the form of dioramas or dreams. In constructing and caring for these ecologies, we begin to cultivate many small gardens: a microcosmos in continuous formation.

Affective Productivism:
Betty Glan in the Soviet Union
Alla Vronskaya

Betty Glan (1904—1992) was born before the Russian Revolution and passed away after the Soviet Union ceased to exist. From 1929 to 1937 she was the director of the Central Park of Culture and Leisure in Moscow, a vibrant site of architectural and cultural experimentation—"the Magnitogorsk of proletarian culture," as it was hailed by the Soviet press. 1 fig.1 Her spectacular career rise was interrupted by the purges of the 1930s, and Glan would spend the next decade and a half in prison and exile. Rehabilitated in the 1950s, she resumed a comfortable, privileged life as a respected mass performance director. In philosopher Giorgio Agamben's terms, Glan's life vacillated between *bios*, the life of a citizen, and the merely biological *zoē*, pertinent to those whose life is not protected by law. 2 This article assesses these transformations, which both reflect the turbulence of Soviet history and exemplify the paradoxes of Soviet culture, which Glan herself helped to shape. In addition to the park, her own self became an equally important project for Glan, one that she tirelessly directed, curated, and chronicled.

Glan's fate was similar to that of another Jewish woman, the activist, writer, and editor Eugenia Ginzburg, who had been an ardent supporter of Soviet power but became a victim of political repression, eventually rehabilitated after Joseph Stalin's death. Ginzburg's memoir *Journey into the Whirlwind* (1967; first Russian publication in 1988) remains among the darkest testimonies of Stalinism. 3 Avoiding all mention of the purges and focusing instead on her work as an organizer of mass spectacles and celebrations before and after her prison sentence and exile, Glan's autobiography (also published in 1988) could not be further in spirit from Ginzburg's. In an homage to Ernest Hemingway's biographic depiction of his life in Paris in the early 1920s, Glan cheerfully and seemingly forgetfully titled her memoir *A Moveable Feast* (the literal translation of her Russian title is "Holiday is always with us"). 4 How could someone whose life was ruined by Stalin's repressive machine be so cheerful? In pondering this paradox, the present article views Glan's biography from the standpoint of Hayden White's *Metahistory* (1973), which suggests that all history is, in essence, a form of fiction. At issue is not whether a historical text is truthful but to what genre of historic fiction the narrative belongs, and that, for White, is a question of metahistorical analysis. 5 Moreover, detached writing about history, making history through one's life, and chronicling that life through one's memoir are poetic gestures.

Alla Vronskaya is Professor of the History and Theory of Architecture at the University of Kassel.

1 V. Mentsinger, "Napisat' istoriiu parka," *Park kultury i otdykha*, no. 23 (10 September 1932), 1.

2 Giorgio Agamben, *Homo Sacer: Sovereign Power and Bare Life* (Stanford, CA: Stanford University Press, 1998), 4.

3 Eugenia Ginzburg, *Journey into the Whirlwind* (New York: Harcourt, Brace 1967).

4 Hemingway's *Moveable Feast* (1964) was published in Russian as *Prazdnik kotoryi vsegda s toboi* [Holiday that is always with you], trans. M. Bruk, L. Petrov, and F. Rozental' (Moscow: Progress, 1966). The Russian translation of the title avoids the Christian connotation of the English original. Glan, in a collectivist spirit, modified the title to *Prazdnik vsegda s nami* (Holiday is always with us). Betty Glan, *Prazdnik vsegda s nami* (Moscow: Soiuz teatral'nykh deiatelei, 1988).

5 Hayden White, *Metahistory: The Historical Imagination in Nineteenth-century Europe* (Baltimore: Johns Hopkins University Press, 1973). I am indebted to Adam Jasper for making me think about Glan's staging of her life in terms of White's historiographic method.

6 Glan, *Prazdnik vsegda s nami*, 10.

7 Glan, *Prazdnik vsegda s nami*, 11–12.

Glan was born Berta Naumovna Mandelzweig into a rich Jewish family in Kyiv. Her grandfather was a singer and artist, and her father was the chief manager of a food factory. The family had likely been baptized to assimilate into Russian imperial society. 6 From early on, Betty (the nickname she received within the family and that she later officially adopted) was trained in music and foreign languages. She studied at the elite gymnasia founded by Empress Maria, finishing with distinction. There, she became fluent in German and French (later in life she would also learn English and Italian). Simultaneously, Glan studied piano performance at Kyiv Musical Conservatory. Her true passion, however, was theater. In the gymnasium, she cofounded an amateur theater group, directed by a local actor. 7 Betty had four siblings and found a close soul mate in her younger brother, the future acclaimed Soviet writer and journalist Yakov Ilyin (1905–1932), whose successful career in Moscow ended with his premature death from tuberculosis at the age of twenty-seven. A friend of Vladimir Mayakovsky, Ilyin was a member of the Central Committee of the Komsomol (the Young Communists movement) and the editor-in-chief of its popular newspaper, *Komsomol'skaya pravda*. Yakov's childhood friend Grigori Kozintsev, a classmate from an art school in Kyiv, would become Betty's first sweetheart. Subsequently an influential Soviet theater director, Kozintsev was an aspiring futurist artist, and his mother was a cousin of writer Ilya Ehrenburg, a collaborator of El Lissitzky, and a friend of the revolutionary Nikolai Bukharin. 8 These early influences and connections would both guide and haunt Glan's life. But in 1920, when the civil war between the supporters and opponents of the revolution raged in Russia, and when Ukraine and Belorussia where shaken by the Soviet-Polish War, the future of a sixteen-year-old conservatory student was uncertain. To ensure herself a useful profession, Glan took stenography courses.

8 Kozintsev's sister Lyubov, herself a painter who would study at Moscow's Higher State Artistic and Technical Studios (VKhUTEMAS) under Alexander Rodchenko, married Ehrenburg (her second uncle) in 1919. Yakov Ilyin also became a VKhUTEMAS student; however, he left the school after less than a year.

In April 1920, Kyiv was occupied by the Polish army of Marshal Józef Piłsudski. Glan, who had been politically radicalized during her time in the gymnasium, escaped with her communist friends to Odessa, where she found employment as a typist in the election commission of the local revolutionary committee. There, she was assigned as a stenographer to philosopher and aesthetic thinker Anatoly Lunacharsky during his brief visit to the city. Another native of Kyiv, Lunacharsky, in the aftermath of the revolution, became the head of the Ministry of Culture and Education (Narkompros)—a role that carried little political agency but gave him the power to shape the emerging Soviet culture. Impressed with Glan's enthusiasm and her knowledge of foreign languages, Lunacharsky recommended she be hired as the secretary of the

fig.1 Illustrated children's book *Park of Culture and Leisure* by artists Valery Alfeevsky and Tatyana Lebedeva (Mavrina). Published as *Park kultury i otdykha. Risunki Alfeevskogo i Lebedevoi* (Moscow: Gosizdat, 1930)

Alla Vronskaya Affective Productivism

army's political department for the summer of 1920 and invited her to Moscow to join Narkompros and resume her studies later on. Arriving in Moscow that fall, Glan started work as secretary of the Chief Artistic Committee of Narkompros, simultaneously enrolling in evening classes with the French Department of the Higher Courses of Foreign Languages at Moscow State University. fig.2 Soon she moved to work in the Communist International (Comintern). In the mornings, before her regular working day, she also worked at the Moscow Airplane Factory, organizing cultural events and teaching the children of factory workers. "But," she asked in her memoir, "can one consider that an overexploitation or too long of a working day for a seventeen-eighteen-year-old? There was so much happiness in that whirlpool, and the feeling of the joy of being!" 9

Giving her whole self to work, and ultimately to others, Glan was inspired by the writer Maxim Gorky's iconic literary hero Danko, who pulled his heart from his chest, using the fire of love that burned within him to light the way out of a thick forest. 10 Those whom Danko saved walked upon his still-burning heart with indifference, but he had not been hoping for gratitude. Gorky's story remains optimistic: Danko's sacrifice was not in vain, for its purpose was not recognition but the salvation of the human race. In the 1910s, Gorky and Lunacharsky, alongside philosopher Alexander Bogdanov, developed these ideas as the philosophy of collectivism, which celebrated life and vital energy, reconciling Friedrich Nietzsche's admiration of strength with Marxism. 11 The new collectivist human was not only strong in spirit and body, noble and brave, but, unlike Nietzsche's individualist *Übermensch*, deeply altruistic. For the collectivists, as well as for Glan later, care for humanity, including sacrificing one's life for the life of the other was the only source of meaning. This ultimate humanist care was heroic, and, conversely, heroism was defined through care. Locating humanism at the core of Soviet revolutionary aesthetics might seem surprising in the light of the brutality of the revolution, the civil war, and ultimately Stalinism, yet the two were intricately interrelated. As Glan's life and writings demonstrate, while the Russian Revolution was presented as a heroic humanist sacrifice, the violence it unleashed was romanticized as a challenge that proved one's commitment to unconditional care for the other.

Glan's adopted last name, which she started using in the early 1920s, honored Thomas Glahn (spelled *Glan* in Russian), the protagonist of the popular novel *Pan* (1894) by Norwegian writer

fig. 2 Glan as a French aristocrat in a play staged during the graduation ceremony of the French Department of the Higher Courses of Foreign Languages, Moscow, 1922. Photograph: unknown

9 Glan, *Prazdnik vsegda s nami*, 29.

10 The legend appears in Gorky's short story "Old Izergil" (1895).

11 On the role of Nietzsche in Russian revolutionary culture, see *Nietzsche in Russia*, ed. Bernice Glatzer Rosenthal (Princeton, NJ: Princeton University Press, 1986); Edith W. Clowes, *The Revolution of Moral Consciousness: Nietzsche in Russian Literature, 1890–1914* (DeKalb: Northern Illinois University Press, 1988); Bernice Glatzer Rosenthal, ed., *Nietzsche and Soviet Culture: Ally and Adversary* (New York: Cambridge University Press, 1994); and Bernice Glatzer Rosenthal, *New Myth, New World: From Nietzsche to Stalinism* (University Park: Pennsylvania State University Press, 2002).

Knut Hamsun, who in 1920 was awarded the Nobel Prize in literature. [12] Exemplifying vitalist ideals, Hamsun's Glahn rebels against social norms and conventions, turning instead to nature and cosmos. Similarly, Hemingway's young self as depicted in *A Moveable Feast* is poor but full of life, health, energy, and youthful idealism. Applied to the writing of history, such Nietzschean idealism, according to White, exemplifies the genre of romance, "a drama of self-identification symbolized by the hero's transcendence of the world of experience, his victory over it," "a drama of the triumph of good over evil, of virtue over vice, of light over darkness." [13]

12 Knut Hamsun, *Pan* (Copenhagen: P. G. Philipsens, 1894).

13 White, *Metahistory*, 8—9.

Aesthetic thinkers associated vital force with true creativity. Lunacharsky's collectivism departed from pan-idealism, a philosophy developed by his former classmate at Zurich University, Rudolf Maria Holzapfel, who devised a hierarchy of human feelings and states that culminated with the ideal. In the pan-, or universal, ideal, which served everyone, Holzapfel found the maximum development of individual creative personality, which alone could build a new society. Revolution, Lunacharsky professed in the spirit of Holzapfel, had to unfold each person's individuality, bringing joy and playfulness — moreover, it was joy and playfulness that sustained the revolution. This is why, as the head of Soviet culture and education, Lunacharsky devoted himself to educating spiritually, physically, and culturally developed and enthusiastic builders of socialism. Tireless, energetic, and burning with enthusiasm, Glan was, in his eyes, the new Soviet person par excellence.

How was one to translate this ideal to the masses? In 1924, Glan was appointed the director of the newly opened Krasnopresnensky workers' club. In comparison to other workers' clubs founded in Soviet Russia during these years, the Krasnopresnensky club was underfinanced: receiving little state support, it had to rely on the work of volunteers to care for the building, stage performances, and organize guest lectures and dance evenings. Glan prided herself in being able to attract workers to this activity. Her early directorial success was a costume party and contest that she organized in the club. In a twist of irony, the first prize was unanimously awarded to the costume "When the mistress is not at home" (or "The victim of female equality"): a Primus stove and a pot attached to the belt of a woman, who was "fiercely lulling the baby on the go." [14]

14 Glan, *Prazdnik vsegda s nami*, 33—34.

The private and the professional were entangled in Glan's own life, much of which was that of a single mother. In 1925, after studying by correspondence, she received her second higher-education degree, graduating as an economist and diplomat from the Department of Foreign Relations of the Faculty of Social Sciences of Moscow State University. She then moved to take a position as secretary to the Soviet delegation of the Communist Youth International (KIM) and the editor of the Russian edition of the KIM's bulletin. Through the KIM, she met young Yugoslav communist Milan Gorkić, whom she married at the end of 1925. Born Josip Čižinski, Gorkić came from a Czech family that shortly before his birth had settled in Sarajevo (Bosnia), where he grew up and became involved with revolutionary struggle. Thanks to the patronage of Bukharin, Gorkić would soon gain power within the international communist movement, becoming the head of the underground Communist Party of Yugoslavia (CPY) in 1932. Spending most of his time in Europe, Gorkić rarely visited Moscow, leaving Glan to take care of their daughter Elena, born in 1928.

The most important project of Glan's life, and one of the most ambitious experiments in early Soviet culture, began at this very time. After a two-year period at the KIM, in 1927 Glan returned to her work at the club of the Moscow Aviation Factory, which had by then been rebuilt as a state-of-the-art flagship palace of culture, boasting a six-hundred-seat hall, the largest in Moscow. This experience proved to be valuable when, in May of 1929, the head of the Moscow City Soviet, Konstantin Ukhanov, invited Lunacharsky to become an adviser for the first Soviet Park of Culture and Leisure. [15] The park, which had opened in 1928 on the site of the All-Russian Agricultural Exposition designed by architect Ivan Zholtovsky in 1923, was in need of architectural transformation. More important, it needed a program that would serve not only this park but all other parks of culture and leisure to be created throughout the country. At Lunacharsky's suggestion, Glan was appointed the park's first director, tasked with developing its program. She was excited about the opportunity, later recalling, "Lunacharsky was my political and spiritual mentor, whose influence crystallized my worldview and life principles; now he became my theoretical and practical supervisor in an endeavor to which, as it seemed to me then, I had already aspired for years." [16]

The Central Park of Culture and Leisure became the laboratory for developing the principles of a socialist urban public space where workers could recuperate after long workdays. In his novel *Ten Horse Powers* (1929), Ehrenburg had offered a poignant critique of how industrial capitalism — especially Fordism, which drove the division of labor to perfection — dehumanized and mentally crippled workers:

"The worker does not know what is an automobile. He does not know what is a motor. He takes a bolt and puts a nut. The neighbor's raised hand already holds the setting. If he loses

15 Glan, *Prazdnik vsegda s nami*, 25–26.

16 Glan, *Prazdnik vsegda s nami*, 26.

ten seconds, the car will move further. He will be left with the bolt and [salary] deduction. Ten seconds is a lot and very little. Ten seconds can be enough to recall one's whole life and not enough to take a breath. He has to take a bolt and put a nut. Up, right, half circle, down. He does this hundreds, thousands of times. He does this eight hours straight. He does this his whole life. He does only this." [17]

In response, Ilyin's most successful novel, *The Big Conveyer* (published posthumously in 1934), offered an alternative vision of the relationship between human and machine. Factory work, Ilyin believed, did not have to be dehumanizing. Quite the opposite: it offered an opportunity for creativity and active and engaged labor. "Nonsense," Ilyin replied to Ehrenburg through his hero Bobrovnikov,

"Those who write this do not know or did not see other forms of physical labor. Isn't the work on a textile loom monotonous? Does the shuttle beat in different directions and not one? Stamping, molding, hammering, loading sacks in a port—any physical work is monotonous in essence. It is absurd to blame the conveyer for monotony. Only handicraftsmen can be afraid of it." [18]

Similar to Soviet labor theoreticians Osip Yermansky and Peter Palchinksy, who critiqued Taylorism from a humanist perspective, offering their own versions of labor management and organization theory (both were influenced by Bogdanov's collectivist theory of organization), Ilyin argued that industrialization was fully compatible with humanism. [19]

The program of the park was developed in response to these discussions. Glan wanted to create a space that would support humanist industrialization, ensuring that factory work stayed close to Ilyin's rather than Ehrenburg's vision. Transforming the debilitated and exhausted factory workers into the mighty men and women of the future, the park offered educational opportunities that elucidated to workers the meaning and significance of their work and enabled their physical recuperation. In 1933, the park was officially named after Gorky, who paid a much publicized visit in 1934. In the early 1930s, Glan also met with Gorky on other public and private occasions, discussing the program and activity of the park.

As the newly appointed director, Glan was unhappy with the decorative scheme of Hungarian artist Béla Uitz, who had painted all park pavilions in red—the color of the revolution. This approach was, she found, too formalist and hostile to the architectonics of buildings. "The park urgently needed a new outlook. It needed an artist! Contemporary, colorful, having a feel for space and nature," Glan decided. And, "Of course, one has

17 Il'ia Ehrenburg, *10 l.s.* [1929], https://www.rulit.me/books/10-l-s-read-402852-1.html (accessed July 14, 2019).

18 Yakov Il'in, *Bolshoi Konveier* (Khabarovsk: Dal'giz, 1936), 10.

19 See Loren Graham, *The Ghost of the Executed Engineer: Technology and the Fall of the Soviet Union* (Cambridge, MA: Harvard University Press, 1993).

20 Glan, *Prazdnik vsegda s nami*, 47.

to search first and foremost among theater artists." [20] The avant-garde work of brothers Vladimir Stenberg and Georgii Stenberg in the Chamber Theater of Alexander Tairov was, Glan quickly realized, what could save the park. The Stenbergs' work in the park took two years, and by the 1931 season the park was transformed; it became cheerful, optimistic, and playful.

"Its theaters, sports pavilions, the library, the children's village, the café, which were all painted in light colors — white transitioning to blue, beige, lemon-yellow (with colorful pictures of smiling children, running athletes, theater masks) — now looked taller, lighter, and more elegant. The beautiful wooden caryatids on the variety theater by [sculptor Sergey] Konenkov became noticeable and prominent, intricate gazebos and small stages — latticed and transparent.

Having highlighted the buildings with spring brightness, the Stenbergs decorated all alleys and grounds with an unusual banner ornament. Already earlier, many red flags had been hanged on the [park's] territory on holidays, but this time a new decoration system, comprising flags and banners of different shapes and sizes — long, vertical, attached to poles and lamps, wide horizontal on several buildings, and small triangles, waving on the wind on the spires of low buildings.

For the first time flags of other colors — light and dark blue, white, orange, were used. [Contrasted] with the background of greenery, they looked surprising and cheerful.

But particularly beautiful the green and flower decoration of the park looked in combination with fountains, pools, streams, waterfalls. In the evenings, greenery, water, sculpture, skillfully lit, seemed completely different than during the daytime — so enigmatic and magic." [21]

21 Glan, *Prazdnik vsegda s nami*, 47—48.

At first sight, Glan's dismissal of modernist seriousness and her preference for a vibrancy and richness that would soon be labeled as "kitsch" by the likes of Clement Greenberg, prefigures Stalin's notorious motto, "Living has become better, comrades. Living has become happier" (1935), and socialist realism as the new aesthetics of Stalinist imperialism. However, what the case of the Park of Culture and Leisure actually demonstrates is that, far from being a manifestation of a top-down, coherent, and complete program, socialist realism was a project of many authors, inspired by a variety of sources, modernist and traditionalist, right and left, Marxist and otherwise. If Glan's cheerfulness fit the general direction of socialist realism, her love for the magical and the playful stood apart from the nascent artificiality of the official aesthetics.

Glan's favorite means of architectural expression were color, greenery, water, and light. Among her most cherished architectural projects in the park was the Green Theater (1929–1933) by architect Lazar Cherikover. fig.3 The largest open-air theater in the country, the Green Theater seated twenty thousand people and was equipped with modern audio and light technology. Proud of its modernity, Glan loved it for the magical effect created by the stage set of trees and the ceiling of night sky. In 1935, she asked Alexander Vlasov, who replaced Lissitzky as the head architect of the park, to design the Island of Dance—a ballet stage on a pond—and an open-air amphitheater with eight hundred seats on the bank. The figures of dancers were mirrored in the water, lime trees provided the stage set, and hundreds of fountain streams served as the curtain, reflecting the rays of setting sun and, after sunset, of colorful projectors. The Water Theater

fig.3 Advertisement poster for the Green Theater, Central Park of Culture and Leisure, Moscow. Public domain

became a perfect stage for the *féerie*—a nineteenth-century genre of magical extravaganza advocated by Gorky's friend, writer Aleksey Tolstoy, and revived by Glan in the park. 22

    In the park, Glan's authority was maternal. As the director, she hosted the visits of important foreign and domestic guests, directed theatrical performances, and supervised all other work. Many years later she would recall how once, on a Sunday, her daughter Elena, who was then five, was brought to visit her in the park. The girl found her mother inspecting the park in the company of its board of directors. The group moved through the park, noting what needed to be done. Turning to the author of

22 For a discussion of the concept of *féerie*, see Alla Vronskaya, "Objects-Organizers: The Monism of Things and the Art of Socialist Spectacle," in *A History of Russian Exposition and Festival Architecture, 1700–2014* (London: Routledge, 2019), 151–67.

fig. 4 Cartoon.
Source: Archive of
the State Museum
of Architecture,
Moscow, Russia
(MUAR), collection
of Mikhail Korzhev.
From: *Bulleten'
rabochikh i
sluzhashchikh Parka
kul'tury i otdykha
im. Gorkogo*, no. 2
(November 26, 1929).
Image courtesy of
MUAR

architectural guides Petr Portugalov, Elena said, "You are evil, you torture my mom: you don't leave her alone even on a Sunday." "Ah, what if it were us — it is she who doesn't leave us alone," Portugalov retorted. 23 "We cannot without mommy," a cartoon published in the park's internal bulletin in 1929, depicts Lissitzky (in the middle) and two other unidentified male employees holding Glan's skirt as they push their sledge up the park's celebrated sledding and skiing ramp. **figs. 4 and 5**

23 Minutes of the meeting of the veterans of the first Gorky Central Park of Culture and Leisure (1974), 27—28, in Central Moscow Museum-Archive of Personal Collections (TsMAMLS), Fond L-33, opis' 1, delo 53.

The park received many famous Soviet and foreign guests, including Nikita Khrushchev, then the secretary of the Moscow party organization. **fig. 6** Another guest, Romain Rolland, a known enthusiast of Holzapfel's philosophy, visited the park in 1935 and could not hide his excitement about its mission:

"I wish that the world of the West, which conceitedly drapes itself in 'humanism,' which intends to satisfy the pride and dispel the boredom of a narrow group of selected few, came here to learn the true and noble humanism, which nurtures all humanity, rejuvenating the body and soul." 24 The elevation of workers' lives from *zoē* to *bios* was the goal of the park.

24 Glan, *Prazdnik vsegda s nami*, 117.

Glan's faith in humanism was put to a hard test when she was arrested in June 1937, following Bukharin's arrest earlier that year. At the same time, Gorkić was ordered to travel from Paris, the seat of the underground headquarters of the CPY, to Moscow, where he was immediately detained and executed in November. His replacement as head of the CPY was Josip Broz Tito, a collaborator of Stalin's secret police (NKVD). Glan's trial took much longer, lasting until April 1939. In jail, she again met Khrushchev, who was examining prisons in the company of the head of Moscow NKVD, Stanislav Redens. In his memoirs, Khrushchev recalls their uncanny encounter:

fig. 5 El Lissitzky, poster for the ski ramp at the Central Park of Culture Leisure, Moscow, 1934. Public domain

"It was terribly hot, being summertime, and the cell was terribly overcrowded. Redens had warned me that we might meet so-and-so and so-and-so, that personal acquaintances had ended up there. And sure enough, an intelligent and very active woman I had known was sitting there — Betty Glan. Today [in 1967], it seems, she is still alive and well. She had been a director of Gorky Park in Moscow. But she had been not only a director; she had also been one of the founders and creators of that park. I didn't go to diplomatic receptions back then, but as someone who came from a bourgeois family Glan knew the etiquette of

high society, and [Maxim] Litvinov always invited her, so that in a way she represented our government at such receptions. And now here I was encountering her in prison. She was half naked, like all the others, because it was so hot. She said: 'Comrade Khrushchev, what kind of enemy of the people am I? I am an honest person, a person devoted to the party.'" [25]

25 Memoirs of Nikita Khrushchev: Commissar, 1918–1945, Vol. 1 (University Park, PA: Penn State Press, 2004), 50.

26 Under Article 58-10 of the Penal Code of RSFSR.

Yet, even as her life was degraded to *zoē*, Glan not only fought to restore its dignity but devoted herself to dignifying others. In December 1939, she was found guilty of counterrevolutionary activity and sentenced to five years in a labor camp. [26] In September 1942, Glan was convicted for the second time and sent to the Volga-region city of Saratov. There, still a prisoner, she became deputy director, as an engineering technologist and economist, of the textile factory of female labor-educational colony (labor camp for underage girls) and the head of the colony theater group. A recommendation letter from the colony director, written in 1944, mentions that, during the three years Glan spent there, she conducted giant "industrial-mass work, contributing to socialist labor education of children and the increase in the productivity of their work"; the letter also praises her for treating "the students well and with attention" and for actively contributing "to their education in the spirit of communism." [27] In August 1946, Glan was released and moved to the industrial center Ivanovo, where she found employment as the artistic director of the lecture program of the Ivanovo philharmonic while simultaneously directing the "cultural and educational work" of the Ivanovo regional party committee. Things seemed to improve, and in 1948 Glan became the director of the Ivanovo All-Soviet composers' sanatorium and simultaneously the head of the house of culture of a collective farm in Cheganovo in Kineshma District of the Ivanovo region. A recommendation from the head of the collective farm mentions her frequent visits, during which Glan helped organize cultural and educational work, "paying particular attention to cultural events that help agricultural campaigns." Glan also invited Moscow and Ivanovo actors and musicians to the farm and lectured the farmworkers about music and literature. [28] Yet, in November 1948 she was convicted a third time, again for counterrevolutionary activity, and sentenced to "special settlement" in the Kazachinsky district of the Krasnoyarsk region in Siberia. There, she created and directed clubs and amateur theater groups in the collective farms Kemskoe and Udachny and in the village of Momotovo. In 1951, Glan moved to the local center, Krasnoyarsk, where she directed the amateur choir and theater collectives of the Spartak shoe factory, the local

27 Zaveduiushchii uchebno-vospitatel'noi chast'iu zav. TVK#1, "Kharakteristika: Glan Betti Nikolaevna," December 5, 1944, in TsMAMLS, Fond L-33, opis' 1, delo 198.

28 Solov'ev and Evgenova, "Otzyv: Glan Betti Nikolaeva," 1947, in TsMAMLS, Fond L-33, opis' 1, delo 198.

textile factory, and the Trade School of Physical Culture, where she also taught music. In August 1954, following Stalin's death, she was fully rehabilitated and released.

Back in Moscow, Glan was able to quickly restore her social circle and return to the passion of her life: organizing mass performances. She became the deputy general secretary of the Union of Soviet Composers and the director of the All-Soviet propaganda department of the Union of Soviet Composers. In 1957 she staged her last great performance, the water carnival of the 6th International Festival of Students and Youth, whose actors included a high-speed passenger boat; motor boats; four richly decorated floating stage-barges two steam ships converted into "islands of friendship and joy of youth"; and river trams with singers, orchestras, and dancers. fig.7 In 1959, retired and with the privileged status of a "personal pensioner," she continued working as a volunteer, no less tirelessly than ever, becoming the deputy head of the Committee on Mass Spectacles of the All-Russian Theater Society. In this capacity, she was instrumental in shaping the opening and closing ceremonies of the

fig.6 Betty Glan showing the park to Anastas Mikoyan and Nikita Khrushchev, 1935. Published in *Park kultury i otdykha: Gazeta-Desiatidnevka* (1930s)

1980 Moscow Olympics. In 1964, she was honored as a "distinguished cultural worker of Russia"; in 1970, she received the award of the All-Union Festival of Theater Performances. Unlike most of her fellow citizens, Glan frequently traveled abroad, both within and beyond the socialist bloc. 29

To put it in White's terms, suppressing the execution of her husband and her own incarceration from her memoir, Glan styled it as a romance. However, the blatant discrepancy between the cheerfulness of the text and the tragic reality of her life relate it to another of White's categories of history writing: satire, "the precise opposite of this Romantic drama of redemption, a drama dominated by the apprehension that man is ultimately a captive of the world rather than its master." 30 While romance, according to White, is based on the poetic trope of metaphor, satire is based on irony — "negating on the figurative level what is positively affirmed on the literal level." 31 Yet, rather than a satire, Glan's memoir is a stubborn defense of romance as a genre not only of writing but also of living and building history — even in the face of the pervasive accusations of hypocrisy that followed in the 1980s.

29 According to her profile in the Union of Soviet Theater Workers, she visited Gorkić's family in Czechoslovakia in 1966, 1968, and 1980; visited Bulgaria, Romania, Poland, East Germany, and France in 1962, 1964, 1969, 1977, and 1981; and Hungary and Canada in 1965, 1967, 1974, and 1978. See TsMAMLS, Fond L-33, opis' 1, delo 198.

30 White, *Metahistory*, 9.

31 White, *Metahistory*, 34.

When, in the wake of *glasnost*, a journalist asked Glan about her gulag experience, she declined to respond directly:

"One cannot reduce life, and not only ours but the life of the entire generation, to one, even if deeply tragic, year. As if we were interesting only insofar that we survived 1937, only in how we lived precisely after the arrest. It is clear today that bright and strong people were destroyed. Write about what made them such, about our youth, happy and joyful. Otherwise . . . otherwise it appears that my life, the books of my brother, and the big and difficult work of Milan was not the most important in our lives." [32]

32 V. Koval', "No iarkikh krasok bol'she u sud'by," *Komsomol'skaia pravda*, unknown issue, in TsMAMLS, Fond L-33, opis' 1, delo 217.

As if she were a Danko whose flaming heart was trampled upon by the Soviet state, to whose enlightenment project she had dedicated her life, Glan refused to acknowledge that her sacrifice was in vain. Declining to consider herself a passive object of vio-

fig. 7 Water carnival, 1957, International Festival of Youth and Students, Moscow. Published in: *Prazdnik mira i druzhby* (Moskva: Molodaia Gvardiia, 1958). Public domain

lence, she insisted on her political sub-jectivity, on possessing *bios* rather than *zoē*. The very project of her life — the concept of the park of culture and lei-sure — aimed to empower the work-ers, whose dignity was crushed by the assembly line, and thereby to elevate their life to *bios*. Denying her this right would have meant repro-ducing the act of violence on the epistemological level. More-over, the very act of self-censoring the memory of her personal tragedy can be seen as the ultimate confirmation of her political agency. And yet, enmeshed in Glan's insistence on her subjec-tivity one can detect an avoidance of responsibility for the zoe-fication of the lives of others, the zoefication that her collectivist philosophy, which postulated altruism as the highest value, in-voluntarily sustained as it was instrumentalized by the Stalinist state. Politicization of *zoē*, Agamben claimed, is the decisive event of modernity. [33] Objectification of *polis*, one could add, is its other, equally sinister, side. The boundaries between romance and satire, as genres of modern history writing, are permeable.

33 Agamben, *Homo Sacer*, 4.

Scientific Board
Tom Avermaete
Eve Blau
Mario Carpo
Maarten Delbeke
Mari Hvattum
Caroline Jones
Laurent Stalder
Philip Ursprung

Editorial Board
Moritz Gleich
Anne Hultzsch
Adam Jasper

Editorial Committee
Gregorio Astengo
Sebastiaan Loosen
Davide Spina
Nina Zschocke

Issue Editors
Torsten Lange and Gabrielle Schaad

Academic Editor
Adam Jasper

Copy-editing
Christopher Davey

Proofreading
Thomas Skelton-Robinson

Graphic Concept and Design
büro uebele visuelle kommunikation, Stuttgart
Maks Barbulović and Andreas Uebele

Production
Offsetdruckerei Karl Grammlich GmbH

Typeface
GT Eesti

Paper
UPM Fine 100 g/sm
MaxiScript 170 g/sm

Cover Illustration
Collage by Milena Buchwalder. Featuring Mierle Laderman Ukeles, *Washing/Tracks/Maintenance: Outside (July 23, 1973)*. Courtesy Milena Buchwalder and Mierle Laderman Ukeles

© 2022
gta Verlag, ETH Zurich
Institute for the History and Theory of Architecture
Department of Architecture
8093 Zurich, Switzerland
www.verlag.gta.arch.ethz.ch

ISBN 978-3-85676-432-6
ISSN 2504-2068

gta Verlag

ETH zürich